D0065461

BUSINESS
@ the **Speed** of **Stupid**

BUSINESS

 **@** the **Speed** of **Stupid**

Building Smarter Companies
after the Technology Shakeout

DAN BURKE
AND
ALAN MORRISON

PERSEUS
PUBLISHING

Many of the designations used by manufacturers and sellers to distinguish their products are claimed as trademarks. Where those designations appear in this book and Perseus Publishing was aware of a trademark claim, the designations have been printed in initial capital letters.

Cataloging-in-Publication Data is available from the Library of Congress
ISBN 0-7382-0542-7

Perseus Publishing is a member of the Perseus Books Group.
Find us on the World Wide Web at http://www.perseuspublishing.com
Perseus Publishing books are available at special discounts for bulk purchases in the U.S. by corporations, institutions, and other organizations. For more information, please contact the Special Markets Department at the Perseus Books Group, 11 Cambridge Center, Cambridge, MA 02142, or call (617)252-5298.

Text design by *Brent Wilcox*
Set in 10.5-point Berkeley by Perseus Publishing Services

First printing, October 2001

1 2 3 4 5 6 7 8 9 10—03 02 01

CONTENTS

ACKNOWLEDGMENTS

We'd like to recognize some of the people who helped us with this book. Before we start naming names, though, let us say that both of us have been privileged to work with and learn from a great many talented people over the years. Rather than try to list them all and certainly overlook someone, we instead just say "Thanks" to all of you. We would like to acknowledge a few, however, who directly contributed to this book. We couldn't possibly rank their contributions, so we'll just use alphabetical order.

Ralph Brainard, a very talented management consultant, co-worker, and friend, contributed the seed that grew into the Executive Thought Framework, introduced in Chapter 12. Tom Griffin, a good friend and all-around great guy, contributed in both words and spirit. Carl Fitch, co-founder and CEO of Immedient, shared his wealth of knowledge and experience in consulting with us. Steve Jones helped with a technologist's perspective, and Frank Mendicino provided insights from a venture capitalist's point of view. Daniel Montano provided insight from the creative agency viewpoint, as well as the powerful observation that because Web software is "free and simple," many think that it must be "cheap and easy" to build.

Mark and Lara Morrison, Alan's son and daughter-in-law, helped with editing tasks as well as providing a technologist's viewpoint on certain parts of the book. Vijaya Naraparredy, a professor at the University of Denver, helped us with business strategy, and Jon Nordmark, CEO of eBags, was a great help, providing a mature perspective on the dot-com world from the inside out. John Raeder, entrepreneur and venture capitalist, provided invaluable guidance and understanding of the successful entrepreneurial mind, and Steve Reynolds, without even knowing it, contributed through key thoughts relating to process. Karl Wimer, marketer extraordinaire, provided valuable feedback in the area of marketing.

We offer special thanks to Christian Smith, vice president of sales and marketing at eProject (www.eproject.com), for allowing us to use eProject's excellent project collaboration system in the preparation of this manuscript. Although designed to support software project collaboration, it worked extremely well as a writing collaboration tool, allowing us to remotely store, manage, and share documents without conflict or data loss.

There are two special people without whose assistance and support this book would never have become a reality. Nancy Stender, our literary agent from Sanford J. Greenburger Associates, Inc., was invaluable in both helping us to formulate our original proposal and providing guidance regarding our foundational approach to the book. Nancy, throughout the course of this effort, has served without complaint as coach, critic, editor, cheerleader, friend, and Mom. Jacqueline Murphy, executive editor at Perseus Publishing, proved flexible, patient, and willing to work with us in making this book a success. Jacque perfectly walked the fine line between keeping us on track and allowing us valuable creative freedom. To both of you, we offer our most sincere thanks.

On a more personal note, we recognize our wives, Dena Burke and Ann Morrison, for their patience, support, and encouragement. Of course, we had to promise that we wouldn't start our next book for a while. Alan would also like to recognize his mother, Lily Morrison, who inspired him to write. This one's for you, Mother.

Last but far from least, we earnestly thank all of those unnamed and unknowing contributors who, through their misadventures in technologyland, provided the material for our stories. We sincerely wish you success and happiness.

Dan Burke
(Dan.Burke@ExecuThought.com)
Alan Morrison
(Alan.Morrison@ExecuThought.com)

Introduction

It is necessary for us to learn from others' mistakes. You will not live long enough to make them all yourself.

—Hyman George Rickover

THE BATTLEGROUND

You are at war, whether you know it or not. Your enemies are loose in the competitive battle space, determined to exhaust you with their agility and crush you with their might. The battle for survival lies in front of you, and the weapons of war that will keep you alive are all based on technology. Are you prepared?

Probably not. If you're like most executives, entrepreneurs, or investors, your knowledge of technology is sketchy at best, a fact that immediately places you at risk, but even if you understand technology, you are still probably not ready for battle. Mastery of technology requires much more than just an understanding of it. It requires a systems-based approach to *thinking* about the employment of technology, an approach fundamentally at odds with the inevitable sense of urgency brought on by the pace of battle. It requires an understanding of not just technology itself but the place of technology and its relationships with other entities on the battlefield. Successfully employing technology is not easy, and if you fail, you die.

In that quiet and lonely no-man's land between the executive or entrepreneur's vision of technological grandeur and successful corporate execution lies a battleground that most fail to traverse:

- Almost 100 percent of the growing businesses in this economy are technology dependent.
- $300 billion is allocated annually to software projects.[1]
- Most technology projects are considered a failure.[2]
- System failures cost e-commerce companies an average of $10,000 per minute.[3]
- Dot-com and related e-ventures have and will continue to drop like flies.
- Venture capitalists and investors have and will continue to lose millions, if not billions.
- Executives, entrepreneurs, managers, and project managers have and will continue to lose jobs and damage their careers at an alarming rate.
- It's all going to get worse before it gets better.

The carcasses of technology endeavors, venture capital investments, and promising careers are strewn in rapidly growing piles along the treacherous "Information Superhighway." It doesn't matter what era or sector your organization surfaced in, if you have a role in this economy you will be both a victim and a benefactor of technology dependence. If these facts do not scare the hell out of you or at least make you nervous, then you are either independently wealthy or some corporate version of Forrest Gump.

Those who will survive and thrive in this challenging environment must change the way they *think* about business strategy and related mission critical technology investments. That is exactly what this book is about: how to *think better* about business and technology and how to gain the wisdom necessary to avoid the huge failures and consequences suffered by the foolish and less battle-wary travelers.

Some time ago, Alan Greenspan stated that our economy was in a state of "irrational exuberance." Even following major market corrections that followed this comment, we still believe this to be true, both of our economy and of our beliefs about the ability of technology to solve problems. As with any mass movement or business trend, the lemming factor around technology and the Internet is extreme. Regardless of the number of carcasses accumulating in plain sight, otherwise intelligent executives and entrepreneurs continue to blindly race down the technology path, driven by greed and a frantic sense of urgency. Astoundingly, no matter how clear or frequent the warning signs, they never seem to realize what is about to happen until they tumble into the abyss of failure.

We are constantly astonished at the extreme naivete of many executives and technologists as they attempt to exploit technology. It is a statistically validated fact that very few of either group understand how to success-fully *leverage* technology to realize real-world benefits for their businesses, employees, or customers. A lever is nothing but a tool, a long bar standing in the corner of your garage. It can do nothing by itself, but when placed on a fulcrum and with sufficient downward force applied, it becomes a powerful tool. Applying this analogy to technology, we find that most people think of technology as *leverage*, whereas it's really nothing more than a *lever*. Technology does not, cannot, and will never work its magic on its own. In and of itself, neither the lever nor technology has any value or capability. It is only when it is seen and used as a tool that its value and power can be exploited. For the lever to work, to have value, it must be integrated into a more complex system. It requires a fulcrum, proper placement of one end under the object to be lifted; sufficient force exerted in the correct direction on the opposite end; and on and on. The steel bar is simple, but properly integrating it into a system to gain true leverage is not so simple. The same is true of technology: It's never as simple as it ap-pears, and to believe otherwise is to set yourself up for failure.

Much of this perception problem is rooted in the Western, and particu-larly U.S., propensity to speak instead of listen, act instead of study, create something completely new instead of adjusting something established. There are fantastic benefits to this worldview and approach. The United States boasts the most powerful and creative economy in the world. How-ever, with few isolated exceptions, the likelihood that we will ever share a reputation with the Germans for superior engineering talents or the Japanese for teamwork and consensus building is remote. Our propensi-ties are particularly disastrous when confronted with managing and im-plementing complex systems or solutions or applying complex tools.

This tendency has caused the widespread trial use and then discarding of many powerful management tools such as total quality management (TQM) and business process reengineering (BPR). Each of these tools has been "tried," has "failed," and has now passed out of favor like the latest fashion apparel. However, closer examination of the "use" of these tools reveals a superficial attempt driven by silver-bullet thinking that never even approached real or sustainable utilization. The results are very predictable. The tool is misunderstood and thus misapplied, perception builds that the tool does not work, and then the tool is rejected. Consequently, most change brought about in organizations, whether through technology, process, or structure, rarely achieves the intended results, and often ends in unintended consequences and disaster. The lack of wisdom, of deliberate thought before action, the tendency to fire before aiming— all are epidemic across our industries and society in general.

Wisdom is the result of learning from mistakes. True learning requires a stable environment that allows us to make decisions and implement them, experience the results of those decisions, and then make adjustments. Because environmental change is constant and dramatic in today's business world, it would seem that learning and attaining wisdom would be impossible, but this is far from the truth. The good news is that there *are* constants in business and technology, even in the midst of extreme chaos. Unfortunately, the sensationalism instigated by the new-era pundits warps our perspectives and obscures these foundational principals upon which all sound business and technology investments rest. However much these new economy prophets preach the "new way," there are unbroken threads of truth that have woven and will continue to weave their way through all eras, economic conditions, industries, and business sectors. There are legitimate solutions for the challenges we all face; we can learn and acquire the necessary wisdom to survive. We can get out of this alive.

ABOUT *BUSINESS @ THE SPEED OF STUPID*

The goal of this book is to provide you with the tools and wisdom to survive and thrive in the modern technology-powered world. Our aim is to surface many of the timeless truths that will always lead to an increased probability of personal and business success. We deliver on this goal through story, analysis, and a framework for strategic thought. Here's how we lay it out.

PART ONE: AT THE SPEED OF STUPID AND ACCELERATING

Each of the ten chapters in Part 1 opens with a story that is in most cases a blend of several real-world cases that we have witnessed or studied. The stories document both large- and small-scale technology-dependent business initiatives that went awry because of simple bad thinking: mistakes made due to specific shades of ignorance, oversight, or faith in the hype surrounding technology. You will briefly get to know the players and key factors making up the context of the decisions made. Immediately following the story we provide analysis and conclusions that capture issues central to the project's demise. Finally, at the end of each chapter we provide a summary table of do's and don'ts related to the success and failure of similar real-world scenarios.[4]

PART TWO: DECELERATING THE STUPIDITY

In Part 2 we examine the "whys" behind our analysis and conclusions in the case stories, the common threads woven through them. We reveal and analyze a unique cognitive framework that will enable you to avoid the problems revealed in Part 1, as well as the thousands of other scenarios that surface in the trenches of battle. This section begins with an examination of the rarely discussed or disclosed root causes of destructive industry trends and perspectives. We then outline a framework for executive thought that will allow any executive, entrepreneur, or active investor to make far better decisions about corporate life and death issues. Finally, we conclude with an approach for practical implementation of the framework in any corporate setting.

DON'T BUY THIS BOOK IF . . .

Eager enthusiasts of management fads tirelessly search for the silver bullet that will slay the latest monster sucking the life out of their corporations. If you are looking for magic solutions, for shortcuts to success, for the one elemental truth that will solve all of your problems, don't buy this book. If, however, you recognize the benefit of being a fly on the wall watching a parade of failed projects and companies pass by, and you also recognize that the lessons learned from these fatalities are worth their weight in gold, this book is for you.

WHAT THIS BOOK IS AND IS NOT ABOUT

This book is not about project management or development "methodologies." We touch upon them, but only superficially and from the perspective of the executive. Project management methodologies are peripheral to our primary purpose, which is to provide better ways to think about and lead strategic technology-centric business initiatives. In addition, most managers and executives simply do not have the time, interest, or perceived need to become experts in the project sciences. Therefore, our goal is to be not methodologically perfect but practically effective.

Most writings that touch on the project sciences focus on the details of project management and attempt to force executives and managers to learn and comply with their rigorous tools. Our approach is just the opposite. We begin from the outside and work our way in. We approach the topic from the vantage point of the executive office, as it should be. Successful mission critical initiatives never begin with project schedules, Gantt charts, or PERT diagrams. They begin with a vision, a sound understanding of corporate strengths and weaknesses, of market factors, the competitive environment, and then take into account the human factors, organizational structures, and business processes that establish the context for execution. We don't in any way intend to minimize the value of traditional project management tools, only to place them in proper perspective. Real business needs and strategy must drive projects, not the other way around.

CASE STORY CONFIDENTIALITY

Determining the proper approach to writing this book was difficult. Our agent and publisher both, for many good reasons, requested that we reveal the names of the companies and characters in our case stories. Although this approach would certainly have lent a degree of credibility to the stories, it was not possible for several reasons. First, we have nondisclosure agreements with all of our clients and would be in breach of contract if we revealed information specific to these clients or their projects. Second, although the stories would clearly be more interesting with the names of widely known companies and executives, these details would lend little if any real value to the problems and solutions presented. Third, the individuals involved in our studies, almost without exception, are highly qualified and capable professionals. All are deserving of the respect and confidentiality we provide all of our clients, regardless of the situations they find themselves in.

OUR WISH FOR OUR READERS

We have learned a tremendous amount from studying and rescuing failed and failing projects and investments. We sincerely hope that this book provides the framework for thought and the practical knowledge needed to ensure your personal and corporate success.

Part ONE

@ the **Speed** of **Stupid** and *Accelerating*

CHAPTER 1

It's About the Customer, Stupid

Most companies of any size have a Web site. Most suck! They suck because they simply fail to communicate with the intended audience. If you have or plan to build a corporate Web site, heed this: It's easy to waste a lot of time, money, and energy building a site that looks great but that fails to converse with your customer. Listen up: A good Web site isn't about you, it's about your customers.

Imagine two scenarios, the first a customer receiving a brochure in the mail, the second a customer sitting across from your best salesperson. What's the difference? Lots! The first is a monologue that tells the customer how wonderful you are, whereas the second is a dialogue, during which your salesperson listens to the customer's needs, pains, and vision, and only then offers suggestions about how your company can help solve the customer's problems. The first ends up in the trash, the second ends in a sale.

A recent book, *The Cluetrain Manifesto,*[1] drives home a very important point about the World Wide Web: It's a dialogue, not a monologue. Most corporate Web sites are monologues. They are about the company, not about the customer, but it doesn't have to be that way. It's easy to build a Web site that first listens to the customer and then responds in terms that are meaningful and valuable. You just have to think from your customer's

---

The Story

Company Name	DSTination
Industry	National technology consulting firm
Products	Technology consulting services
Size	$100 million in revenue, 700+ employees
Issues	Needs to have a corporate Web presence to attract new customers and build IPO interest
Key Players	Sam Zaputa, CEO of DSTination
	Bob Sundin, vice president of marketing

---

viewpoint, putting yourself in your customer's shoes. If you want your Web site to be successful, stop talking and listen.

Sam Zaputa, CEO of DSTination, Inc., stared intently at his vice president of marketing, Bob Sundin. He hadn't hired Sundin and didn't have a lot of confidence in him but was stuck with him. Sundin was a friend of the founder and chairman of the board, and Sam was the consummate corporate animal. He would have to wait and let Sundin fail, something that was certain to happen eventually. Until then, Sam would make the best of it.

"We believe we can have the site up in three months at a cost of about a quarter-million. We're forecasting that the site will bring in about twenty-five prospects per month resulting in somewhere between $1 and $5 million in additional revenue per month, not bad for a quarter-million investment." Sundin paused, uncomfortable under the CEO's gaze. He knew Zaputa didn't like him and dreaded times like this when he and his work were under the CEO's scrutiny.

Zaputa shifted and leaned forward. "Look, this site has to be first-rate. It's got to be classy; I want sizzle. It has to attract customers, but don't overlook the fact that our investors are going to depend on the site to help position us with Wall Street for the IPO. We've got to build a site that will convince the big institutional investors that we are a major player in the e-solutions professional services market. Does that make sense?"

Bob nodded and said, "Sure. I've got some great copy guys ready to start work, and our graphics people have already started on the creative. We'll storyboard it and get it in front of you within two weeks."

Two weeks later Bob presented his team's work to the CEO and several board members and investors. Zaputa had been involved all along driving the content of the site, but this was the first time the board members and investors had seen it. They had a lot of comments, some of which would require changes to the design, but all in all seemed pleased with what they saw. Bob breathed a sigh of relief as he left the boardroom. He smiled at his team leader and commented, "Looks like we're off and running."

Things went well, with most of the work progressing according to schedule. The required servers and software exceeded the original budget estimate, but the CEO approved the increase under the condition that, "It had better be good." Bob was particularly proud of the work that his copywriters were doing. He almost got Goosebumps when he read:

> By combining imaginative strategy, trend-setting creativity, and cutting-edge technology, we have created an unequaled eSolutions company that is ready to be your partner for success.

The site was finished on schedule and previewed at the quarterly board meeting. Bob sat proudly while Zaputa navigated through the site. Projected on the big screen in the boardroom, the site was simply spectacular. The board members smiled and nodded, and Zaputa performed in his usual brilliant manner. When the presentation was finished, the chairman said, "That was awesome, Sam! Great job! Tell your team 'Thanks' for me." Zaputa smiled and nodded.

The official site was launched with an extensive print media and Web advertising campaign, with "www.DSTination.com" boldly splashed across the pages of major industry magazines and Web sites. During the first month of operation, the number of visitors far exceeded Bob's most optimistic forecast. When he reported this to Zaputa, he received a rare smile from the CEO. "Maybe he's not such a bad guy after all," Bob thought.

A week later Bob's phone rang. "Come to my office. We need to talk about the Web site." Bob hung up and headed for the CEO's office. Zaputa was sitting at his desk, studying a computer screen covered with numbers and graphs. "We're not getting the results from the site that you forecast," Zaputa began. "It's been up for over a month and I'm not seeing any increases in contacts from prospects or new leads for the sales team. You said 'twenty-five per month,' right?" He looked up.

Bob shifted uncomfortably and answered, "Well, are we sure we aren't getting contacts through the site? I mean, how do we know if calls are coming in because of the site or because of something else?" Zaputa looked at him without expression. "We ask, right? You should know that. We'd better start seeing some results soon, or otherwise you're going to have some explaining to do to the board."

The next day Bob rounded the corner into the break room just as one of the company's most senior project managers said, "It doesn't look like the company *I* work for. Hell, you can't even tell from the site what we do!" Bob pretended not to hear. Back in his cubicle, he brought up the site and studied it. He had to admit that the home page didn't expressly state what the company did, but it was a well-designed page: great graphics, great copy, and lots of eye-catching animation. Yet the words, "It doesn't look like the company *I* work for," haunted him.

Bob could tell that Zaputa wasn't happy when he next saw him. "As if Mondays aren't bad enough," Bob thought. Zaputa leaned forward. "You have a problem. The chairman played golf Saturday with Vick Miller, president of FTV. Apparently Vick asked if we still did Oracle work. He said that his CTO had pointed out that our Web site doesn't say anything about Oracle. In fact, he went on to say that he later visited our site personally and wasn't sure if we were still in the technology business! Needless to say, the chairman isn't happy, nor am I. No wonder we aren't getting any prospects from the damn site—they don't know what we do!" Zaputa paused.

Bob tugged at his ear nervously and began, "Well, I . . ." Zaputa waved his hand and interrupted, "Look, I want a plan on my desk by Wednesday on how we make the site work for us. I don't care what you have to do—I want it by Wednesday! The board meets on Friday and I want to have answers. You said the site would result in new contacts and increased revenue, and they're going to ask why nothing is happening."

Bob and his team put everything aside and went into crisis mode. Working almost around the clock, they came up with a plan to revise about half of the copy on the site, putting in specifics about what the company did. They did some drawings showing a cleaner graphical approach and worked on improvements to the navigation scheme. The result would be a much simpler and easier-to-use site, one that Bob felt would be more effective. Yet at the same time he was beginning to feel uneasy. Finally, late Tuesday night he looked at the revised storyboard for the site and asked himself, "If I were a potential customer, looking for professional help on a technology project, would I choose DSTination?" He had to answer, "No." There was no getting around it: The site was about DSTination, not about what DSTination could do for the customer. There was no compelling value proposition. "Marketing 101," thought Bob. "Oh well, too late to worry about it now. I'll just have to take my medicine tomorrow morning."

Surprisingly, Zaputa was pleased with the proposed revisions. He directed a few changes, but none was significant. Bob and his team put some finishing touches on the package for the board meeting and gave it to Zaputa's secretary for distribution. Bob knew he was prepared, but he was still nervous. Deep down he knew that the changes wouldn't have the desired effect. He could now see the site from the customer's viewpoint, and he didn't like what he saw.

Entering the boardroom, Bob noticed two unfamiliar faces. It didn't take long to find out who they were. The chairman opened the meeting. "It has come to my attention that our site isn't drawing prospects as we had projected, and is apparently confusing our existing customers as well. I decided that we should have someone from outside our organization take a look and give us an independent opinion. We have two guests from One-Web Marketing here today with their assessment. They've looked not only at the existing site but at the proposed changes as well. Gentlemen, the floor is yours."

The next thirty minutes were humiliating for Bob. The consultants started on the revised home page, pointing out a variety of ills but focusing on the fact that the site talked to the visitor but didn't listen. They went on to explain that a successful Web site has to be a dialogue, allowing the customer to control the interaction. There has to be something on every page that speaks in the visitors' language, offering something of value in return for their time and attention. "You pay for mouse clicks and view time by giving the viewers something they need," one said. They labeled the copy that Bob and his team had worked so long on as "frankly, marketing fluff." Angry at first, Bob slowly became depressed. The chairman, his friend, avoided looking at him. Zaputa sat on the edge of his chair, nodding in agreement with every conclusion, occasionally casting a serious glance toward Bob. Bob knew that this wasn't going to go away; his future with the company was fading by the second.

The next Tuesday morning, Bob sat across the desk from Zaputa. He was trying to explain how he and his team would redesign the site, but

Zaputa interrupted. "Look, look . . . That's all in the past. We've got to move forward. I've decided to turn the site over to One-Web. Furthermore, I'm going to make a few organizational changes, as a part of which I'm going to move you into the advertising department and have you focus on traditional media advertising. You've got a lot of experience there and should do a great job. Does that make sense?" Bob opened his mouth to say "No," but didn't.

ANALYSIS AND CONCLUSIONS

Hundreds of thousands of companies have built and are building Web sites just like the one DSTination launched. Most of them are vanity sites, nothing more than exercises in pompous bravado and self-worship. Your customers need to know how great you are, but only after they ask. First, you need to listen to them, hearing who they are and understanding why they're there. Later, after they come to believe you have what they need, they will ask for your credentials, at which time, with a single click, you can give them your best marketing spiel.

Consider this analogy. Suppose you went to a new attorney with a legal problem. Suppose that the attorney spent the first half-hour of your time telling you about his degrees, his famous clients, cases he has won, and so forth, all without ever asking who you are or what you're there for or anything else about *you*. Would you want him to represent you? Of course not! It would be obvious that you're not important to him, nor is anyone else, for that matter. All of the things he's telling you might be important later, after you've told him your problems and you're convinced that he understands and can help you. At that time, it would be nice to know his qualifications and experience, but only then; up front, you aren't interested. You just want to know that he cares about and understands your problem and can help you solve it.

The same is true of corporate Web sites. DSTination's was a quality site that spoke eloquently of the company's qualifications, experience, and mastery of industry buzzwords. But the site never gave viewers the opportunity to say anything, to identify themselves and express their needs. The site spoke well to potential investors but not to potential clients. Had the worth of the site been measured by increased market valuation of the company rather than increased revenue through sales, it might have been judged a success, but as a sales-driver it was a failure—and sales was the primary motivator behind the site investment.

Let's examine the three key issues surrounding this "failed" project and how DSTination could have enhanced its conversation with prospects and improved its return on investment.

Does the Customer Care?

Bob fell into a common trap. When Zaputa told him that the site should both attract customers and impress investors, alarms should have gone off. What marketing executive would accept the assignment to create a single marketing piece designed to sell customers and communicate information to investors and analysts? The problem here is audience confusion. DSTination created a site that reveled in its own press, but potential customers didn't care. This concept is extremely simple to grasp: Build your product and your message for your intended audience. For some reason, whenever it's time to build a corporate presence on the Web, the collective IQs of brilliant executives drop and a self-worship service begins.

DSTination was not alone in this foolishness. It is safe to say that most corporate sites are exercises in self-adulation and ego gratification. If you have any doubt about this, just take a brief survey of corporate sites you are aware of. If you really want a laugh and you know who they are, drop in on the world's leading Internet "solutions" companies.[2] When you survey these sites, pretend to be a potential customer and ask yourself the following basic questions:

- Does the site succinctly state, without me having to search for it, what the company does?
- Can I quickly determine if this company offers what I'm looking for?
- Does the site attempt to find out about me, my company, the market segment I'm in, my needs, or my interests?
- Am I, the "customer," the center of the site, or is the site simply a long and useless verbal barrage about the company and its accomplishments?
- Do I receive value in return for every mouse click and for the time I spend on every page?

Table 1.1   Questions Every Corporate Web Site Must Answer

Customer Question	Meaning of This Question
Do you know who I am?	Before you start running off at the mouth, you'd better make an attempt to understand who I am, maybe not by name, but by profile: industry segment, business needs, product interests, and so forth.
Do you understand my needs?	You'd better quickly convince me that you understand the unique problems and issues experienced by my business and/or industry; otherwise, you're wasting my time. I should not have to work hard to determine if you can or cannot solve my problem.
Do you have something of potential value to me?	I'm busy, and a lot of your competitors would love to have my business. You have but a few seconds to interest me in what you have to sell—or I'm gone!
Can I trust and depend on you?	Okay, now that you've got my attention, convince me that I should trust you with my business. Tell me about how great you are, your customers, your partners, your processes, and so on. It's okay, I asked!

- Am I confronted by a copious cornucopia of boisterous buzzwords and a cacophony of multi-syllabic circumlocution—or does the site speak clearly and concisely in terms that are meaningful and of interest to me?

DSTination's problem was that potential customers answered "No" to all of these questions. They were met with a lot of business jargon and marketing fluff about the intellectual capital of the company, its approach to solving problems, and other assets the company had at its disposal—and they left. These are points that should be covered and that the potential customer eventually may want to know about, but they were presented without the viewer having asked. Investors, market analysts, and potential partners might be interested, but not a potential customer looking for a solution to a problem. If your purpose is to attract real customers, you must focus on the customer and listen to and understand its questions. Table 1.1 is a list of very basic but powerful questions every corporate site should answer.

To be successful in the competitive domain, you have to establish your presence, your total image in the marketplace. Your Web site can be a key part of this, assuming you do it right. Do it wrong and it will damage your image and detract from your ability to compete. Given this fact, what should DSTination have done differently? Well, Web site design is a topic large enough to fill several books of this size, so we won't try to outline a complete site design methodology.[3] We will, however, offer two observations about DSTination's mistakes that will help you ensure that your Web site enhances your market presence.

Who Are You? A simple approach that DSTination should have taken is to focus on the questions: "Who are you?" and "What are your needs?" Probably the best way to frame the first question is in terms of the likely audience segments into which viewers will fit. Simply offer the viewer the opportunity to indicate which segment he or she is in by clicking an appropriate link. Likely audience segments for DSTination are customers, investors, and potential employees. The home page should have offered links that, with a single click, would have sent these audience segments to a personalized domain within the Web site intended for them alone.

What Are Your Needs and Interests? Once the "Who are you?" question had been answered, DSTination should have moved to the next step, initiating a conversation to answer the question "What are your needs?" For example, the top-level page of the "customer" domain could have "asked" the customer (by offering appropriate links) whether he or she wanted to learn about industries that DSTination has experience with, solutions that DSTination can deliver, or technologies in which DSTination is competent.

Figure 1.1 illustrates how these categories might be organized from an information architecture perspective. An important point to note is that, whether the viewer selects industries, solutions, or technologies, he or she arrives at the same information, but the presentation is personalized to fit the viewer's perspective and natural thought processes. This design is customer- rather than product-centric.

INFORMATION ARCHI-WHAT?

Figure 1.1 illustrates something very fundamental to but unfortunately rare in the Web world: logical, conversational, customer-centric information flow. In contrast to this approach, the design of most corporate sites

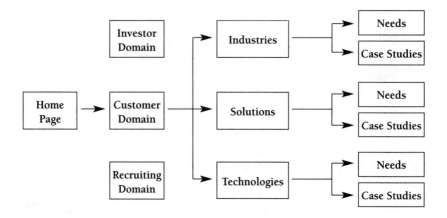

Figure 1.1   Identifying Customer Identity and Needs

is driven by what the competition is doing. The executive sponsors assume that because their competitors are doing it, it must be right. In a recent discussion with a dot-com executive, we pointed out that his company's site had four different navigational schemes, only one of which was built around a natural customer-centric flow. The visual experience is like that of walking into a room and having four salespeople begin talking to you, all at once and all at full force, each without concern for the chaos he or she is creating. The executive responded that he was happy with it because it incorporated the look and feel of sites from several other successful companies and that it just felt good to him. The problem here is the assumption that an arbitrary approach to site design is valid. It is not, unless you are aiming for chaos and confusion. Just as the choice of sentence structure shapes the effectiveness of written or oral communications, the structure of site information flow is critical to the ability to communicate with the intended audience.

Unfortunately, this problem is worsening by the moment with the advent of creative agency influence on the Internet and the misuse of excellent tools such as Macromedia Flash®. To be clear, Flash is a powerful tool for manipulating graphics and text delivered over the Web. However, most uses of this tool reveal an obsession with being "cool" and entertaining, demonstrating a total lack of understanding of the impact on the user. Bob Sundin, the vice president of marketing in our story, was excited when he reviewed his new site because he was rightly proud that through this medium he could say great things about his company in unique ways. What he failed to grasp was that half of his intended audience, the potential customers, were not interested in what he was saying, and that he was speaking to them in a manner that was unnatural and meaningless both to customers who knew his company and to prospects who had no idea what DSTination had to offer.

Who's Minding the Store?

Bob's initial exuberance over the many visitors to the site was simply the euphoria of ignorance. Did Bob know who any of these visitors were? Did he capture any of their names or other information about them? Did he know where they came from? Did he know how much time each person spent on the site and where he or she spent that time? Did he know when or why visitors left the site? The answer to every question was "No."

This problem is not unique to DSTination; in fact, it is more often than not the case. For some reason, when it comes to the Web and technology, companies seem to abandon commonsense activities that would rarely be overlooked in a brick and mortar scenario. Would any legitimate brick and mortar proprietor make a significant investment in marketing programs without measuring the response? Would that same proprietor ignore customers when they enter its stores? This is exactly what most companies do with their Web sites. It is exactly what DSTination did.

No corporation seeking to recoup and benefit from its Web investment should be without tools like WebTrends[4] (www.webtrends.com) or similar software to gather and analyze Web statistics. This type of software will provide you with critical information such as

- How many people have visited your site,
- Who is in your site,
- Who has been in your site,
- Where they came from,
- What they looked at,
- How long they looked at whatever they were looking at, and
- Which page they left from.

Without this kind of critical information, it is impossible to determine the effectiveness of your attempts to communicate with your prospects. Your customers' behavior is talking to you, but you're not listening.

DREAMING VERSUS FORECASTING

Bob was dreaming when he spoke the fatal words, "We're forecasting that the site will bring in about twenty-five prospects per month resulting in somewhere between $1 and $5 million in additional revenue per month, not bad for a quarter-million investment." Where did Bob find these numbers? Was it from experience? Was it from standard industry ratios? Well, it was neither, because these numbers don't exist. Bob got the numbers from the same place that most people in his shoes get them; need we say more?

There are many dangerous myths lying in wait for unwary followers of the Web-land prophets. A common and widely held misconception is the idea of magic conversion ratios that convert the number of hits on a site to projected customer leads, e-commerce sales, or whatever. Let's be clear: This type of thinking is 100 percent certified crap. It has led to millions of dollars of lost venture capital, thousands of dot-com layoffs, and hundreds of devastated entrepreneurs. Even with the recent debunking of these fables by the press, people like Bob continue to believe in them and use them.

Here's the issue. Bob didn't have any idea what the return on investment would be. He did not consider how or why people would come to the site. He did not know what they would do when they got there. Bob didn't have a clue. Should Bob then have just given up and gone home?

No! What he should have done is requested funding for a proof of concept pilot effort. He should have commissioned a high-quality, lower-cost effort that would have allowed him to learn from the behavior of customers and prospects and then determine a larger strategy for the future based on real data. Companies regularly use test marketing for their physical products; why not do the same with their "intellectual" products, their Web sites?

The DSTination case by no means covers all the issues surrounding why Web efforts typically fail to yield expected benefits, but the failure

Table 1.2 Do's and Don'ts for Corporate Web Sites

Never	Always
Never try to build generic or all-purpose communications. If you don't specifically aim our message at something, you won't hit anything!	Always understand and talk specifically to audience segments you are trying to reach in ways that make sense specifically to them.
Never use a monologue if you are trying to have a dialogue. Stop telling and start listening.	Always let your viewers "drive." Offer navigation links that allow viewers to quickly zero in on the infomation they need. And remember, every mouse click tells you something if you're listening.
Never lose sight of the value and impact of predictable information flow. There is no substitute for straightforward communication.	Always screen every graphic and every textual element of your design with one key question in mind: Does this element enhance or detract from predictable communications? If you cannot firmly answer "yes," get rid of the element.
Never assume that your site is having the effect you intended, and that your viewers are doing what you intended. This is like opening a storefront and then going back and taking a nap. Pay attention.	Always use Web site monitoring and statistical analysis tools to validate your assumptions—they are probably wrong! It is rare when customer behavior is predicted and that prediction perfectly follows. You must observe and adjust. Experiment!
Never build a site around popular Web myths. Remember that there's nothing magical about the Web. It's just another means to converse with your customer.	Always build your site around facts. If you don't have the facts, pilot the project and get the facts, then build from there. Listen, listen, listen.

points are extremely common and at the core of many corporate site problems. Table 1.2 recaps the simple do's and don'ts for corporate Web sites.

There is no disputing that the Web can be an extraordinary medium for enhancing conversations with customers and prospects. The problem is that humans have a natural tendency to talk rather than listen, and this medium, for whatever reason, seems to intensify and draw out this stupidity. Shut up and listen!

CHAPTER 2

The Simplicity Trap

If something looks simple, it must be, right? Of course not! We all know that simplicity in appearance or operation doesn't in any way imply simplicity in design or construction; in fact, the world is full of things that appear simple but are in fact very complex. So why is it that the simplistic appearance and ease of use of the Web makes people believe that Web software must be simple? Who knows? The fact is that this erroneous belief is a trap into which the overconfident and unwary stumble every day. Particularly susceptible are those who have been involved in creating what is known as a "brochureware site," which serves up only static pages consisting of graphics and text. Such sites are indeed simple to build, requiring straightforward creative ability and little technical knowledge. Unfortunately, add the seemingly simple requirement that the site interact with the user and complexity increases by orders of magnitude.

The best software looks simple and is easy to operate, but this simplicity is a façade masking the true complexity of the system. Nowhere is this truer than on the Web. Online shopping, for example, has been reduced to a few mouse clicks, but the systems that provide e-commerce capability are extremely complex and costly to implement and maintain. *Beware:* Your experience with the simplicity and ease of your brochureware site is a trap waiting for you as you approach your first transaction-processing software project.

"Okay, I don't have much time, so let's get on with this. I've been told that the corporate Web site you did for us was excellent, something I can't vouch for, since I neither know nor care to know anything about

---

The Story

Company Name	SSE Productions
Industry	Production company specializing in sporting events
Products	Film, video, and still photos
Size	Under $60 million annual revenue
Issues	Current manual payroll and expense reimbursement processing for temporary workers is slow, costly, and error prone
Key Players	Becky Williams, operations manager for SSE
	Doug Keefover, independent consultant specializing in creation of Web sites
	Don Tyler, independent consultant specializing in database design
	Ken Shaffer, independent consultant specializing in Web page design and ASP programming
	Mindy Cox, subcontracted consultant experienced in integration with accounting systems

---

Web sites. Anyway, our COO told me to contact you about helping us solve a problem we have with our temporary workers. You should probably take notes, since this is complicated and I don't want to have to repeat myself."

Becky Williams was all business. Impatient and temperamental, she usually got her way. Now she fought impatience, waiting while Doug opened his notepad and took out a pen. She then continued, "Whenever we have a location shoot, we send a skeletal crew of regular employees with the equipment and then supplement them with on-site temporary workers. On a typical shoot, we'll usually have more temps than regulars. These people have to get hired, scheduled, paid, and have their expenses reimbursed, all of which is my responsibility. They fill out paper forms—job applications, scheduling requests, timesheets, expense reimbursement requests, and so on—that get faxed back to me here. My people have to check the forms for errors, get any errors they find corrected, and enter them into our accounting system. We run two to three weeks behind most of the time, especially in the busy periods. It's a *very* labor-intensive process with lots of room for error. What I need is a system that will let the temps fill out forms online and send them here for my people to review and process. My COO tells me that a Web program is what I need, which is why you're here."

Doug glanced up and nodded. This was exactly the kind of project he had been looking for. He had designed and built several corporate-image Web sites, all fairly simple and straightforward, and he was anxious to do more. He had been hoping for something a little more complex, something that would require a database and some real programming, and this sounded perfect. He would have to hire some contract help to do those parts, but that wouldn't be a problem.

Becky continued for another fifteen minutes, with Doug feverishly taking notes. She gave him copies of all the paper forms, explained some rules about how the forms had to be filled out, and told him about the common errors. She said that the screens should look as much like the forms as possible because both the temps and her employees were used to them. She impressed on him the fact that she wanted this done quickly because another busy period was fast approaching. Finally, she told him that her COO was going on vacation the following week, so she needed time and cost estimates ASAP so that she could get approval before he left.

Becky paused, waiting until Doug stopped writing and looked up. "Any questions?" she asked. Doug replied, "Not at the moment. Tell you what. Let me go away and digest all of this and if I have questions, I'll call you, okay?" Standing, Becky replied, "Whatever. I'll expect your estimates by close-of-business on Thursday." Doug stood and replied, "Sure. No problem." The meeting was obviously over.

Walking to his car, Doug called Don Tyler, a database expert he had met some weeks before. He briefly explained the system and asked Don if he would be able to help. Don replied that he could create both the database and the data access objects. "Great," said Doug. "I know another guy named Ken Shaffer who has done a lot of ASP (Active Server Pages) programming who can do the actual Web pages. With the two of you, and me to do the project management and some of the creative stuff, we should be able to pull this off. Can you meet Ken and me for lunch today?" Don said he could, and they agreed to meet at a local restaurant at noon.

Over lunch, Doug gave Don and Ken copies of the paper forms and explained the system. Don and Ken agreed that it sounded like a great project, one that they definitely wanted a part of. Ken suggested that, given the complexity of the screens and the database accesses needed to implement them, he would need help. He suggested another ASP programmer he had worked with before, and Doug agreed. Leaving the restaurant Doug said, "If you guys can do the estimates on the database, the access objects, and the Web pages by noon tomorrow, I can do the rest, and then I'll roll everything together and get it to the client by Thursday." Don and Ken agreed.

At four o'clock on Thursday afternoon, Doug sat in Becky's office. His proposal was for a four-person team consisting of himself, Don, Ken, and the other ASP programmer Ken knew. "We should be able to have the site up in five weeks at a cost of about $80,000. I suggest we do this on a time and materials basis, which will save you money in the long run." With that, Doug slid a one-page "Contract for Leased Labor" across the desk. "I'll need you to sign this," said Doug. "Assuming you agree, we can start work as early as Monday." Becky nodded. "I've already talked to the COO and he told me that this is my decision, so I guess we can go ahead. I want to look this over, but you can assume that I'll sign, so you should plan to be here Monday morning at nine o'clock sharp."

Work commenced the next Monday and progressed rapidly. The only problem the team encountered was difficulty in getting as much of Becky's time as they needed. They had to rely on e-mail and voice mail for most of their interactions with her, and it sometimes took a day or two for her to respond. Despite this, Doug was pleased and began to feel comfortable that they would complete the site on time. Then, two weeks into the project, his phone rang. It was Ken.

"Don't get me wrong. Don's a great guy and has forgotten more about databases than most DBAs know, but he just doesn't listen. We tell him what we need in the way of access objects, but when we get them it's as if he didn't hear what we said. They don't provide all the data access necessary, plus they're hard to use—we usually have to access two or three objects to get to the data we need. All of this is causing us a lot of extra work, so we're having a hard time staying on schedule. You've got to do something or we aren't going to make the delivery date." Doug agreed to talk to Don and hung up. "Just what I need," he thought, dialing Don's number.

"Doug, the problem is that this system is a lot more complex than these guys have ever dealt with. They don't understand this, so they're blaming it on me. Hell, I don't like having so many objects either, but to do otherwise would be poor design that would cause problems later. It isn't simple because it isn't simple, if you know what I mean." Don paused, and Doug took the opening to respond. "Okay, Don. I know next to nothing about any of this, and since you're the most experienced of the three, I'm going to trust your judgment on this. Maybe you can meet with the programmers and explain to them why things can't be simplified, okay? Help me out here." Don agreed and they hung up.

Two weeks later, things had not improved. Don and Ken took turns calling Doug and complaining, each blaming the other and each warning that the project was falling behind. Finally, at the end of the fourth week, Doug met with the team and together they worked through the project status. From this, they came up with revised estimates to completion. Doug wasn't feeling so comfortable any more.

The next Monday Doug met with Becky and broke the bad news. "Our best estimate is that it will take us an additional three weeks, eight in total. That's also going to run up the costs some, to around a hundred thousand. I'm sorry, but the system is just more complex than we expected." Becky was furious, and let Doug have it for what seemed like an hour. Finally, she calmed down. "Look, I don't want any more screw ups on this. You'd better stay on top of it and bring it in at the end of eight weeks, or we are going to have serious setbacks." Doug assured her that he was confident there wouldn't be any more problems. In the back of his mind, he was hoping he was right.

Doug was rising to leave when Becky said, "Oh, by the way. We're going to be upgrading the accounting system from version 4.5 to version 5.0 next weekend. I don't know if that's going to affect you or not. Is it?" Doug stood looking puzzled, and then said, "I don't know what you mean. We aren't doing anything that touches the accounting system. I can't see why it would matter to us." Becky frowned and cocked her head, obviously confused. "What do you mean that your aren't 'touching' the accounting system? I presume you have to connect with it to get data in and out, right? It seems to me that a new version might affect that." Doug slowly sat back down. His felt cold, his stomach suddenly in a knot. "Now wait a minute. Are you saying that you think we're actually feeding data to and from your accounting system?"

The next fifteen minutes were some of the worst in Doug's life. He couldn't imagine how he and Becky could have miscommunicated on something this important. Becky had apparently assumed all along that Doug knew that the Web site had to integrate with the accounting system. Doug, on the other hand, had never even imagined that she expected that. "It's not an option!" exclaimed Becky. "That was the whole point in doing the system. I can't believe that you could possibly have thought otherwise."

Finally, Doug reluctantly agreed to do the integration, but told Becky that it would cause a lengthy slip in the completion of the system. "How about we move that out into a 'Phase II' of the project?" he asked. "Look," said Becky. "Four weeks from now, I want the Web site up and working *and* it had better be talking to the accounting system, or you are not going to get paid. I don't pay people who don't deliver." Doug realized there was no point in arguing, so he told Becky that he would meet with the team and see if they had any ideas on how to get it done on time. With that, he left.

Don summed up the team's reaction clearly. "You're crazy, man! I've been involved with that kind of integration before, and it isn't pretty. Even with an upgrade, that old accounting system they have was never intended to work with anything else. You have to brute-force your way in and out. If we're going to try this, we need help."

Doug contacted a local consulting firm and explained his need. As luck would have it, they had a programmer available who had quite a lot of experience doing integration work on accounting systems. The programmer, Mindy Cox, reported to work the next day and quickly assessed the systems. The next morning she handed Doug a three-page document and said, "Here are the obvious things that we'll have to do to integrate the two systems. I can guarantee you that there are more, some of which we won't discover until we're under the covers." Doug looked at the list and his heart sank. Even with no experience in the area, he knew from the length of the list that another schedule and budget slip was in his future, and he knew it would be painful.

Doug, Mindy, and the other three team members met that afternoon. They went over the change list and eventually came to agreement on who would do what, and in what order. They then did quick estimates on the tasks and concluded that the effort would add at least another three weeks to the project. Doug told them of his meeting with Becky, and that he wasn't ready to "go back into the lioness's den" just yet. He asked them to increase their efforts on the site by increasing their work schedule to ten hours per day, six days per week. They grudgingly agreed.

Doug called Becky the next morning and told her that the integration effort would add at most a few days to the project, pushing the delivery date to the end of the ninth week. Becky protested but, to Doug's surprise, remained calm and accepted the slip. Doug then warned her that the "burn rate" had gone up due to hiring the additional programmer and having to put everyone on overtime. That was more than Becky could handle. "Your big fat profit on this project just got skinny. I'm not paying for another programmer *or* any overtime. You said four people working normal hours, and that's all I'm paying for. You're going to just have to eat the rest." Doug tried to argue but lost the argument to a loud click—Becky had hung up on him.

Unfortunately, the integration effort turned out to be more complex than first thought, so much so that at the end of the eighth week, Doug found himself once again on the phone with Becky, telling her that the site wouldn't be finished on time. Becky blew up. "Look, I am sick of this. I want a definite completion date and definite cost. The way this is going, you'll still be around this time next year and will own half the company!" Doug answered, "Becky, I assure you I want this project to be over as badly as you, but it's turned out to be so complex that we can't even give you a good estimate on when it will be done. Almost every day the team seems to discover something new. I really don't know what to tell you."

"Well, I know what to tell you," Becky replied. "I'm not going to pay you another penny until the site is working, and if you decide to do something foolish like stopping work, you'll find yourself in court so fast it will make your head spin. I want my site up and working, integrated with the accounting system, and I want it by the end of the month." Doug protested, telling her that he had to be paid so that he could pay his team, but Becky responded by saying, "That's your problem, not mine." Again, a loud click—another argument lost.

Over the next three weeks, the team got the site working—barely. It seemed as if everything that could go wrong did, and then some. At the end of the period, Doug made the decision, over some protest from the team, to go live with the site. As expected, there were problems, most minor and easily fixed, but enough to cause Doug to have to keep his entire team on the project. Doug watched as his profit margin shrank below zero.

After two weeks, the system seemed to stabilize and Doug breathed a sigh of relief. Only one hurdle was left, to complete the end-of-month processing through the accounting system. Doug watched as the processing started, hung around for about twenty minutes, and then walked down the street to a coffee shop. He had just gotten his latté when his cell phone rang. It was Becky. "You'd better get back here fast. Something's wrong. The end-of-month run has already taken twice as long as normal, and it's still going. I think you've screwed up my accounting system."

By the time Doug returned, the payroll and expense reimbursement registers were printing. Becky was standing next to the printer, looking at the printout and shaking her head. As Doug walked up she turned to him and said, "I was afraid of this. Look at this—here's a temp getting paid three times for the same thing, and here's a guy that I know we fired, but he's showing up as still working for us. And look at this, here's someone named 'Ax3bz' being paid over $20,000. *Hello?* I don't think we have anyone by that name on the payroll." Doug felt sick.

Doug called Don and Mindy, who came in and began studying the data in the accounting system's database. After about a half-hour, Don pushed back his chair and said, "I hate to tell you this, but we have a real problem. The database is pretty much hosed. I can go through and clean up some of the obvious issues, but there's just too much inconsistent data to know what is right and what's wrong. I don't think it's worth the effort." "Ah, crap. I was afraid of that," said Doug. "Let's go find a conference room and see if we can figure out what to do. No, better than that, let's get out of here so that we can talk without being interrupted by Becky. Let's walk down to the Coffee Haus."

For the next hour the trio brainstormed how they might recover. Doug's phone rang three times, all three from Becky, and he ignored it each time. Finally, Doug sat back and threw up his hands. "Okay, so there's no way for a fix without manually cleaning up the data. So what do we do? Mindy?"

"Well, our worst-case fallback is to restore the accounting system from backups made the day before we started feeding our stuff into the database. We would then use the recovery feature of the accounting system to reprocess everything the accounting people have done, after which we dump the transaction log from our system and manually enter all of the transactions in the log that appear to be 'reasonable.' It's an ugly solution, but it's fairly safe." Doug sat for a moment, and repeated the phrase "fairly safe" in his mind a few times. Rubbing his temples with his fingertips, he sighed and said, "Okay. I'll go see Becky. Don, call the other two guys and get them in here. We're all going to have to pitch in to get this done."

Four days later, after almost nonstop work by Doug, his team, Becky, and the accounting department, the database had been restored and all of the transactions from the site log had been manually entered, after which the end-of-month processing was restarted and ran successfully. After a lengthy period of checking the output, Becky turned to Doug. "It looks right, but I'm going to have my people check everything with a fine-tooth comb. I can tell you this: We aren't going to go through that again! You've got another month to get everything working right, and you'd better not screw it up this time."

Exhausted, Doug headed for home. As he turned onto the highway, his cell phone rang. Digging it out of his coat pocket, he looked at the display and saw "Becky Williams." He hesitated, and then flipped it onto the passenger seat. After a moment, it stopped ringing and then shortly thereafter it beeped—Becky had left a voice mail. Doug sighed. "Why did I ever take this gig?"

ANALYSIS AND CONCLUSIONS

This project, truly a project from hell, was a classic example of both developers and the project sponsor being completely ill-equipped and unprepared to identify the complexity of the effort, let alone understand how to mitigate it. The frequency of this type of foolishness is increasing dramatically as more and more projects are sponsored and managed by nontechnical professionals and staffed by zealously ignorant technologists. These factors, coupled with the current widespread misconceptions about Web technologies, promise that the frequency of these types of failures will continue to grow at an exponential rate. Following are a few key things our unfortunate characters could have done to avoid the mess they found themselves in, and how you might avoid finding yourself the owner of an expensive but worthless system.

AN EXPEDITION WITHOUT A GUIDE

How did Becky select Doug for this project? Did she determine if he had prior experience with the level of software development she was requiring?

Did she determine if he had any experience at all beyond graphic design of Web sites? No. She simply assumed that because he was a professional in the realm of Web technology he could do anything required in the development of a Web application. It does not take much to understand that this was foolish and irresponsible on her part and on the part of those like her who fail to perform due diligence on the technology projects they commission. Just because someone has the words "Web" or "Internet" in his or her resume does not make that person qualified to solve the specific problems you are facing, even if he or she has years of experience in the area of expertise.

To be fair to Doug and his team, all of them were competent professionals and could have performed well given proper leadership and direction. Without it, the outcome was predictable. Although each member had a reasonable amount of experience in his or her specialty, no one on the team possessed basic project management or application design and architecture skills. Without these skills and experience, the team was traveling in unknown territory without a map or compass. When they got lost, none of them had the necessary tools to find the way out. Becky essentially found an eager explorer in Doug and commissioned a predictably fatal expedition to a place none of them was prepared to go.

NAVIGATING WITHOUT A MAP

Another key problem in this story was Doug's complete lack of any framework to deal with the complexities of this project. In his case, the presence of a sound software development process would not have solved the problem of inexperience, but it might have helped Doug realize early on that he was in way over his head. At the very least, Doug should have documented Becky's requirements and had her sign off, acknowledging that the document represented the extent of the work he would do for her. It is likely that she would have noticed the absence of accounting package integration, and Doug would have recognized early on much of the true complexity of this project.

BEWARE BACK SEAT DRIVERS

Doug made a fatal mistake at the beginning of this project that should concern both technology professionals and the buyers of their services.

Doug allowed Becky to dictate her role and level of involvement and availability to the project. If you hire a technologist to solve a problem and expect him or her to manage the project, then go into hiding as Becky did, you are asking for trouble. Because of the inherent complexity of transactional systems, much care must be taken up front to ensure that all parties have a clear understanding of what the system must do. Both graphic and verbal descriptions are a powerful way to mitigate project-crippling misunderstandings. In this case, Becky's dictatorial nature imposed an approach on the project that would not work in any scenario, and even worse, Doug allowed her to do so. Any experienced technology professional or project manager would have insisted that the vision and scope of the project be defined and documented up front. Instead, Doug allowed Becky to set the project into motion without first establishing rock solid clarity about project direction and desired outcomes. Becky dictated an approach and set a tone that ensured the project's eventual failure.

HYPE-BASED OVERCONFIDENCE

Revolutionary technology gains have been defined as a solid 10 percent or more increase in productivity or other key financial measures. Airplanes, for example, represent a revolutionary leap in transportation. Computing hardware is another example of continuous quantum leaps in efficiency. Do we have similar gains with the Web? Certainly we do, but only in the area of information delivery, not in the area of transaction facilitation. This bears repeating: The Web and related technologies have not solved traditional problems developers have faced for years with building complex transaction-oriented systems, and most e-commerce systems are just that. Anyone who claims otherwise is simply deluded, or even worse, attempting to deliberately deceive. One of the most influential thinkers in software in the late twentieth century was Frederick P. Brooks, Jr. In his renowned and timeless work, *The Mythical Man Month,* he states, regarding the complexity of software:

> Software entities are more complex for their size than perhaps *any other human construct* because *no two parts are alike.* . . . [I]n this respect software systems differ profoundly from computers, buildings, or automobiles, *where repeated elements abound.*

Digital computers are themselves more complex than most things people build; they have a very large numbers of states. This makes conceiving, describing, and testing them hard. *Software systems have orders of magnitude more states than computers do.*

Likewise, a scaling up of a software entity is *not* merely a repetition of the same elements in larger size; it is necessarily an increase in the number of elements. In most cases, the elements interact with each other in some non-linear fashion, and the complexity of the whole increases much more than linearly [emphasis added].[1]

Becky, her COO, and Doug all shared the same radically erroneous perceptions regarding the complexity of Web software and transactional systems. Becky and her COO's perceptions were based on the apparent ease of the development of SSE's corporate brochureware site and whatever other media and professional influences had echoed this message of ease and simplicity. Doug's perception was similarly based on ignorance. Although he had greater exposure to the world of software development, he had no direct experience in working on a transaction-oriented Web site. He seriously underestimated the difficulty and was not equipped with the necessary training, experience, or tools to surface and deal with this complexity.

Any time a Web site must interact with a user or database, perform complex logic, or exchange information with other software applications, it has moved out of the world of static content and into the world of transaction-processing software. What Becky and her boss failed to understand was that a transactional system is significantly more complex than the information delivery and display on their brochureware site. Their ill-fated confidence was further bolstered by the fact that Doug seemed to be perfectly comfortable with their assumptions.

Technology project sponsors must understand the difference between static and dynamic applications. This concept bears repeating: Brochureware sites consist of primarily static[2] information display, such as text in a browser. These sites are basically online ads that provide product and company detail. Dynamic or transaction-oriented sites are those sites that interact with the user or other systems to facilitate a transaction or service. Using experience with a static site as a basis for estimating the time and cost of building a dynamic site is akin to using experience building a toy balsa wood airplane to estimate the effort needed to build an F-16 fighter. The skills required are vastly different, the core logic is exponentially more complex, the execution far more difficult, and the consequences of mistakes or oversights much more severe.

CONSULTING FEE STRUCTURES AND PROJECT BEHAVIOR

A brief word is in order here about approaches to project fee structures. In this case, Becky absorbed 100 percent of the risk on this project by allowing Doug to work on a time and materials basis. Put simply, this meant that if Doug were wrong in his estimates, Becky would pay more than she expected. Assuming Becky had the ability to understand that Doug was talented but inexperienced and that she still wanted him for the project, she should have attempted to mitigate this risk by asking Doug for a fixed fee bid. This would have accomplished two things: First, it would have likely frightened Doug into a less confident state and forced him to pursue greater detail and accuracy up front regarding project parameters and expectations. Second, as Doug pursued greater detail in project definition, this would have caused friction early in the project for both parties and may have signaled to both of them that they were heading for trouble.

There is no perfect project fee structure that could have magically solved the problems of this or any effort; however, fee structures can help surface issues and place risk ownership in the right place to drive healthy self-protection mechanisms and increase project rigor. Fee structures always dictate where the risk on the project rests. It is ludicrous to absorb risk beyond your capacity to mitigate it. If you totally outsource a project as Becky did, there is no reason for you to absorb the risks of a time and materials approach. Conversely, if you want to maintain a high level of control and management of a project, no project sponsor with an ounce of real experience would agree to a fixed fee project. Although not an exciting topic, project fee structures can be a powerful tool when leveraged by a wise sponsor.

CONCLUSION

The Internet is simple, right? We can just throw together some Web software and solve our problem, can't we? By now, you know that this is obviously bad thinking. Table 2.1 lists a few key points to remember when working with these "simple" software projects.

Ultimately, there were many problems with this project that doomed it to failure from the start, but the core issue was the parties' lack of understanding that Web software is software, and software is complex and difficult to develop. It is an indisputable fact that building quality transaction-oriented software that truly meets the needs of you and your customers is just plain old time-consuming difficult work, regardless of whether it is based on Web technology or whatever the next latest-greatest technology savior may be.

Table 2.1   Do's and Don'ts for Outsourcing Software Projects

Never	Always
Never engage a consultant on a project who cannot clearly demonstrate experience with similar projects, software, or systems. This was plain and simple negligence on Becky's part. Although Doug will take all the blame, what Becky did was equivalent to putting her five-year-old son behind the wheel of her car on the freeway and expecting to make it home alive.	Always ask consultants for specific demonstrations of experience in the form of other completed software products, project planning documentation, and references. "Small" projects like this can turn into huge disasters when the wrong person is driving, either on the sponsorship or project management side of the fence.
Never underestimate the complexity of software. No matter how easy it looks, always deliberately attempt to prove yourself wrong by diving as deeply into the details as possible as early in the project as possible. Document the assumptions upon which the project schedule and budget are based. This is often painful work, especially to action-oriented professionals; however, it will hurt a lot less than a failed project.	Always approach software with the assumption that it is difficult to build and manage. With this approach, you might later find that it is less difficult than you expected, but to approach software from an "it's easy" perspective is always a precursor to disaster.
Never, never, never assume that software professionals understand or will incorporate undocumented requirements. Becky assumed that Doug would foresee the integration of this application with the accounting system. Even if Doug was experienced, he might not have understood	Always document and get sign-off on requirements. One of the most powerful methods of exposing misunderstandings between team members is deliberate and constant communication feedback loops. The most effective method in closing these loops is paper and ink with a sig-

(Continues)

(Continued)

the requirement without Becky calling it out. Although sound software development processes might have surfaced this requirement, it was utter incompetence on Becky's part to make the assumption that Doug would just "know" it to be necessary.

Never underestimate the power of risk ownership and risk sharing. Good service providers will always be willing to share in the risk-reward equation. Time and materials contracts are not a bad thing, but by definition they ensure that the customer owns 100% of the risk. If you want a lot of control, then you should own the risk; if not, change the fee structure of the project and be prepared to allow the service provider to dictate project approach and fully manage the project to completion.

nature block at the bottom. Using this method can at times be uncomfortable, but it rarely fails to get a project sponsor and a project manager on the same page.

Always structure project fee parameters around a deliberate approach to risk management. If you want to completely shed the performance risk of a project, structure a fixed fee arrangement and get out of the way. If you want a high degree of involvement and control, structure some form of time and materials agreement. However, this approach assumes you have the experience necessary to identify and mitigate risk and absorb significant project cost overruns when faced with unforeseen complications.

CHAPTER 3

Technology Myopia

As we write this, the business landscape is littered with the rotting re-mains of thousands of technology ventures. These deaths seem to have many unrelated causes but in reality share several common threads. Young executives with strong technical backgrounds but little business experience led many of these startups. These technocrats may have been brilliant in the latest technologies, but without critical business experience and educa-tion, they made dangerous executives. They often confused product with business, accepting a popular myth that if they built a world-class technol-ogy product, the world would beat down their doors to buy it.

John Raeder, a well-known entrepreneur and venture capitalist, re-cently observed[1] that there is a continuum of technology-space business concepts ranging from "pure marketing plays to pure technology plays," and that most failures occur at one of the extremes. To succeed requires striking a balance somewhere in the center of this continuum, a balance that requires experienced executive leadership. Obviously, any business betting its success on technology must have great technology; however, it may not be so obvious that the very focus required to deliver great tech-nology, when applied to executive management, can also doom the busi-ness to failure. Technology must take a back seat to core business and cus-tomer needs, not the other way around. Getting these priorities out of order practically guarantees that you'll end up with a great product and a ruined business.

The Story

Company Name	Provithon, a spin-off of ParCor Networks
Industry	Technology
Products	ASP focusing on a complete e-commerce solution
Size	250 people (mostly consultants) and $0 revenue
Issues	Opportunity to capture large share of e-commerce outsourcing
Key Players	Richard Bohl, president of Provithon
	Mikhail "Mickey" Dubrovich, CTO of Provithon
	Kristi Moore, director of marketing for Provithon
	Carolyn McLean, chair and CEO of ParCor

Carolyn McLean built ParCor Networks into a leading provider of a range of network services including broadband, co-location, and server and network management services. As a result, ParCor was on the inside of the early ASP boom, providing services to several of the early players. Carolyn studied the ASP market aggressively, absorbing everything she could about an industry that appeared to be the next big technology wave. After careful deliberation, she prepared and presented a proposal to the board, pointing out that ParCor's experience and vast network capability could provide a huge competitive advantage in this new market. "This is the next big thing and, unlike the dot-com wave, in the ASP model there are real customers with real money to spend on a recurring basis." She continued, making a convincing argument that their best course would be to fund a new company and give it enough independence to be able to move quickly. The meeting ended with the board's pledge of support.

Carolyn immediately began a search for a chief executive officer (CEO) for the new company. She recognized the importance of time to market and felt that someone with experience as a top dot-com executive would understand this and have the qualities needed to make it happen. She quickly found what she was looking for in Richard Bohl, chief technology officer (CTO) of one of the most successful dot-coms in the region. She was struck by his energy, charisma, and mastery of technology, and convinced him to accept the position of CEO of "Provithon," as the new company was called. She gave him free rein in making final staffing decisions, suggesting only that he give serious consideration to any ParCor personnel who applied.

Richard's first official act as CEO was to call Mickey Dubrovich, his assistant at his previous company. Mickey was one of the most brilliant people Richard had ever known, and he couldn't imagine a better choice for CTO of Provithon. Mickey agreed and, over the next three weeks, Richard and Mickey built their executive team. Many were former co-workers, and practically all had experience in one or more dot-com startups. A notable exception was Kristi Moore, who Carolyn recommended to head up marketing. Richard and Mickey weren't convinced that she was the best choice for the position but felt that it was a good political move to honor Carolyn's suggestion.

While other members of the new executive team dealt with a myriad of new business details, Richard, Mickey, and their senior architects basically went into hiding. Several weeks later they emerged with a detailed architectural design for the entire system. By building a robust infrastructure based on ParCor's existing network and data center operation and by leveraging ParCor's proven network operations and server management processes, they would have a sound platform for the applications. The core application suite would provide all the necessary software to host an e-commerce business end-to-end. This suite consisted of three e-commerce applications, a customer relationship management (CRM) application, components from two enterprise resource planning (ERP) packages, and an accounting package. Provithon's programming staff would integrate all of these applications, resulting in a seamless package of services.

Richard and Mickey presented the system architecture and project timeline to the team. They emphasized that only best-of-breed hardware and software components were being used, which brought smiles and nods from the technically astute members of the audience. Their timeline showed five months of development, with the first "live" customer by December. Finishing their presentation, they opened the floor to questions. There were a number of questions about the technology, the schedule, and the budget. Kristi listened quietly until the very end. She finally raised her hand and, after Richard nodded at her, she spoke. "First of all, I have to admit that I don't really understand all of the technology, so maybe my question doesn't even make sense, but how do we know that the set of products we've chosen are what our future customers are going to want? I mean, shouldn't we do some basic market research and find out what people want, how much they're willing to pay, and whether they're actually interested in buying our services?"

Richard stared at her blankly for a moment, opened his mouth, then closed it without speaking. Mickey's gaze could best be described as a glare. Finally, after what seemed like an eternity to Kristi, Richard answered. "That's a very good point, Kristi. Actually, we have a very senior technical team with enough experience in the field to know what our customers are going to want, but if you'd like, you can talk to some of them and verify that." Then, turning back to the rest of the room he said, "Any other questions?" Kristi flushed.

Work commenced immediately. Because of the massive integration effort required, Mickey brought in four consulting firms, two to help build the infrastructure and to set up the network and server operations, and two others to integrate the applications. Initially there would be forty consultants working on the system, but Mickey warned Richard that there would probably be double that number before they were finished. Because of their best-of-breed strategy, the application components chosen were ridiculously expensive, but ParCor was used to spending hundreds of millions on infrastructure and thus had little reason to question the exorbitant costs.

Two months later, things were going poorly. The integration project was behind schedule and over budget, and there were more than a hundred consultants on the project, with the number increasing almost daily. It was simply taking a lot more effort than anticipated to get things connected and working together. Richard found himself having to get involved and help Mickey, who was swamped. Both were working long hours, and it usually wasn't pleasant work. It was on such a day that Kristi walked into Richard's office with a big smile on her face. She excitedly told him that she had a very strong prospect that she would like Richard and Mickey to meet. The prospect was Berners, a leading national retail clothing chain, and the company was ready to sign as soon as a couple of things could be worked out. "What are the 'couple of things' that we need to work out?" asked Richard impatiently. "Well, I'm not sure I understand, which is why I want you to meet with them, but I believe they want us to replace one of the e-commerce applications with something else—uh, I don't remember the name. They also said they have an ERP application from another vendor in place already, so they want us to use it instead of what we have right now. The timing is ideal, because they want to be up by December 1, which fits our schedule perfectly."

Three days later, Kristi, Richard, and Mickey met with Berners's director of information technology (IT). On the way to the meeting, Richard was confident that he could convince Berners that the applications Provithon had chosen were better than what Berners wanted. Leaving the meeting, his confidence had been shattered. "Mickey," said Richard. "He's not going to budge on this. If we want the business, I don't think we have any choice. This is going to be a huge contract, so it's worth the time and cost to try to please him." "Oh, great!" replied Mickey. "You mean that instead of working eighteen hour days six days a week, I'm going to get to go twenty-four by seven? Look, this is going to cost us a lot. To hit the December deadline means that we're going to have to bring in an army of consultants." Mickey argued more, but he knew he had already lost. He knew that ParCor's board was getting nervous about the absence of good prospects and was beginning to put pressure on Richard, so they couldn't lose this one.

The next two months were like a bad dream. Integrating the components to meet Berners's requirements turned out to be far more difficult than anticipated. In particular, the ERP components they wanted were from a small vendor who hadn't designed them to work with other applications. Consequently, the job of integrating them into Provithon's suite required more than twenty programmers working long hours of overtime. The deadline was only a month away when the team began testing. Nothing worked—nothing. Richard was worried.

"I need to talk to you about something," said Kristi, standing in Richard's door. Richard nodded toward a chair. "I've sent you a couple of e-mails about this, but I guess you haven't had time to read them, or to answer my voice mails." Richard looked annoyed. "Kristi, what do you want?" She continued, "My sales team and I have been working really hard to close business, but we keep running into the same problem. Every time a company starts to warm up to us, they look at the set of applications we've chosen and start asking if we can change this or that. It's just like Berners: They have their own ideas about what they need, and don't seem inclined to change their minds. I know that you and Mickey are busy, but I really need your help on this."

Richard cut her off. "Look. I appreciate your problem, but neither Mickey nor I have time to help you right now. Talk to me after December 1; until then, I just don't have time. Hell, you're a salesperson. Stall them. Make promises. Lie to them. Do whatever it takes." Kristi could see that there was no use in arguing, so she left. "Stall until after December 1," she relayed to the sales team.

Late on the evening of November 15, Mickey walked into Richard's office and plopped down. "How's it going?" asked Richard, not really wanting to know. "It's not going," answered Mickey, "and I don't think it's going to go, at least not by December 1. It isn't possible. We might as well stop kidding ourselves and admit it. Tell Berners that we can probably have them up by January 15." The next ten minutes were the most uncomfortable in Richard and Mickey's relationship, as Richard brought up one idea and then another, and Mickey quashed each. Finally, Richard said, "Okay, I'll call Berners tomorrow and give them the bad news. This is going to cost us, you know. A six-week slip will cost us about a million and a half in penalties, unless Berners just happens to be in a nice mood."

Two days later Carolyn received a call from ParCor's general counsel. "I just got a call from an attorney representing Berners. It's about Provithon, whom I'm about to call, but I thought I'd give you a courtesy call first. Apparently Richard called their director of IT and told him that the system is going to be six weeks late. Berners's attorney wants to meet with me and discuss payment of the nonperformance penalties built into the contract. You may recall, there is a penalty of $250,000 for each week we are late, or $3 million if we default." When they finished their conversation, Carolyn dialed Richard's number. "I just got off the phone with our attorney, about a call he received from Berners's attorneys. We need to meet, today if at all possible. I want you, Mickey, and Kristi in the meeting. Call me with a time." She hung up.

At the meeting, Carolyn summarized the situation: "So just to be clear, you're telling me that it is impossible for you to deliver on time, that you can't deliver before the fifteenth of January. Is that correct?" Richard nodded. Carolyn was about to continue when Mickey interrupted. "Actually, I'm going to have to be honest with you. The way things have been going, I'm not at all sure we can make January 15. I certainly wouldn't bet anything on it that I couldn't stand to lose. Maybe mid-February or early March; I really don't know anymore."

There was a long silence while Carolyn studied Mickey's tired face. She then turned to Kristi. "So tell me about sales. Who else do you have in your pipeline?" Kristi glanced at Richard, then began, "Well, we have four potential clients that I think I could sign, one of which is even larger than Berners, but each wants significant changes to the system, and I don't know what to tell them."

Carolyn spoke, "Mickey, are we in a position to promise changes to these clients?" Mickey replied, "This is the first I've heard about these four clients. Kristi, why didn't you talk to me about them?" Richard interrupted. "It's my fault. We were so busy that I didn't want us to stop and lose focus, so I told Kristi to stall the clients until after we delivered Berners. At the time, I thought we would deliver by December 1, but now things are different. I guess we can meet with them, but I just don't see how we can do estimates and work up contracts with Berners hanging over our heads. We can try, I guess."

"Not so fast," said Carolyn. She stood and began pacing. "Let me see if I understand. It seems to me that there are four important points. First, the Berners system will be at least six weeks late, thus costing us at least $1.5 million in penalties, probably more. There is, in fact, a possibility that the total penalty could exceed the $3 million default figure, making default the least costly avenue. Do we agree?" She paused to observe three nodding heads, then continued, "The second point is that signing even one additional client is at least six weeks off, probably more, and each will require a significant additional investment to bring into production. Is that correct?" Again she saw three nods.

"Third, assuming we have to continue to make changes for every client, we will end up with multiple systems to maintain and enhance, meaning that our ongoing system maintenance and support costs will be a lot higher than we projected. Agreed?" She continued without pausing. "Finally, your business plan called for profitability in the sixth quarter of operations." Carolyn stopped and, looking at Richard, said, "That's not going to happen—not even close. Correct?" Richard nodded and replied in a somber tone, "That's correct."

Carolyn stood at the window and looked out for a moment and then, without turning, said, "It appears to me that we should consider defaulting on the Berners deal. That's probably our safest and least expensive bet. Furthermore, we need to take a hard, honest look at how, or maybe a better word is whether, we should continue operations. Shutting down would be a huge write-off, but it may be our best choice." Turning back to the table she continued, "I want you to get back to me by tomorrow afternoon with specifics on everything we've discussed. I want realistic estimates of when the Berners system can be made operational and how much it's going to cost. I also want to have projections on sales, the cost and time required to bring up new clients who want modifications, updated figures on maintenance and support, and a revised projection on when Provithon will be profitable. I'll call a special board meeting for Friday and we'll decide what to do." She picked up her things and left.

The next Friday, Richard, Mickey, and Kristi sat in the boardroom while Carolyn revealed the grim story to the board. She had slides and charts and masterfully laid out the dilemma. The board members then began a grueling two hours of questioning, with most of their questions directed to Richard and Mickey. Finally, Carolyn said, "Well, I think we have the facts. Thank you for your time. Now if you three will excuse us, I'll call you when we decide what we're going to do."

Two hours later Richard's phone rang. It was Carolyn. "We aren't really certain what the long-term outcome will be, but we've decided that the best thing in the short term is to default on the Berners deal. I want you to suspend all development immediately. Send the consultants home, cancel anything you've ordered, and stop payment on everything you can. Our attorneys will contact Berners and try to negotiate down the $3 million penalty. I want to meet with you and your management team first thing next week to determine if there is any way to keep the company afloat. Any questions?" They talked for a few more moments, then Carolyn said, "Oh yes, I almost forgot. Tell Kristi to call ParCor's vice president of marketing—she knows him. He wants to talk to her about options in case this doesn't work out. I don't know the details, just tell her to call him." With that, she hung up.

Richard sat in his office, dreading the call to Mickey that he knew he had to make. He was also dreading what he knew this meant for Mickey and him. Unlike Kristi, he was pretty sure ParCor wouldn't have any "options" for either of them. He sighed, picked up the phone, and punched "Mickey" on the speed dial.

ANALYSIS AND CONCLUSIONS

No bones about it: The goal was an end-to-end e-commerce solution; the outcome was an eight-figure screw up. As always, it seems a bit too easy to pick a problem apart with hindsight; however, the true root causes of a problem are rarely as obvious as they seem. Richard and Mickey really made some excellent decisions at a micro level. Their best-of-breed strategy was viable, given their assumptions. Carolyn's recognition of the need for technology-savvy leadership was dead-on for a company almost solely dependent on successful technology execution. Ultimately, there was a true need in the market for e-commerce technology infrastructure solutions. So where did they go wrong? Let's take a look.

PRODUCT, PRODUCT, PRODUCT . . .

Most entrepreneurs who start businesses from the ground up are product-centric. This is natural, normal, acceptable, and, in many cases, necessary. How else can you get a business off the ground, sell to people who have never heard of you before, and make a profit? The entrepreneur at this stage must believe in and focus on the product or service. The irony is that the same myopia and focused energy required to successfully launch a new product, service, or business have put many entrepreneurs out of business.

Why? In this case, it is because of a serious misperception of market demand. The product may have perfectly solved a specific and legitimate need, but if the timing is not right, if the need is narrowly distributed, or if the price is not right, the product will not sell. If the entrepreneur does not have sound judgment about the actual demand for the product, then regardless of the quality of the idea, the entrepreneur is doomed. In contrast, the successful venture typically has one advantage over the unsuccessful: the ability to accurately identify true business trends that are large enough to justify developing a product or service.

It is almost impossible for a business executive involved in the market every day to tap into a true mega-trend, so how likely is it that someone from outside the market would be able to do so? NOT VERY! In fact, it is absolute to-the-core stupid to think that this is even possible. So then why in the hell would any sane executive or investor place a technologist at the helm of a business in which he or she has no prior related business experience? As strange as it may seem, many dot-coms and technology-centric ventures have done and continue to do just that. Brilliant technologists who have great instincts about how to solve previously defined needs with technology are thrust into situations where the needs are not defined, only to find themselves fried by the intense heat of market forces.[2] Now, to be fair, Richard and Mickey were set up by Carolyn's faulty assumption that ParCor's core competencies could be leveraged, making it easy to gain a dominant position in the burgeoning ASP market. However, their lack of experience served to dramatically amplify the problem to the tune of tens of millions of dollars.

"Okay, you start coding while I go see what the customers want." This is a classic cartoon line designed to illustrate the tendency of technologists to consider customers' needs lightly, if at all. This is exactly what happened here, but on a massive scale. The market did not want the product, but the builders of the product were obsessed with giving it to them anyway.

TECHNO-CENTRICISM

Another twist on the product-centric theme is techno-centricism, the tendency of many technologists to operate as if the world revolves around and serves them and their technology rather than vice versa. This too was at the center of the mindset of this team and at the core of their product-centric zeal. It is utterly amazing, but predictable, that their first few weeks on the job were spent designing technology architecture. The obviously false belief behind their zeal was that if the technology were world class or best of breed, people would buy it. This demonstrated an extreme lack of understanding of the true nature of business and the market. Had they spent some time studying the market and understanding what potential customers really wanted, they would have identified the varied needs and could have adjusted their business plan accordingly. As it was, they attempted to build an incredibly capable "one size fits all" system that turned out not to fit anyone.

A good example of this can be found in the ERP world. You are unlikely to find a single large ERP system implementation that was simply installed out-of-the-box without modifications. Why? Because ERP systems touch and affect so much of what is unique to each organization's business infrastructure. There is no single system flexible or full featured enough to meet 100 percent of the needs of every business. So when a company like Provithon integrates two ERP systems, an e-commerce system, a CRM system, and so forth, then tries to sell it as an end-to-end solution, that company is in incredibly perilous waters! The application suite the team ultimately proposed would essentially affect almost every single iota of any customer's business infrastructure. ERP systems are hard enough to implement by themselves; this team created a monster similar to the Hydra of Greek mythology. No one—not the best technologists in the world, not the smartest business people—could have made this idea work as they designed it.

Richard and Mickey chose a best-of-breed strategy that drove the price of their services through the roof. Who then would be able to pay for this service? Probably only the Fortune 1000, or maybe the Fortune 5000. Wouldn't you think that such companies would already have huge investments in existing ERP, CRM, or other core packages that would significantly overlap the functionality Provithon provided? This market segment is even more likely to have existing systems or components that are already heavily integrated into their organizations. Richard and Mickey were not just out of touch on this one, they were nowhere near reality.

Investors and entrepreneurs must be wary when elevating brilliant technologists to executive status. They are not brilliant technologists because they spend time in the marketplace understanding customer needs and marketing solutions. They are brilliant technologists because they immerse their entire being in technology, largely ignoring the market. Let technology leaders drive technology, and business leaders drive business. They must and can work together, but they will rarely survive roll reversal.

BIRDS OF A FEATHER FALL TOGETHER

One huge mistake made by Richard that contributed to the company's market-related blind spot was to quickly and comfortably surround himself with fellow technocrats. Carolyn wisely inserted Kristi but, because of

Richard's bias, to no effect. Richard did not understand or appreciate his own weaknesses enough to rely on Kristi for understanding and perspective that he did not have. Frank Mendicino, a technology venture investor, recently commented, "Startup companies are human chemistry experiments."[3] Without the right balance of talent, drive, and teamwork, the team can draw a company so out of balance that it is doomed to fail from the start.

NINE WOMEN AND A BABY

Another critical mistake that revealed Richard and Mickey's inexperience was their handling of labor on the project. Their constant addition of consultants cost them millions of dollars and only served to put their project farther behind. Although both of them were very experienced technologists, neither had experience building or integrating this many systems of this magnitude. Neither had been around the block enough to intuitively understand the old software development adage that nine women can't have a baby in a month.

CONCLUSION

Ultimately, a few minor but critical strategy adjustments would have solved many of this team's problems. There was legitimate market need and demand for a product like the one they were building, and there was sufficient talent on the team to produce the product. Table 3.1 is a summary of the traps they fell into and what they should have done to turn this multi-million-dollar loss into a successful venture.

Every day, in every major newspaper, there are ads for CEO, CIO, and CTO positions from new and existing companies. Too often, the ads read more like ads for programmers than for executive business leaders. This is a deadly mistake. Leadership skills required at the executive level are radically different than those required for building and managing quality software and software integration projects. Get the right people in the right roles or you will find yourself facing insurmountable problems.

On an equally important plane, many dot-com failures have come at the hands of product-centric zealots who foolishly ignore the wisdom

Table 3.1 Do's and Don'ts of Technology and Leadership

Never	Always
Never hire a technologist to do the work of a business leader or manager. It would have been better to hire a technology-illiterate but business-savvy leader of a lingerie company than to hire a technologist to head this one up. Without a basic understanding of even the most basic questions to ask, Richard was completely ill-equipped to lead this company.	Always recruit leaders who understand the market. There are a handful of world-class technologists who are also world-class business people, but this is an extremely rare combination, and you and I are not likely to meet one in our lifetime. Find business talent to run the business and technology talent to support the technical execution.
Never build an executive team around a single skill set. It would have been smarter for Kristi to run this company than Richard. At least their product set would have been more likely to meet demand. In hindsight it is obvious that this team was lopsided.	Always build balance on your executive team. Don't be fooled into thinking that because a company's product is technology dependent, the deck should be stacked with technologists. Technology companies, to survive and thrive, must have people like Richard and Mickey. However, they should build the technology, not run the business.
Never assume that labor will solve large systems integration problems. This is certainly a side note in this story, but it represents a mistake that is often repeated. Because of the nature of technology, there is a point at which adding bodies causes more problems than it solves. In this case, adding bodies radically inflated the burn rate and caused significant confusion and frustration on the project.	Always staff projects to critical path. Staffing decisions should be made on the basis of deliverables, project scheduling, and actual staffing needs. If you ever see a team growing rapidly without clear documentation and thought behind it, put a stop to it quickly—you are in trouble.

gained by marketers of the past. They get a truly great idea, sell it to unwary investors, and then launch in a blaze of glory right into a brick wall. If the damage were limited to the entrepreneur, that would be fine. But if you have ever had to hand a pink slip to a friend, the thought of this foolish melee is enraging. There is no excuse for the stupidity that the dotcom dummies have thrust upon the industry. There is no excuse for arrogantly ignoring tried and true marketing and business practices. The "new rules" are simply a recipe for disaster, and those who continue to propagate them are completely irresponsible.

CHAPTER 4

Ready, Aim, Aim, Aim . . .

Launching a significant technology venture within an aging corporate structure can be an uphill battle. Although leveraging corporate assets can be powerful, particularly when contrasted with the constant scrapping required of most entrepreneurs, the support always comes at a cost rarely obvious at the outset. Many "internal entrepreneurs" learn a painful lesson: Aging organizations seldom understand how to take advantage of opportunities in a market moving at lightning speed.

Although the time-to-market madness exhibited by many recent Web ventures proved to be wrong and had deadly consequences, it remains true that one of the single most significant risks faced by technology or Web-centric ventures is the ability to get to market and gain revenue traction quickly enough to survive. There are two reasons for this. First, if you are going after a market niche that is currently unpopulated, you're probably in a race to be "first to market." There are a lot of smart people out there looking for ways to capitalize on the Internet, so you can't assume that you're genetically superior or the sole owner of your idea. If you fail to get to market quickly, you risk becoming a "me-too" venture with little appeal to investors and little competitive differentiation for consumers.

Second, if you are entering a market in which you already have competition, you can't afford to slowly ramp up at the normal pace of business. In the traditional business world, there is almost always room for another competitor, so you can start your business, do some advertising, and once

---

The Story

Company Name	Wheeling National Bank
Industry	Banking
Products	Consumer and commercial banking services
Size	280 banking locations in 3 states
Issues	Difficulty in reselling repossessed vehicles
Key Players	Jim Billings, director of consumer credit for the home office branch of Wheeling National Bank
	Larry Barling, Wheeling's president
	Terry McGee, programmer for Wheeling

---

you have cash flow, begin to slowly grow your business, often taking years to achieve respectable size. This will not work in the Web-world. You've got to have a "vertical launch," achieving "escape velocity" quickly, or you'll watch your money dribble away on ever-escalating expenses, never achieving sustainable revenue or market share momentum. Let's take a look at a real-world example.

"I'm really sorry, Ms. Johnson, but I've got no choice. You haven't made a payment in four months, and we can't carry your loan any longer. Would you please bring the car in before 3:00 today?" Jim Billings, director of consumer credit for Wheeling National Bank, closed his eyes. He hated this part of his job. He remembered Sheila Johnson, and how excited she had been when she signed the loan papers. It was her first new car. "If you want it, come and get it!" came the reply. The line went dead.

Jim opened his eyes. Larry Barling, Wheeling's president, stood in his doorway with his arms folded. "Bad day?" he asked. "Yeah," said Jim, "another repo." Larry slipped into the chair in front of Jim's desk and said, "Another one? That makes about twenty for the quarter in this branch alone. The numbers don't look good. We've got to get smarter about our loans, but we've also got to figure out a way to recoup more from our repos."

"Funny you'd say that. A couple of days ago I went to one of those auction sites and discovered they had a section of the site devoted to selling used cars, so I clicked around for a while. I was surprised—the prices people were offering were really pretty high. I had the thought that we might list some of our repos there. I'm not sure that it's a good idea, but it might be worth looking into. I planned on asking Terry about it." "Hmm . . . it doesn't strike me as a great idea," said Larry, "but let me know what Terry thinks."

Terry McGee was one of those people who seem to live technology. Six months after joining the bank, Terry single-handedly created the Wheeling Web site, a site that was admired by everyone who saw it. He sprawled in a chair in Jim's office. "Sure we can! I can help you list a car or two right now; wouldn't hurt to try." Jim agreed, and with Terry's help, listed a 2000 Cherokee and a 1999 Intruder on eBay™. Jim knew that if they could just get wholesale plus $500, they would do okay. Less than an hour later a bid came in on the Cherokee. Jim smiled; maybe this would be the solution to his problem.

Three days later, Terry was in Jim's office after the auctions closed. Both cars had sold, and for more than Jim could have gotten through traditional channels and with far less effort. Jim was looking at a list of autos, talking about which cars to auction next, when Terry interrupted him. "Hey, let's start an auction site of our own," he said. He paused for effect. Jim stared back blankly. "Look, eBay is an incredible auction site," Terry continued, "but I think we could offer some things they can't. One big advantage we would have over them is that we offer loans. We could set it up so that the bidder could fill out a loan application as part of the bidding process, and by the time the bidding was over, the loan would probably be approved. We would overnight the papers to the buyer, who would sign and return them, and the car is sold. What do you think?" Jim smiled. He really liked Terry.

That afternoon, Jim and Terry sat in Larry's office, first explaining their eBay experience, then outlining their idea for a Web site. Larry remained silent until they finished. "Interesting idea, fellows," he said. "Now let me build on it for you. If this will work for our bank, it will also work for other banks and credit unions and anybody else who has to do repos. We could let them list vehicles on the site, charging a listing fee plus a percentage of the sale price, and we would get the financing. I like it." He paused and smiled, then continued. "Tell you what, guys. If you want to try to pull this off, bring me a business case. I need to see how much the up-front investment would be, plus revenue and cost figures for the first three years. I want you to include everything, right down to paper clips. Jim, you know what it needs to look like. If I like what I see, I'll take it to the board and see what they think."

Over the next three weeks, Jim and Terry put in long hours, mostly after closing, building the business case. Jim did most of the work building the revenue model, and Terry drove the cost detail. It wasn't the kind of work he enjoyed, but he hung in there. "Hell, I could build the site in less time than it's going to take us to get approval," he grumbled. Jim agreed, but he knew that they had no choice.

When they took the business case to Larry, he said, "Look, guys. You don't have any basis for your revenue figures. I mean, revenue is dependent on the number of people who will come to the site, and you're guessing at that. I can't take this to the board. You say you're going to concentrate on radio ads, right? Well, then you need to do some research on the effectiveness of radio ads and then do visitor projections from that. That's the only way you can get at solid revenue figures."

Jim and Terry were both tired, and Terry was feeling impatient. Terry's face was flushed as he began, "You're right. We could do all of that and more, but would it change the fact that this is a great idea? I mean, we know this is going to work. Let's just get the site up and we'll be able to *see* the visitor numbers and revenue." Jim interrupted, "Terry, there's a lot of truth in what you're saying, but Larry's right. We can talk to our ad agency and come up with improved projections. Larry, we'll get back to you next week."

They were back in Larry's office a week later. Jim presented the new revenue projections, which were even higher than the ones of the previous week. Larry had a lot of questions, and disagreed with a couple of their assumptions, but finally leaned back in his chair. "Okay, let's leave the revenue question for now. How about costs? This worksheet is based on what you call outsourcing to a hosting company. I presume that outsourced means that we would be using someone else's equipment, right? What if we bought our own servers instead? What would that do to costs? It seems to me that we could save money by doing it ourselves."

This was Terry's area, so he spoke. "I've considered that. We could buy servers, but we need a fat data pipe to the Internet so that we'll have the bandwidth we need for all the graphics and photos on the site. That means that we would have to put our servers at a co-location facility. We would also have to maintain the hardware and software ourselves, which means we would have to hire people. The total cost of that would probably exceed the cost of using a hosting company, plus they have all the security and system maintenance procedures figured out, making a site they host more secure and reliable than one we could build ourselves. Hosting is our best bet."

Larry sat expressionless for a moment, then leaned forward. He put his fingertips together. Jim knew what that meant. In a measured voice, Larry responded. "You said 'probably.' You're guessing again. This isn't about computers—it's about money. We're a bank—we don't guess about money. You guys might as well face the fact that we're not moving forward until you give me facts!"

A month later, Jim and Terry left Larry's office smiling. "Finally!" Terry exclaimed. "No time to relax, though," said Jim. "We have to get Larry's changes on paper and create a presentation for the board. We've got a lot of work in front of us."

Jim was sweating. He had barely started his presentation to the board when he was interrupted by questions. It only took a few moments for him to realize that several board members knew nothing about the Web, so Jim's presentation simply wasn't making any sense. He had spent the last hour trying to explain how online auctions worked, what hosting and co-location meant, their revenue model, and several other things. Larry looked on without speaking. Terry tried to help a couple of times, but mostly stayed silent. Finally, the chairman said, "Well, I think we've spent enough time on this. Gentlemen, thank you for all you've done. We'll discuss this and get back to you with our decision."

Jim was depressed. Terry tried to cheer him up, but Jim was having no part of it. "Hell, we just wasted two months of hard work. Those old bastards wouldn't know a Web opportunity if it bit them on the butt. Crap!" Jim left work early, complaining of a splitting headache.

Three days later Larry stepped into Jim's office. "Congratulations, the board has approved funding to get the project moving. They're giving you a budget of $25,000 to get started." "Did you say twenty-five?" Jim asked. "Yes," replied Larry. "They said that they wanted to see what the site was going to look like before they invest any more. Isn't twenty-five enough to get you going?" Jim stood. "No. Hell, the business plan showed the Phase One site costing over $150,000. What am I supposed to do with $25,000?" "Well," Larry interrupted, "I'd suggest you start by working on your attitude." He turned and left.

Jim and Terry sat in Jim's office. Jim fidgeted with a pencil. "Okay," he said. "We agree that it doesn't make any sense to start building the site on $25,000. So what do we do?" "Well," Terry replied, "the way I see it, the board just doesn't understand what we're trying to do, plus they don't seem to have much confidence in our ability to do it. One way to get past that would be to build a prototype that showed them what the site would look like and how it would work. Maybe if they saw something tangible they would understand."

"Can we do that for $25,000?" Jim asked. "Sure," Terry replied, "but understand, it won't be a working Web site. It will look like one, but most of the functionality will be faked. That shouldn't matter, so long as Larry and the board understand that it's just a prototype. I could do the entire thing myself but it will take forever due to my workload. To speed things up we'll have to contract some of the work to a Web firm, but I will do as much of the work as I can to keep costs down." "Okay," said Jim. "I'll talk to Larry and see what he thinks. In the meantime, figure out who you want to contract with and see if you can get an estimate from them. If we're going to do this, I want to get it done fast."

Three weeks later Jim and Terry stood behind Larry as he "opened" the Wheeling "Repo-Junction" Web site prototype. They and one contractor had worked long and hard getting the prototype finished. Larry had been on vacation for the last two weeks of the period, so this was the first time he had seen their work. Larry frowned and said, "*Repo-Junction*? Who came up with that? Sounds like a South Broadway used car lot. And where did you get this color scheme? Our bank colors are blue and white."

An hour later Jim and Terry stood in the hallway outside Jim's office. "I guess it would be safe to say that he didn't like it, huh?" said Jim. "Like it? He hated it!" exclaimed Terry. "You know, sometimes that guy really pisses me off. He's the pickiest damned person I've ever met, and he always seems to wait until the last minute to tell you what he doesn't like. Here we are almost three months into this, having spent most of our money, and we're no closer to having a site up than when we began. What do we do now?"

"Well, a lot of what we have is still useable. We just have to make some changes. We'll spend the rest of the money getting the graphics redone, and we'll just have to do the remaining work ourselves," said Jim. "Do you really think it will do any good?" asked Terry. "I mean, I'm not sure we can ever please Larry."

After two long weeks of after-hours work, Jim and Terry once again stood by as Larry navigated the prototype site. He quickly found fault with first one thing and then another. After about ten minutes, Terry burst out, "This is a freaking waste of time!" and stomped out. "What's wrong with him?" Larry asked, looking genuinely puzzled. "He's tired," replied Jim, "and so am I. Larry, this doesn't need to be perfect. It's a prototype, intended to give the board some idea of what we're proposing." "I'm not asking for perfect," Larry replied, "but it has to be a lot better than this."

The next day Terry resigned, leaving the prototype project stranded. Jim met with Larry, asking for more money to bring the contractors back in to finish the job, but Larry declined. He also refused the idea of showing the prototype as-is to the board, saying, "It's just not ready for the boardroom. If you want the board to see it, you're going to have redo it." Jim left, shaking his head. He didn't know what to do.

The next morning Larry walked into Jim's office and spread a newspaper on Jim's desk. He pointed at an article and said, "Check this out." The story headline read, "Broadview Auctions Repos Online." Larry quickly scanned the article. It was about a new Web startup named "Repo Central," funded by Broadview Trust, which was auctioning repossessed autos.

While Larry waited, Jim opened a new browser and typed the URL. The home page was similar to the one Jim and Terry had designed—better looking, perhaps, but similar. After a moment of navigating through a few pages, he said, "Damn. They've beaten us. They're doing almost exactly what we wanted to do. Hell, here's even a page where other banks and credit unions can apply for membership. Damn!" "Well," said Larry, "at least that solves our Web site problem. All we have to do is join their site and let them do all the hard work. I don't mind that."

After a few more moments, Larry left, leaving Jim staring at his computer screen. He felt exhausted. How many hours had he spent on this, and it was all wasted.

ANALYSIS AND CONCLUSIONS

Was this chapter hard to read? It took extreme restraint to avoid severe editing. However, that would have made the point less obvious and would have defeated our purpose. Our only solace was the hope that those of you who have lived or are living a similar scenario would hang in there and get this far and perhaps pick up a tip or two that will help you survive.

Jim and Terry were bright individuals but absolutely clueless when it came to the internal business and external market realities of launching a Web-based venture. However, their idea was powerful, and if they could have been better prepared for battle, they might have succeeded. Let's dive in and dissect the traps they fell into.

FAILURE TO UNDERSTAND THE BATTLE SPACE

Jim and Terry had a great idea that surfaced out of real pain and problems, and they had a legitimate solution via Web technologies. Terry, in particular, was a talented technologist and showed accurate insight at several key points within our story. Unfortunately, not unlike many of these scenarios, the problem was not in the isolated realm of technology but in the broader understanding of market forces in the Web space.

Jim's first and most damaging oversight was his failure to accurately assess his organization's ability to move quickly in support of a Web venture. If he had taken a moment to step back and gain a better perspective, he would have recognized the need to gain support for a spin-off, a nimble, entrepreneurial organization rather than another department within an aging bureaucratic company. Unfortunately, Jim did not recognize this dot-com killing risk and thus suffered the consequences. Wheeling had not created a new product or service in years. It was ludicrous to expect it to move quickly in this case.

The risk of not getting to market quickly often significantly outweighs all other business and technology risks and is frequently ignored or severely underestimated. This underestimation is particularly common for ventures attempting to launch out of mature and often out-of-touch industries. When attempting to spin off a Web venture, the manager must be acutely aware of the inherent industry structures and norms and be prepared to mitigate them with offsetting strategies. In Jim's case, a sound approach would have been to gain agreement from Wheeling to create an entirely new organization outside of the excessive control systems of a larger, more established organization. Note that in this story we are talking about a Web venture, but the same is true in other fast-growing areas of technology where entrepreneurs are attempting to develop and spin off new products and services.

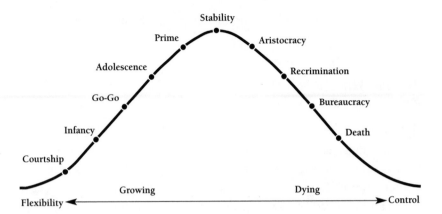

Figure 4.1   *Source:* This perspective is directly derived from Dr. Ichak Adizes's seminal work, *Managing Corporate Lifecycles* (Paramus, NJ: Prentice Hall Press, 1999), p. 322. © 1999 by Ichak Adizes. Reprinted with permission.

Corporations are simply a group of individuals organized around common goals. Because of this, the lifecycle of an organization mirrors the collective maturity of the individuals in it. Consequently, there is a relatively predictable path that all organizations follow to a greater or lesser degree. Figure 4.1 is an accurate reflection of the maturation phases of any organization that lives out a complete, normal lifecycle.

Wheeling was an organization in the aging phases of corporate life. These phases are generally characterized by excessive internal operational issues, with the goal of mitigating all personal and corporate risk. Consequently, when faced with the need to flex, move quickly, and respond to the market, Wheeling did not even know how to act. Because of this, Wheeling was not able to accurately understand or capitalize on any new idea, let alone one so far out of its comfort zone. So how would we advise Jim?

CAREER COUNSELING

If Jim had a true entrepreneurial bent and job offers elsewhere, we would have advised him to take one of them. Trying to pursue an entrepreneurial venture within a rigid corporate structure is an extremely painful and often career-limiting move. A technology-centric venture is hard enough to get going in the best of cases, let alone trying to launch one when your organization is trying to squeeze the life out of you from day one.

TEST THE WATERS BEFORE
YOU ASK YOUR BOSS TO THROW HIMSELF IN

If Jim did choose to follow this risky path, he should have pursued it in a way that anticipated and significantly mitigated the risks that the board would naturally surface. From the beginning, he and Terry took an all-or-nothing stance. They didn't know what to do when they were provided with partial instead of complete funding. However, this is exactly what they should have asked for in the first place. They should have pitched a safe, short-term pilot project that would allow them to get to market quickly and prove the concept with real cash flow. The trick would be to get the site up with limited but essential functionality, leverage current advertising channels and customers, and show Wheeling how "painless" it is to make money over the Web. The next big hurdle would be to get sufficient funding to ensure adequate speed and momentum toward the acquisition of market share in their segment.

A related aside is that Jim, other than some minor Web surfing and talking with his internal technical guru, did zero research in the auction world. He didn't know the space, he didn't know the players, he didn't know typical industry margins, he didn't know who was winning or losing and why, and he didn't even know if anyone else was doing what he was proposing. On top of that, Larry also missed this point entirely, an unforgivable oversight for a senior executive. Does the Web make people stupid, or what?

LEVERAGE THE WORK OF OTHERS

Many Web ventures have failed at the hands of exuberant developers and ignorant managers who are unaware that they are building something that already exists. Again, within an operationally focused organization like Wheeling, risk is perceived as a very bad thing, to be avoided at all costs. The team could have greatly mitigated the perceived risk by proposing a partnership with eBay or some other organization that had already heavily invested in the necessary technology infrastructure. We can't stress this enough. Some of the best ideas and companies have gone down the tubes because they chose a "build" rather than a "buy" or "partnership" strategy.

CONCLUSION

Although this story was more about company politics and market strategy than technology, the fact is that every project faces some degree of political risk. In this case, that impact was unanticipated and fatal. Table 4.1 summarizes what should have been done.

Table 4.1   Do's and Don'ts of Technology Project Sponsorship

Never	Always
Never attempt an internal project without a clear understanding of where your organization is in its lifecycle. Without this invaluable perspective, you are not likely to effectively position and thus gain support for your idea. A good approach to this is to assume you are coming in from the outside pitching a brand new business idea to an investor. With this approach you are much more likely to recognize and mitigate internal risks and thus provide your sponsors with a far greater feeling of comfort and predictability.	Always give serious thought to the maturity of your organization when selling an idea, especially an idea that might be perceived as high risk or "new." What is most important to your organization: saving face, mitigating risk, conquering new markets, or increasing market share in existing markets? Leverage the same momentum and mental models toward the selling of your idea. The step from being an employee of a company to launching a new venture within a company is huge. You must understand where you are if you are to successfully communicate, sell your idea, and enjoy the benefits of sustained support.
Never launch a techno-centric venture without a clear understanding of the market space. Jim failed to gain a clear understanding of the market and was thus extremely vulnerable to serious business speed and scalability problems.	Always understand the battle space you are going to compete in. Following is a short list of questions you must ask and answer: • Who is already in the space? • Who is winning and why? • Who is losing and why? • Has anyone invested in parallel technologies or ideas that might support your venture with minor adjustments? • Who is getting all the venture capital dollars, and why?
Never build when you can buy or form a partnership to gain the functionality or	Always attempt to find partners in your space that can provide you with the func-

(Continues)

(Continued)

business advantage you need. Your well-intentioned internal technology team will always tell you that they can build it faster, better, and cheaper. This is rarely, if ever, true. It is never true if several companies in the space have already heavily invested in R&D on the problem and are willing to work with you. Don't spend your money on development when you could spend it on marketing, sales, or necessary business infrastructure.

tionality you need. If there are none in your space, stretch a little and review other industries that may have similar problems and solutions to them. Believe it or not, most of the time you will find a product or organization you can lean on to get you off the ground much faster and in a much more predictable manner. If Jim and Terry had taken this approach, their path to profitability would have been much more clear and convincing to the Wheeling board.

The entrepreneur starting a technology-based company from the ground up faces huge challenges and has only a small chance of success. It is natural for the "intrepreneur" to believe that starting a venture within an existing company provides fewer challenges and greater chances of success. Nothing could be farther from the truth. The challenges and risks are different, but both scenarios should be approached with equal trepidation and a healthy dose of paranoia. To do less practically guarantees disaster. If you don't know the market, and you are oblivious to the dangers within your own internal battle space, you are just plain wasting your time.

CHAPTER 5

Mars and Venus

John Gray[1] is not likely to write a book on this one, but the gulf that separates artists and engineers is at least as wide and deep as that between men and women. Artists and engineers think, act, and work differently, and often don't even like or respect one another. "So what?" you ask. "Why should I care?" Well, it wouldn't be a big deal, except that anyone building modern software needs the talents of both groups, and the conflicts between them are increasingly at the root of software project failures. Whenever they have to work together, there will almost always be a clash of cultures. Compromise and balance are necessary for these two groups to work together successfully, but this particular compromise is difficult to achieve.

Artists focus on the "creative" aspects of building a site, whereas engineers focus on "technology." Cohesive teams made up of creative and technology professionals are creating the great software of our day, but it's not as easy as it sounds. The almost-assured collision between the two groups presents a management challenge that is often unanticipated and thus unmet. Our story documents just such a situation, one in which a pre-initial public offering (IPO) company stakes its future on a composite team of artists and engineers, but no one manages the mix.

The Story

Company Name	CommMerica, a growing pre-IPO cell phone reseller
Industry	Communications, retail
Products	Cell phones, service contracts, related products and services
Size	$10 million
Issues	Need to put "sizzle" on company to enhance IPO
Key Players	Samuel Goldman, VP of marketing for CommMerica
	Dan Hopkins, owner of Hopkins Creative, a creative marketing design firm
	Amy Butler, project manager for Hopkins Creative
	Lynn Armstrong, project manager for Zorbix, a Web technology firm

---

"Great work, Dan. My thanks to you and Amy, and to your team. It took you a while, but you've finally captured the look that I was after. This is exactly what I've needed to show investors. I'm getting tired of drawing pictures on legal pads—this is great!" Samuel Goldman, vice president of marketing for CommMerica, a fast growing wireless services reseller, leaned back and crossed his legs. He was obviously pleased with the portfolio of Web page layouts before him. It had taken Amy and her team five weeks to reach this point, a process made painful by Samuel's perfectionist nature, but Amy was proud of the result. Samuel continued, "Okay, so Dan, tell me about this company you want to bring in. Who are they, why do I need them, and how much are they going to cost me?"

Dan Hopkins had founded Hopkins Creative, a marketing-oriented creative design firm, four years earlier. The company had grown rapidly and now had an enviable list of clients. Dan's focus on customer satisfaction had paid off; most of his new customers came through referrals, a fact of which he was very proud. CommMerica was one such client, and Dan was determined that Samuel would remain a happy customer.

"The company is Zorbix," he replied. "They're a subsidiary of an engineering firm, specializing in the back-end technology side of Web site creation. They're the best there is at building e-commerce sites, which is the kind of expertise we need to design and build the customer account management part of your site. We could probably get it done without them, but we'd have to bring in contract programmers and it would probably actually take longer and cost you more. Trust me, it's in your best interest that we bring Zorbix aboard."

"Dan, this has nothing to do with trust and everything to do with business. This site is going to put the sizzle on our IPO. Without it, we're just another 'me-too' wireless company. This site has to be done right and delivered by January, so anything that might affect our ability to do that is serious business—like hundred-million-dollar business. If you say you need this Z-whatever-their-name-is company to give me my site on time, then do it. Just make sure that they understand the situation."

The next day Dan and Amy contacted Zorbix and explained what they needed. That afternoon in a conference call, Zorbix and Hopkins agreed to divide the project into two subprojects, a "creative project," which Hopkins would handle with Amy Butler as project manager, and the "back-end technology project" to be handled by Zorbix. Lynn Armstrong, an experienced project manager for Zorbix, would lead the technology project. Amy would have overall project management responsibilities, with Lynn reporting directly to her. They agreed that since the Zorbix team was located halfway across the continent, they would have regularly scheduled conference calls on Monday and Thursday of each week, beginning the next Monday. In the meantime, Amy would send all the project's work products, including budget and schedule estimates, to Lynn for her review.

The next Monday morning at the agreed-upon time, Lynn called the conference number Amy had e-mailed her. She entered the proper code and was greeted by an auto-message telling her that she was the first participant. Ten minutes later, she called Hopkins's main number and got their receptionist, who said that she had not seen Dan or Amy yet. Lynn left a message to have them call and returned to her desk. Forty-five minutes later, Amy called. Amy started an apology, but Lynn interrupted. "Your e-mail said 10:00 A.M. Eastern time, which is when I called. Did you mean Central Time?" Amy noticed the edge on Lynn's voice. "No, I meant Eastern. I'm really sorry, but traffic was terrible this morning. How about we reschedule for 2:00 P.M. Eastern time? That will give Dan time to get here and settle in. Will that work?"

Lynn hung up the phone and took a notebook from the shelf above her desk with "CommAmerica Project Log" printed on it. She glanced at the entry she had made earlier, recording the failure of the Hopkins team to make the conference call. She then entered the date and time, and recorded a brief summary of her conversation with Amy. She flipped to a tab entitled "Lost Time," entered the date, a start time of 9:00 A.M., and an end time of 1:00 P.M., then under "Reason" she wrote, "Amy and Dan failed to make the morning conference call. We have rescheduled to 1:00 P.M." She returned the notebook to the shelf, carefully aligning it with the other notebooks there.

The conference call didn't go well. Lynn, setting the mood, opened by saying that at Zorbix, people make meetings, even if they have to conference in on their cell phones. She then began to grill Amy with questions about the project: How had the budget and schedule estimates been arrived at, what were the specific deliverables, when were they due, who would sign off on the deliverables, who was tasked to do what, how much was budgeted to each activity, how were costs going to be captured and measured? At first, Amy tried to reply to each question, but found it difficult because she had no real answers. After a while she became withdrawn and silent.

Then Lynn moved on to the work products that Amy had sent her. She asked why Hopkins had produced their example pages on paper rather than as actual HTML pages. Amy tried to explain that Hopkins had always done layouts as storyboards, but Lynn ignored her and continued. She pointed out numerous shortcomings in the pages, particularly in the area of navigation and their use of colors, and stated that the copy was, in her opinion, "weak." At that point, Dan interrupted and said, "Look, Lynn. It's obvious we have different opinions on this project, but the simple fact is that the site we've proposed is what CommMerica needs. Samuel agrees, and we're wasting time talking about it. We're in control of the creative project, and you've got the technical project. I think you should focus on your job and we'll focus on ours." After that, there was a short discussion on what needed to be done next, and the call ended. Lynn replaced her logbook on the shelf.

Over the next three days Lynn and her lead architect worked out the task-level details of the technology project, including who would do each task, how long each would take, the interdependencies with other tasks, and external dependencies, particularly those relating to Hopkins's creative project. When Lynn completed her budget and schedule estimates, she found both almost 50 percent higher than Amy's figures. Lynn led off with this on the Thursday conference call.

"I'm not sure how you came up with the budget and schedule estimates for the back-end project, but as you can see by the plan we sent you, your estimates are way off." As Lynn paused, Dan interrupted. "Actually, Lynn, I'd like to ask you to walk through the detail with us. There are a number of items that aren't clear."

The next hour was a long one. Lynn went through her project plan line by line, explaining what each meant, why it had to be done, how she had come up with the estimated task duration, and what the dependencies meant. Dan and Amy had a few questions at first, but then fell silent. When Lynn finished, there was a lengthy pause, after which Dan said, "Okay. Tell you what, we need to talk about this and get back to you tomorrow morning."

The next morning Amy called. "Dan couldn't make it in this morning. He asked me to relay to you that we can't ask the client for a 50 percent increase in budget for the technology component. He asked that you go through your plan and see what you can eliminate, then get back to us." Lynn's voice was taut and cold when she spoke. "Look, there are no optional tasks in the plan. If you'd like to go back to the client and find out what features he can do without, we'll gladly revise our estimates. I've got another call coming in. Get back to me when you decide what you want to do."

Lynn hung up. She sat for a moment, then called her lead architect. "We're probably going to have to cover for Hopkins," she said. "Let's keep all of the graphics we can, as well as the general look and feel they came up with, and start from there. Get our design people together and come up with a revised plan. Assume we are going to take over all of Hopkins's assignments. I just have a feeling that this thing is going to blow up soon, and I want to be prepared to move."

Amy sat across from Dan. Dan was speaking, "Amy, we have no choice. I'll talk to Samuel and see if we can get a 25 percent increase for the back end. Maybe that will be enough for Lynn. If not, we'll just have to take the rest out of our margin. I can't see a way around it." Later that day Dan called Samuel. Blaming Zorbix, he asked Samuel for a budget increase to cover the "overrun." Samuel was livid. "The budget is not negotiable. I want everybody in my conference room Monday morning at ten o'clock, and they'd better come armed with facts. I used to be a consultant myself—I know how this game is played. You get the customer to the point where they have to depend on you and then you start demanding more. There is no way that is going to happen to me. I want the facts!"

On Monday morning, Samuel walked into the conference room with deliberate nonverbal intensity. He paused and looked around the room. Lynn was sitting at the opposite end of the table, looking strangely calm. Samuel was angry. "Okay, now what is this crap about a budget overrun?" Lynn, without speaking, opened her briefcase and pulled out a stack of bound documents. She passed them down the table and waited until Samuel opened his, then began speaking in a calm, purposeful voice.

Lynn reviewed what had transpired to date, placing emphasis on the lack of rigor in doing the original budget and schedule estimates. She then went through Hopkins's design, pointing out numerous problems. Dan and Amy interrupted several times, but Lynn simply ignored them and continued. She then went through the project schedule task by task, explaining each and pointing out what would happen if any were eliminated. Finally, she passed out copies of pages from her logbook and went through her interactions with Hopkins, showing how ineffective they had been at managing the project and pointing out the amount of lost time that was attributable to them. She summarized, "Look, we're a professional software engineering firm with a proven track record on projects like this. I'm sorry to have to be so blunt, but this project has been and continues to be badly mismanaged, and until that is corrected, we're all wasting our time and," turning to Samuel, "your money."

After a moment, Samuel looked up from the papers he had been studying. Looking at Dan, he said, "So?" Dan hesitated, looked at Amy, and then said, "Samuel, we've worked with you for several years. You know us, and you know you can trust us. Maybe we aren't as methodical as Zorbix, but we have always delivered on our commitments. Lynn has surfaced some things that we definitely need to look at, but I don't see that this changes anything. I suggest that Lynn, Amy, and I get together this evening and work through these issues and report back to you tomorrow morning." Samuel nodded, and then said, "I agree, but I'm going to follow my gut and make a change. I'm going to make Lynn the overall project manager. You and your people have done a great job on the customer experience part, but that's behind us. Most of what remains to be done is in Lynn's court, so it makes sense for her to take the lead." Dan frowned and shook his head slightly, but remained silent.

That afternoon, Lynn took charge. She made it clear that from then on the team would conform to Zorbix's approach. She gave each of them a copy of the "Z-One Process" documentation and suggested that they familiarize themselves with it as quickly as they could. She went on to explain that their process required that complete project documentation be created and kept up to date. The first document that had to be completed was a "Preliminary Analysis & Design" document. "My team completed their part some time ago, but the creative section is empty. You have a week. Nothing on the creative side moves forward until it's complete."

Over the next week, Amy and her team worked to complete their part of the document, but they had no experience and found it difficult to put on paper what they usually held in their minds. They became confused and discouraged when Lynn called and told Amy that she was returning their first draft. "You have holes in here I could drive my car through. I want the update by Monday. If you don't complete it by then, I'm going to have to escalate this to Goldman." When Amy repeated the conversation to her team, her design lead interrupted and said, "Screw this. I'm off this project, one way or another. I'll quit before I'll do any more work for that . . . " He stopped, but everyone completed the sentence in their own minds. Amy and Dan tried to reason with him, but to no avail. Rallying the remainder of the team, they worked through the weekend, finishing the document late Sunday afternoon. Amy apprehensively e-mailed it to Lynn.

An hour later Amy got a call on her cell phone. It was Lynn. "The document you sent me is better, but is still missing key components. We don't have time to wait on you any more, so I'm going to have one of my people finish it. Your next job is to finish the page templates and get them to us by Friday morning. You've put us behind schedule, and *my* projects don't get behind schedule." Amy tried to tell Lynn that it wouldn't be possible to complete all the templates by Friday, but Lynn cut her off. "This is not negotiable. If you can't get them done by Friday, just say so now and I'll put my creative people on it." Amy backed down. Later that evening she called her team and asked them to please get to work early the next morning, because they had a deadline to make.

Lynn opened the conference call the next morning by announcing that Samuel would be joining them. "I just talked to him and he's going to be a few minutes late. I thought that since he's our executive sponsor, he should attend these meetings." Samuel joined a moment later. Lynn then proceeded to do a status update, during which she informed Samuel that Hopkins's difficulty with getting the analysis and design document done had put the schedule in jeopardy, but that by working overtime they would catch up by the end of the week. She made it clear that the critical item for the week was the completion of the page templates, and said that Amy had assured her that they would be done by Friday morning. Amy said nothing.

Amy and her team spent a grueling week completing and refining the templates. They finished late Thursday night and e-mailed them to Lynn. Amy told the team to take the next day off, something she planned to do herself. Her cell phone rang the next morning at 9:30. She saw that it was Lynn and ignored it. A few minutes later, she picked up the voice mail that Lynn had left. "I received your templates and forwarded them to my team. They told me that they are unusable and I have to agree. It would be easier for my people to redo them than to try and use them as they are. Call me and tell me what you're going to do. If I don't hear from you by noon, I'm going to pull the template tasks over to our side and have my people do them."

Amy called Dan and explained the situation. Dan assured her that she shouldn't worry. He said he would call Samuel, explain the situation, and have Samuel call Lynn and calm her down. He called back in about a half-hour. "Well, it seems that Lynn got to Samuel before I did. He was pissed, and told me that Lynn's team has already done page templates in anticipation of us not delivering. He said that as near as he could tell, we weren't adding any value to the project, so we could consider our part of the contract terminated. He went on to say that because of our screw ups, the site might not be done on time, which would probably mean they would delay their IPO. He said that if that happened, he might have to take legal action, but that in any case, they're going to withhold payment of what they owe us until the site is up and working. At that time, he will decide what, if anything, he owes us. Maybe he'll calm down, but it doesn't look good right now."

They talked for a few minutes longer and then Amy hung up the phone. She knew that Hopkins couldn't stand to lose the revenue, much less be sued, and felt that she was to blame. She sat staring out the window for a while and then turned to her computer. She began an e-mail. "Dan, please accept my resignation from Hopkins Creative. I've sincerely enjoyed my stay, but given the failure of the CommMerica project, for which I accept full responsibility, I must resign. I hope you can forgive me and that we can remain friends. Thanks for everything. Amy."

ANALYSIS AND CONCLUSIONS

Okay, this one looks pretty simple. The Hopkins team were dopes and the Zorbix bunch heroes, right? Wrong! Wrong! Wrong! Zorbix, and Lynn in particular, was the primary cause of the failure and the resulting serious damage to CommMerica's IPO chances. Had Samuel recognized the volatile mixture he had assembled he might have been able to extract the best of what both firms had to offer. Instead, he was blindsided and fooled by what he perceived as sloppy work on the part of Hopkins and professionalism on the side of Zorbix. The approach used by Zorbix appeals to control-oriented managers like Samuel because it appears they have all of their ducks in a row. The fact is that there is a time to align, weigh, adjust, space, and perfectly groom ducks, and there is a time to get the damn work done. Zorbix and Samuel equated the two, a fatal mistake.

PROJECT RISK AND THE CELEBRATION OF DIVERSITY

"Creative companies" and the artists who inhabit them are relatively new to the technology scene. Prior to the Web, no one cared much how a user interface looked as long as it worked efficiently. With the Web came a need to make the interface look good as well as work efficiently. Enter the artist, and the improvement was magnificent! No one has any desire to return to the green-screen days. Modern Web-based interfaces are not only highly functional but also pleasant to work with. A quality interface and quality technology work together to produce Web sites and applications that not only meet customer's needs but are a delight to use. We need and benefit from the artist; that's not the problem. The problem is the naive assumption on the part of management that culturally divergent individuals will be able to work together to achieve quality outcomes.

As indicated above, the chasm between these two groups is plenty big enough to drive a project into. The conflict between the two groups arises on several problematic fronts in the software development arena. As discussed in Chapter 2, both artists and ill-informed customers regularly underestimate the value that true engineers bring to the table on projects like these. However, in this case, Amy and the Hopkins team accurately recognized the limits of their own capabilities and attempted to mitigate this with the addition of a quality engineering team. That was the beginning of the end for them, not because they should not have acquired help, but because they acquired help that they, as we will see later, could not manage.

Let's be perfectly clear: The problematic group on this project was the Zorbix team and Lynn in particular. Lynn, as is typical of those with her skills, was very methodical and controlled. She preferred to move at a much more deliberate and planned pace than Amy, but instead of seeing the opportunity to effectively collaborate and bridge the experience gaps with Hopkins, she used her experience to expose and damage their reputation. Lynn was too shortsighted to see that her approach damaged the customer and project as well as Hopkins's reputation. It is the nature of an engineering-focused technology professional to try to make every activity conform to accepted best practices, with the goal of eliminating all possible software quality risk. Although this may seem wise at first glance, too much of a good thing can often be as bad as none.

It can't be overemphasized that great software comes from teams where free-flowing creativity and solid engineering practices are in balance and where that balance is continually monitored and managed. Without this balance, many things on the engineering side will become excessively elevated. For example, what was the greatest risk on this project? Was it software quality? Was it integration with other systems? It was neither. The greatest risk on this project was that the software would not be delivered on time to support CommMerica's IPO bid. Having said that, of the two teams, which would be most capable of getting a site up quickly that looked fantastic, even if all the functionality wasn't quite ready for prime time? The answer, of course, is "Hopkins." Lynn obviously did not appreciate the business risk on this project or she would have demonstrated far more deference to Hopkins. As the story ended, Zorbix was leading the project down a very slow and methodical path that did, in fact, minimize risk due to technology but could not possibly deliver the system in time to support CommMerica's IPO.

Who's Leading the Charge?

Some of the problems with this project were classic and just happened to be exacerbated by the differences between these two groups. Although Lynn drove this project into the ground, Amy set the stage for this by her hands-off approach to project leadership. Amy, as many in the creative world do, held to the egalitarian ideal that seeks to maximize individual autonomy and creative freedom. This approach works well for a very small team in cases where project complexity and risk are low, but it totally disintegrates when the complexity rises to the level illustrated in this project.

In keeping with the immutable laws of physics, structure mitigates complexity and chaos. In this project we clearly see the damage of both extremes. Amy dropped the reigns and expected the project to guide itself: too little structure. Lynn picked up the reins and brought the project to a screeching halt: too much structure. Neither party had the experience to choose and apply the appropriate degree of structure and control necessary for this project to succeed.

Tom Peters, reflecting on the topic of teamwork, has observed that humans have strong and conflicting desires to both be a part of something bigger than themselves and also express their gifts and talents as individuals. This conflict often shows up in the form of competing leadership theories. The egalitarians will fight for "creative freedom" and total autonomy, whereas those with a hierarchical or structural bent will seek the order brought by structure and process. As is typically the case, the middle ground resulting from a realistic assessment of project risk and compromise yields better results than either extreme. In this case, Lynn ultimately

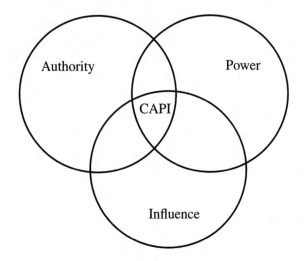

Figure 5.1   Coalesced Authority, Power, and Influence

tipped the balance toward excessive structure, and the project ended up
on its back.

For any project of the size and scope of this one to succeed, well-defined
and documented roles are critical. Roles must be clearly defined within
the authority structure of the organization. Ichak Adizes, in his work on
organizational lifecycles, identifies three areas that must be understood
and managed for anyone to define and succeed in his or her role in a project or organization: authority, power, and influence. The definitions of
these three terms follow:[2]

- *Authority* is the right to make a decision, to say "yes" and "no" to
  change. This right is formal and inherent in a person's job, independent of his or her connections or education.
- *Power* is the capability to punish and reward based on performance.
- *Influence* is defined as a person's ability to cause people to act without invoking authority or power.

An individual will be able to effectively manage and coordinate a project only to the degree to which that individual has coalesced authority,
power, and influence (CAPI). Figure 5.1 illustrates these critical factors
and the degree of CAPI as represented by the overlap in the middle.

At the beginning of this project, Amy had all three, but chose not to exercise authority or power, choosing instead to try to direct the project using only influence. Because of industry culture and her leaning toward an egalitarian model, she assumed that the project would succeed if it were broken into two components, allowing the creative and technology teams to operate autonomously. It obviously did not turn out that way. That was Hopkins's mistake, but when Lynn took over, she made a similar mistake, choosing to exercise authority and power but not influence. This proved even more disastrous, because Hopkins's team became "deer in the headlights" when faced with Lynn's dictatorial and controlling nature. The reason we come down so hard on Zorbix is because the company actually had the tools and expertise to manage a complex project, but instead of using its tools and experience to rescue the effort and help Hopkins succeed, it used them to destroy Hopkins and the project.

For projects like this to succeed, all players must be constantly and aggressively aligned toward a common goal. This does not mean that individuals cannot have freedom to execute in the manner they prefer, nor does it mean that a manager cannot treat each individual with dignity and respect. It simply means that there must be someone leading the charge who is exercising and providing sufficient CAPI, constantly ensuring through communication and course correction that everyone on the team, as well as the team sponsors, is moving in the right direction and performing as necessary for the project to be successful. The bottom line here is that this alignment is impossible without leadership that both has and exercises sufficient CAPI.

CONCLUSION

The fundamental makeups of artists and engineers are at polar opposites in terms of approach, perspective, and often attitude. This project provides examples of both excessive and insufficient project structure. Table 5.1 summarizes perspectives that would have armed Samuel with the tools he needed to see and manage the real problems on this project.

The wise manager recognizes that the creative firm's talent and value lies in the emotional appeal and visual communications aspect of a Web site. If that's all the site has to do, let the creative firm have free rein, but if you also have to conduct business with the visitors to your site, you need some technology-savvy help: Engage a technology firm. Clearly identify the greatest risks your project faces, structure your teams accordingly, and then manage the mix. Not only will you improve your chances of succeeding, but the team members may actually end the project on speaking terms.

Table 5.1   Do's and Don'ts for Working with Artists and Engineers

Never	Always
Never underestimate the difficulty of managing the conflicts between artists and engineers. Both are necessary but solve different problems. You must know which problems are most important to solve if you are to create the proper team mix and resulting authority structure.	Always, when setting up a project team, be very clear about goals, responsibilities, and scope of each member or role. Then, manage the hell out of the idea that the team members must be cohesive and complementary for the product to be of high quality. Project sponsors must never allow this structure to be broken by accepting finger pointing or blame shifting between team members. Everyone on the project team is responsible and accountable for delivering the product, and any personal agendas or behavioral conflicts that get in the way must be dealt with immediately.
Never allow dual leadership structures in project teams. Don't buy into extreme egalitarian nonsense. Someone must be appointed and supported to lead the charge, set the tone, and manage the risk and deliverables to completion.	Always build project structure that supports the mitigation of risks that pose the greatest threat to your project. If the greatest risk is software quality, engineering disciplines should be preeminent on the project, whereas if visual appeal and speed are most important, it might be wise to let the creative team lead the charge. Most of all, always heed the need for deliberate thought and design around team structure, leadership, and project roles.
Never allow process or excessive rigor to become a substitute for thinking. Lynn is the type of person who gives process rigor and engineering a bad name. Her insistence on arbitrary levels of adherence to micro-level process rigor blinded her, and	Always apply process rigor, engineering techniques, and other risk mitigation tools in the context of strategic risks and issues. Most risks on mission critical projects are not found within the realm of the technology itself. You must carefully

(Continues)

(Continued)

always blinds those like her, to the larger issues that fell outside of her rigid project management framework. Her constant critique of what otherwise was sufficient quality work from Hopkins was based on standards that had no relevance or value to the project or CommMercia's ultimate goals. Lynn's behavior and approach was almost solely responsible for CommMercia's eventual IPO woes caused by their delayed offering on the market.

identify project leaders who understand the larger context of their efforts and know how to make the necessary trade-offs for project success. Always apply risk-mitigating effort on actual identified risks, applying rigor only to the degree that it is truly required. Any rigor applied beyond that level is costly, wasteful, and sure to cause damage elsewhere in the project.

CHAPTER 6

Ready, Fire, Aim!

"**D**o it right, do it fast, and do it cheap." Since the beginning of time, humankind has been trying to get the most for the least, and to get it *now*. Since the beginning of time we've always arrived at the same painful conclusion: There's no such thing as a free lunch. Anytime we try to optimize any one of the three, we de-optimize one or both of the others. The wise manager recognizes this and strives to achieve a balance among the three that best facilitates the success of every project.

Unfortunately, not all managers are wise—smart perhaps, but not wise. Our story is about one such manager, a brilliant and effective businessman who demanded "right, fast, and cheap" but who failed to maintain the proper balance among the three. The result, far too common in the fast-paced world of technology, placed undue emphasis on "fast and cheap" at the expense of "right." As you might guess, the outcome wasn't pretty.

Dean Fowler was a successful sales executive with Farbe & Hoyle Publishing. He set sales records for several consecutive quarters, reaping rewards in the form of exceptionally high commissions, yet Dean wasn't happy. He tired of his job and began spending considerable time brainstorming and evaluating business ideas that would allow him to escape the mayhem of corporate sales. Finally, he found what he was looking for.

His idea was a Web site at which aspiring authors could prepare proposals and submit them directly to publishers, eliminating the need for an agent. His extensive knowledge of the publishing industry made it easy to

---

The Story

Company Name	Covenire Publishing
Industry	Publishing
Products	Web-based service to aspiring authors and publishers
Size	Startup
Issues	Limited capital
Key Players	Dean Fowler, founder and former publishing sales executive
	Tom Ferrero, technology project manager

---

prepare a business plan that showed clear profitability within the first year of operation. He gained the support of a retired publishing industry executive, who agreed to be Dean's "angel" investor and provide enough seed funding to bring up the first version of the site and establish a customer base. At that time, with a proven site and solid cash flow, they planned to approach other investors for additional funding.

Dean was well aware of his lack of knowledge about technology, so his first goal was to hire someone to lead the technology effort. After interviewing several candidates, he hired Tom Ferrero, an experienced project manager who was just completing his third Web project. Tom would be hired as project manager, with the understanding that if he performed to Dean's satisfaction, he would be promoted to CTO of the new company. Tom accepted and soon he and Dean moved into newly rented space. Tom began assembling his development team and project plan.

Most of Tom's experience had been with a highly regarded consulting firm, one that insisted that every project conform to the company's software development process. As a result, Tom's plan very naturally followed the same four-phase, cyclical approach used in his old company. This process looked something like Figure 6.1.

Tom's plan was to spend the first three weeks establishing the "vision and scope"[1] of the first product release, after which he and his team would spend six weeks doing detailed design. Only then would they begin actual construction of the site, a task that would take another six weeks, followed by three weeks of testing and stabilization. Tom felt that his eighteen-week estimate to build the Phase One version of the site was reasonable. He was totally unprepared for Dean's response.

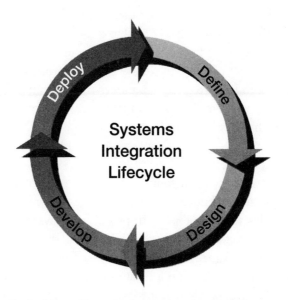

Figure 6.1   Typical Four-Phase Software Development Process

"Eighteen weeks? You're kidding, right? Eighteen weeks is out of the question. I want the site up in half that time—even less if possible! Every day we waste is a day of lost revenue, plus you never know when someone else is going to pop up with a similar idea and beat us to the punch. Salaries alone would run almost $200,000 over eighteen weeks, and that's just to get the site up. Hell, we only have a quarter-million in seed money. I thought you understood that!?"

Over the next hour, Dean went through Tom's carefully thought-out plan line by line, challenging every task. Each time Tom tried to explain why they needed to do a particular task, Dean argued and usually overruled Tom. When Dean finished, he had lined out over half of the tasks in the plan, especially in the early phases having to do with vision, scope, and design. When they finished, Dean leaned forward and looked Tom directly in the eyes. "Look," he said, "all I want is a Web site. Don't treat this like a monster mainframe project. Just build me a damn Web site!"

Tom spent the next morning redoing his project plan. He didn't like what he ended up with but felt he had no choice. That afternoon he gathered his team together and explained that they were going to move ahead aggressively, that they were going to skip a lot of the normal front-end tasks and move quickly into construction. He also told them that they would be doing a lot of things in parallel that are normally done in series, so they needed to be sure to communicate with one another. Even with the best communications, Tom knew that there would be a lot of misunderstandings that would result in confusion and rework, but he didn't know what else to do. Dean made it very clear that he had to cut whatever corners he could to get the site up.

Four weeks later, the team completed the first fully integrated version of the site. It came up, but barely. Things were in the wrong places, many of the data fields were improperly displayed, and several core functions didn't work. It was clear that the graphical user interface (GUI) designers and the database designer hadn't agreed on data definitions, resulting in many fields that were the wrong length or wrong type or wrong value. Even worse, it was apparent that the team didn't share a common understanding of what the site was supposed to do.

"Okay, guys," said Tom, "we have to get this clean enough to show Dean by next week. I've tried to show him page mockups, but he wants to see the full site up and running, and he's getting impatient. I know it means we're going to have to burn the midnight oil, but we have no choice." Tom could tell from the looks on their faces that they were discouraged and didn't exactly relish the idea of working long hours chasing bugs, but he knew he could count on them.

A week later Tom and his team demonstrated the site to Dean. Tom brought up the home page, projected on a screen in the darkened conference room. He had just started going over the elements of the page when Dean interrupted. "So if I'm a publisher and I come to this site, what do I do?" he asked. Tom hesitated, and then asked, "Why would you be coming to this site if you were a publisher?"

The next hour wasn't fun for Tom or anyone else. It turned out that Dean expected a number of features that weren't included in the site design. In addition, he pointed out a number of things that were missing from screens, functions that hadn't been thought of, as well as usability and visual appeal problems. He was angry, but contained himself until after the meeting, at which time he asked to see Tom in his office. Once be-

hind the closed office door, Dean unleashed on Tom, going as far as suggesting that maybe he should be replaced. Tom tried several times to point
out that the omissions and problems were a result of the shortcuts he was
directed to take, but Dean wouldn't listen. He obviously blamed Tom and
wasn't interested in excuses.

Over the next three weeks, Tom's team worked long and hard, cleaning
up a lot of problems and implementing some of the missing features that
Dean had pointed out, but the site remained unstable. With one week to
go before the scheduled go-live date, Tom caught Dean in his office. Closing the door he began, "Dean, we aren't going to have the site ready by
next week. In fact, my development lead and I have gone over the site and
it's our opinion that we have at least another month of work in front of us
before the site's ready."

Dean's response was predictably unpleasant, but after a while he calmed
down. "Okay, here's our problem. Our plan was to begin reducing the size of
the development team by now. Instead, it's looking like we're going to have
to keep them around for another month or so. At that rate, we're going to be
out of money before we get the site up. Do you not realize what that means?"

Tom didn't think that Dean expected an answer, but he shook his head
anyway. Dean continued, "It means that we're going to either have to go
back to our investor for more money, or approach the venture capitalists
(VCs) without a functioning site, customers, or cash flow. I don't think
our investor has the money we need right now, and the VCs are going to
be hard to convince, given our current state. We may be in real trouble."

Over the next two weeks, Dean was on the phone or out of the office almost every moment of the day. As he had suspected, his angel investor
didn't have the funds to help. After making his pitch to four local VCs, it
became apparent that without a functioning system, they weren't interested. Dean tried to get a line of credit from several local banks, but had
neither the collateral nor connections to pull it off. Late one afternoon he
called Tom into his office. Handing him a small stack of envelopes, he
said, "These are for you and your team. We're broke, with barely enough
to make the payroll. Without more money, we can't continue, so I have no
choice but to put the project on hold and let you and your team go."

Tom could see Dean's pain, and asked, "Is there anything I can do?"
"Well," said Dean, "you can tell me how the hell you spent a quarter of a

million dollars building a Web site that doesn't work!" They sat quietly for a moment. Then Tom stood. He wanted to tell Dean that it wasn't his fault, that if they had done it right they wouldn't be in this situation, but he knew it was pointless. He turned and walked out the door, dreading the task that lay in front of him.

ANALYSIS AND CONCLUSIONS

Ouch! It was such a great idea, and Dean and Tom and the development team were such smart people. How could this disaster have possibly happened? Well, the ultimate answer lies in the failure to establish and maintain the proper balance among right, fast, and cheap, but it's still not that simple. Let's take a look at some of the specific mistakes that caused the perilous imbalance.

SUPER WILD-ASS GUESS (SWAG)

As with most development efforts, Dean's problems started well before the project began. Where did he get his estimates for how long the site development would take, or for development costs and funding needs? Who knows? What is clear is that his estimates, to put it nicely, were pulled out of thin air.

IGNORING THE DOCTOR

It is amazing how often executives hire experts and then completely ignore their advice. In this case, Dean was smart in hiring Tom, but when Tom laid out the approach necessary to deliver a quality product, Dean summarily rejected it. It is perfectly valid to challenge a project manager's approach with legitimate business objections, but Dean threw out the baby, the bathwater, and the tub. What is most outrageous about Dean's behavior is that if he were confronted with the need for major surgery, there is no way in hell he would even think of questioning his doctor's specific surgical procedures. Dean's approach to Tom was extremely arrogant, foolish, ill advised, and core to the reasons behind this business failure. Hire smart people and listen to them.

IGNORING THE PATIENT

Tom failed to set the ground rules up front with Dean regarding his approach. A few simple questions asked before accepting the project would have quickly revealed that Dean's expectations were way out of line. Once Tom was beyond the point of no return he still could have asked the right questions and reached a semi-healthy compromise.

The problem was that Dean had no prior experience with software development and was thus completely incapable of understanding or appreciating the need for a simple development process to successfully guide the project. By hitting Dean with something he was totally unprepared to deal with, Tom essentially handed him a big fat bitter pill and expected Dean to swallow it with a smile. This approach is extremely common with technologists: They often fail to bridge the gap between the customer's perceptions and the reality of what it takes to execute a successful project. However ill equipped and poorly positioned, it is the expert's role to recognize and bridge the gap in the customer's understanding. Tom clearly failed to do this and was thus well deserving of Dean's wrath.

MARKET HYPE AND TARGET PRACTICE

Dean's naivete regarding the complexity of Web software development is unfortunately a common one, based on market hype surrounding the Web. You have to memorize the rules of the road before getting your driver's license, so doesn't it make sense to know a little about the rules of software development before you careen down that path? Just as you cannot safely drive down a sidewalk to get around a traffic jam, you cannot shortcut basic elements in any modern software development approach. As the title of this chapter suggests, it is a disastrously foolish thing to fire a gun without first aiming it. It is just as foolish to drop hundreds of thousands of dollars down the tubes of a project that has unclear objectives and unrealistic goals.

IMMUNIZATION REQUIRED

Software development and planning processes always feel cumbersome and painful to people in Dean's position. However, they are as necessary as the immunizations required when traveling to foreign countries. The

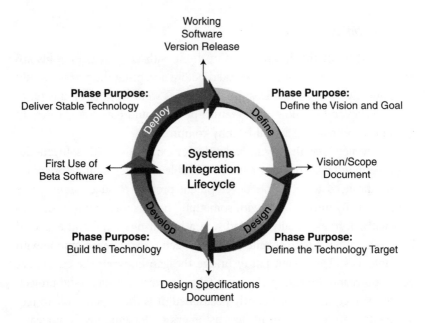

Figure 6.2   Sound Software Development Process

shots always hurt, but the wise patient recognizes that the consequences of not getting immunized far outweigh the pain of the injection. Because Dean had unrealistic expectations, he was convinced he did not need immunization. He ventured into foreign territory with bold ignorance and suffered the consequences.

Despite popular opinion, software development processes are not designed to bring pain without gain. As Figure 6.2 illustrates, they are designed to ensure that the goal is clear to all (definition phase), the target and the path to the target are clear to all (design phase), the software is built to hit the target (develop phase), and the software works as intended (deploy phase). It's just that simple, but not just that easy. Without an understanding that the pain is necessary and worth the value of the expected gain, the Deans of the world will always end up with diseased and dying projects.

THE BIG BANG APPROACH

Tom's approach to achieving Dean's goals was in keeping with an extremely common and problematic approach to software development referred to by James A. Highsmith III as "big-bang thinking."[2] That is, Tom scheduled 100 percent of the site's Phase One functionality to be delivered all at once, at the end of the project. Tom clearly failed to adapt his development process to his environment. Had he initially laid out an approach based on short, quick passes through the development cycle, something we call "Micro-Release Cycles," he would have demonstrated growing value to Dean in the form of incrementally increasing functionality and would thus have avoided triggering Dean's "just do it" mentality. Tom's intent to deliver all the planned functionality at the end of the project was just too much for Dean. Tom was asking him to slowly walk across a football field of hot coals; it was too painful, too long, and too much to ask from a personality like Dean.

Another related problem is that it is nearly impossible to imagine up front everything that a software system, in this case a Web site, should do. Even if Tom had been able to get Dean to agree to four full development phases, it is very unlikely that Dean would have been satisfied with the result. Highsmith again makes a profound observation: "The greatest risk we face in software development projects is that of overestimating our own knowledge."[3] We never have definite knowledge of what needs to be done until we're finished and discover how wrong we were. By using micro cycles, implementing functionality a little at a time, Dean would have had the opportunity to continually experience, tune, and refine the content and functionality of the site. By trying to build the entire site at once, Tom basically guaranteed that it would prove unsatisfactory to Dean.

RIGHT, FAST, AND CHEAP

"Action without study is fatal, and study without action is futile."[4] In this case, Dean set out to act without a clear understanding of the effort required to be successful, and Tom failed to adapt his methods to his environment. Dean's propensity to "just do it" and Tom's to "do it right" were polar opposite perspectives that clashed when Dean and Tom had their first meeting. A casual analysis might lightly select one extreme over the other. However, this project truly required a balance among right, fast, and cheap. Tom's misapplication of the software development process emphasized "right." Dean's entrepreneurial drive and limited budget drove his need for the effort to be "fast and cheap." There were many issues that led to this disaster, but the core issue is a failure to find that critical balance among these three factors.

Specifically, how could this balance have been achieved? Table 6.1 lays out Tom's proposed approach juxtaposed against one that would have been much more effective. This table brings us to the ultimate question: Would you rather be eighteen weeks down the path with no budget left to adjust course or four weeks down the path with both time and budget remaining?

CONCLUSION

The imbalance caused by Dean's zealous ignorance, combined with Tom's failure to adapt, proved fatal. Table 6.2 is a summary of how to avoid the

Table 6.1   Achieving Balance in Project Scheduling

Tom's Proposed Approach	Adjusted Approach	Justification for the Adjustment
Three weeks for vision and scoping of the project	Three days to one week of vision and scope	Dean, as do most project sponsors, had an incomplete vision of what the end result should be. A longer vision/scope effort would have only yielded more documentation that would need to be changed later. Dean needed to get quick turnaround on what he thought he wanted to learn and adjust toward what he really needed as expressed through a prototype of the Web site.
Six weeks for detailed design	One week for preliminary design	To place a limit on design time is dangerous, but if we assume that the vision/scope produced by the first step is inevitably going to be off by a significant degree, the same logic applies here. Tom needed to provide quick iterations of real functionality for Dean to experience to gain better understanding of what the ultimate outcome really should be. This is why architects build scale models of their buildings as part of the design process.
Six weeks for construction	Two weeks for development of initial prototype of functionality	Same logic again. This would allow Dean to quickly see progress and determine if he and Tom were on the same page. It is far better to adjust early than to find out at the end of the project that the perception gap was insurmountable.

(Continues)

(Continued)

Three weeks of testing	Two to three days of testing, if that	If we assume that this first release is to build a preliminary foundation and help Dean experience, learn, and surface his true requirements, then testing for a perfect product is a waste of time. Testing in this case should only be done to avoid unnecessary distractions and concerns for Dean. At this stage, it is not even necessary that all the functions work. Leave exhaustive testing for the final release to the public.
Totals		
Eighteen weeks	Approximately four weeks	This adjustment poses far less risk to Dean's need to achieve a reasonable balance among right, fast, and cheap. True, the result of four weeks' work would have been only a prototype, not ready for release, but it would have positioned the team to make one or two more quick cycles to produce functional versions of the site sufficient to take to market. Total time to build the final site would have been significantly less than eighteen weeks, and the resulting site would have met Dean's needs, at least in the short term.

many traps Dean and Tom laid for themselves and to find a healthy balance both in perspective and in the goal of getting it as right, as fast, and as cheap as possible.

A scene from an old movie illustrates the central theme of this story. An injured man sits exhausted against a tree with rifle in hand and only a single round of ammunition remaining. From only yards away a wild boar charges with ferocious speed. The man leans forward, raises his weapon, and waits for what seems like an eternity until the raging animal is inches away. At the last possible moment, the man fires with skull-shattering precision. The animal drops dead at his feet and the man collapses backward in relief. Most projects have a single bullet (limited budget, time, and options) and a wild boar (failure or substandard outcomes approaching at ominous speed). The answer is to think, to steady, to aim, and then to fire—to hit the mark on the first and only chance you are likely to have. Sound software development processes are designed to ensure that you do just that.

Table 6.2 Do's and Don'ts for Software Development Projects

Never	Always
Never use the SWAG method for estimating software projects. Wild-ass guesses result in wild-ass projects. We don't recommend either.	Always seek counsel from development experts even when ball-parking a development effort. If you, like Dean, don't have an internal team to lean on, submit your basic ideas to a development company for an estimate. *Note*: If the company tells you it must be paid for this vision/scope effort, you've probably found a quality firm. Unless you need extremely simple functionality, organizations that willingly throw out estimates with little understanding do so on the basis of a lack of experience. In fact, the best firms will not commit to firm time/cost/feature estimates until after the first phase of a four-phase development process.
Never ignore the experts. You pay big bucks for professionals—listen to them!	Always hire and engage with someone who understands, has lived within, and demonstrates sound thinking about software development. If you hire anyone, consultant or employee, who does not come to the table with something similar to what Tom suggested, run to the nearest exit—you are in trouble.
Never assume that one size fits all with your software development process. Process can become a substitute for thinking. Tom did not think about how his preferred approach would best work in this situation. He just assumed it would work. He was wrong.	Always adapt processes to support business needs. Process is important but it should always be a slave to the business needs of the organization. Sometimes longer cycles are effective, but in the environment of this case, short, quick iterations would have been much more effective.
Never try to launch a complex project without some process structure in place to facilitate and organize the effort.	Always lay out or adhere to a basic development approach that, by its design, drives you to surface, understand, and respond to the specific activities that must occur for your project to be successful. Software development processes are not designed to inhibit progress, but to ensure that progress is made with the least amount of effort, time, and mistakes possible.
Never try to fully optimize right, fast, and cheap all at once. It is a universal and immutable law of the project cosmos that it is absolutely, positively impossible to optimize all three, and those who try always do damage to their teams, their companies, and themselves.	Always recognize and pursue a healthy balance among right, fast, and cheap. Walking a project tightrope without this critical balance is rarely less than fatal.

CHAPTER 7

Over-Gross and Under-Powered

"Don't bite off more than you can chew." How many times have you heard this advice? Probably enough that it really doesn't mean anything to you anymore, but maybe it should. It is a natural human tendency to want everything, and to want it now. The new car, the big house, and the world-class vacation: We want it all, and we don't want to wait. Good for credit card companies maybe, but not for our long-term well-being.

The same holds true in business, particularly the employment of technology in business. We want our systems to be complete and full featured, and we want everything implemented and available ASAP. Unfortunately, most attempts at building and/or implementing large software systems all at once fail. The primary reason for this is that the complexities of software and human interaction do not increase at a linear rate but at something approaching the square of the number of software components and people. Increase the number of software components by a factor of ten and the complexity increases by a factor of nearly a hundred. Likewise, increase the number of people on a team by a factor of ten and the complexity of team interactions increases by a factor of nearly a hundred. This is not theory, it is a mathematical and human reality, and it's a serious problem.

But suppose you persevere and actually get the monster system with all the bells and whistles to work. Guess what: You will quickly discover that user acceptance, getting the people to use the system, is incredibly difficult. People can accept only so much change at once, and the big, com-

---

The Story

Company Name	ComSysCA
Industry	Technology
Products	Networking equipment and software
Size	2,700 employees
Issues	Loss of market share and a pattern of declining sales
Key Players	Jackie Wells, CEO of ComSysCA
	Dennis Rousch, director of sales for Coviat (CRM vendor)
	Rita Arbino, director of sales for HC
	Larry Orr, former CEO of ComSysCA
	Karl Fredricks, chairman of the board for ComSysCA

---

plex system is usually more than they can handle. Such systems are seldom used to their full potential; in fact, they are often unused. It does not matter how well a surgeon performs the organ transplant, or the quality of the organ. If the body does not accept the organ, it dies; so too with complex human integration with software systems.

Jackie Wells had been on the job as CEO of ComSysCA for only a month, having previously been vice president of operations for a smaller but growing competitor. ComSysCA was a highly respected manufacturer of network hardware and software, selling its products both through value-added resellers and directly to end customers. ComSysCA had gained its position as an industry leader through exceptionally well-engineered, high-quality equipment, but recently its competitors were challenging ComSysCA's position in the market. After two quarters of declining revenue, Karl Fredricks, chairman of the board, had to act. He reluctantly removed Jackie's predecessor, Larry Orr, from the CEO position, moving him to senior vice president of product planning and development. He charged Jackie with the responsibility of turning sales around by the end of the fiscal year.

Jackie immediately began the task of identifying the source of the sales slump. What she found wasn't pretty. Repeat sales had fallen in recent years, opportunities to up- and cross-sell were regularly if not always lost, and the products the company was selling seemed out of date and didn't meet customer needs. Jackie concluded that ComSysCA was simply out of touch with its customers. She identified the root cause as the lack of a comprehensive customer relationship management (CRM) system. Her previous company had a CRM system that had been operational for more than three years, a system that provided instant and consistent information about customers, the products they were buying, and how those products were being used. Jackie was convinced that ComSysCA's problems would be solved by such a system.

"To summarize, in order to sell and service our customers, we have to know them—and we don't. We hardly know who has bought equipment from us, much less why they bought it and what they are going to need in the future. We have three major and seven minor databases that all record some form of 'customer,' none of which contains complete demographic or customer relationship information, plus no two of them agree." Jackie paused for effect, noting that Karl was nodding. She continued, "My recommendation is that we select and implement a true CRM application as quickly as possible. Getting our customer data under control will improve customer satisfaction, resulting in increased repeat sales, plus we'll be able to implement up- and cross-sell strategies that we can't even think about now. In view of the fact that more than 60 percent of our sales come in the fourth quarter, we need to act now. With the board's permission I'd like to move on this as quickly as possible with the objective of having a system operational within three months." Karl looked around the room. Satisfied that there were no questions, he smiled and said, "Thanks, Jackie. I believe we all agree with you. Let's get this thing moving."

Jackie approached Dennis Rousch, director of sales for Coviat Corp., maker of CR-Manager, a leading CRM software package. Jackie had known Dennis as Coviat's account rep to her former employer. "Dennis, think of this as shock treatment. This is a great company with a great set of products, but it's dying. I've got to radically change the way we view and manage our customers, and if that means that the company has to endure pain, so be it. I really don't give a damn if they like it or not—it's for their own good." Jackie paused. "Well, Jackie," said Dennis, "you know that our system will do everything you could need, so it's just a matter of inking a contract and getting it done. I've got the perfect team coming off a big project at the end of the month, one with experience in your industry, so people won't be the problem. We'll be ready to go when you are."

Dennis's team showed up two weeks later. Jackie worked closely with them at first, outlining the specifications for the system. Taking cues from her previous experience, she rattled off a long list of features that included forecasting, pipeline reporting, purchase history, lead sharing, complex commission calculations, integration with ComSysCA's ERP software, data cleansing and import from existing databases, and so forth. In spite of numerous objections from the Coviat project manager (PM), Jackie insisted that she have all this implemented within three months. Dennis kicked his PM under the table each time he tried to slow Jackie down. Dennis knew that because of the huge scope, this would be a model implementation of CR-Manager, one that would bring big commissions for him and international exposure for Coviat.

Two months later, on the date the system had originally been scheduled to enter user acceptance testing (UAT), Jackie met with Dennis and the Coviat team. "Okay, let's hear it. Give me the bad news," said Jackie. She had received word from both the accounting and management information systems (MIS) teams that the project was running into serious integration and configuration issues. After a moment of anxious silence, the Coviat PM spoke. "Well, we've made a lot of progress. The core application is up and running and most of the configuration has been worked out, but I'll have to admit that we're not as far along as we had hoped. We are running into some serious data conversion issues and the constant change requests are killing us. It seems like everyone we talk to has a different idea on what the system should do and how it should do it. There are just too many people involved. I know the changes seem like simple configuration changes, but each time we shift course we loose momentum. We're getting there, but it's going to take a bit longer."

Jackie ignored his comments and opened her Day Timer™. "How much longer?" she asked. Dennis answered, "Well, Jackie, you've been around this kind of thing before. You know how hard it is to be exact about dates, particularly with all the changes. Every member of the team is pulling twelve hour days to bring this thing home." "Look, Dennis," interrupted Jackie. "I told Karl we would have the system operational in three months, on schedule and within budget. I'll be damned if I'm going to go back and tell him that we don't know how long it's going to take or how much it will cost. I want answers, and they'd better be answers you're willing to live with, because I'm going to hold you to them this time.

You've got until close of business tomorrow." She slammed her Day Timer™ shut, rose, and walked out.

Dennis delivered the revised estimates late the next day. "At this pace it's going to take us another three weeks to get to UAT. We are running into a lot of unexpected usability and process issues with your sales and accounting team leaders. We'll eat about half of this overrun, but the remainder is due to requested scope changes. I'd estimate that you should add at least $75,000 to the cost, maybe $85,000, to be safe." Jackie grimaced. She knew that Karl wasn't going to like this.

Jackie sat at her desk, phone to her ear. She had just broken the bad news to Karl. "Jackie, this is going to look really bad. This CRM deal was your idea, your first major decision since joining us. For it to come in late and over budget isn't going to sit well with the board. I'll do what I can to soften the blow, but you'd better be prepared for some tough questions at the next meeting."

The board meeting was tough, but Jackie was prepared. She focused on how the forecasting and pipeline views would help in scheduling production runs and minimizing on-hand inventory, along with other system benefits related to sales team efficiency, and how these benefits would far outweigh the costs, even with the overrun. It wasn't pleasant, but she made it through and work on the project continued. The Coviat team missed their projected UAT date by a week, something Jackie didn't like but couldn't do anything about. At least the system was working and would enter production as soon as the UAT process was complete. Unfortunately, the UAT wasn't going smoothly.

Dennis was frustrated. "Look, Jackie. The system is working like it's supposed to. The users are becoming a serious problem. I don't know if they're confused or what, but they're entering bad data, complaining about the views, and although they've all been through training, they don't seem to understand how even the most basic functions work. I don't know what the problem is, but it sure seems like they're trying to sabotage this project." Jackie was at a loss. She had to agree that the users certainly seemed backwards, especially for a technology company. She had talked to several of them about the system and heard a lot of complaints about it being confusing, too complicated, providing incorrect information, and so forth. When she had tried to dig deeper the users constantly compared the system to their previous manual methods. They simply did not want to use the system or to break their old comfortable routines.

Eventually the system was declared operational, almost two months beyond the originally projected go-live date. Jackie was relieved to be able to put the problems behind her and go on to other things. Her relief didn't last long. Rita Arbino, director of sales, sat in her office. "All it does is get in the way and keep people confused. I don't understand how sales is supposed to collaborate with marketing on campaigns. I don't know how to get access to customer purchase history. Isn't there some way to simplify this thing? We never ran into these problems with our old systems."

Jackie stiffened. "Look, Rita. We spent a lot of money giving you and your people the best system in the industry, so using it is not optional. I want people to use the system—period! I'll tell you what. From now on, to get a commission for a sale, everything has to be entered in the system—everything—company info, contacts, activities, opportunities—everything. And as for the marketing group, they need to understand that using the system is going to be a basic requirement for them to keep their jobs."

A month later Jackie stood before the board. New sales prospects had fallen almost 25 percent in thirty days. "The problem seems to be resistance to the new CRM system on the part of the sales force. Some decline in sales can be anticipated as part of a normal learning curve, but this is excessive. I'm working closely with Rita Arbino to solve this problem—one way or another, if you know what I mean. I assure you that this is a temporary slump that will resolve itself quickly."

It didn't. Three weeks later, Jackie was surprised to see Karl in a conference room with Rita and the sales staff. It didn't take long for her to find out what the meeting was all about. "Jackie, as you know, I've been friends with Rita for a long time. She and I had lunch a couple of days ago and we naturally talked about the fact that sales are in the toilet. Her opinion was that the new CRM system is so complex that using it the way you directed is taking so much of her staff's time that they don't have time left to sell anything. I have to admit that the system is pretty complex, from what I've seen. I'd like to hear your position on this, and what you plan to do about it."

Jackie explained that the system was not complicated, that the problem was really the reluctance of the sales staff to learn something new. She related how the sales staff at her previous company had used almost exactly the same system, and had loved it. "Karl, you hired me because sales were down and no one here seemed to know what to do about it. I know what needs to be done, and I'm doing it. The salespeople are lazy; it's as simple as that. They just don't want to invest the time and energy needed to ramp up on the system and run the sales operation the way it should be run. We just have to stay tough on them for a while. They'll learn the system and we'll begin to see results."

Karl wasn't convinced. "We've spent over a million dollars on this software, and now you're telling me that we have to force the sales staff to use it. I don't understand that kind of logic. If the system is so darned great, where are the benefits, and why is it so difficult to use? I've known these people a long time. They aren't stupid or lazy or anything of the kind. I am frankly offended by your comments. They're loyal employees who are always willing to go the extra mile for the company. I honestly don't think they're the problem."

"Karl, I resent the implication that the CRM system was a bad decision. If you have so little confidence in me, maybe I should resign." Jackie knew from the look in Karl's eyes that she had gone too far, but she was totally unprepared for what he said next. "Jackie, I think you're right. The board and I aren't happy with your performance, so why don't we cut our losses and call this off. I appreciate your offer to resign, and I accept. I'll see to a severance package for you, and will be happy to serve as a reference for you."

ANALYSIS AND CONCLUSIONS

Believe or not, in the real-world situation from which this story was created, things were far worse. This project blew a $3 million hole in the company's budget and set it back months in sales momentum. It is easy to identify a host of issues that contributed to the loss, including runaway scope, large systems integration issues, and most important, human integration issues. Thousands of companies have invested millions in "automation" projects for accounting, warehousing, sales force, purchasing, software development, and so forth, with little or no return on investment and often huge losses in productivity. Why is this so? Let's examine a few key issues that surfaced in this story and find out.

Technology Is Our Savior

From the start, Jackie demonstrated a common misconception, that technology by itself could solve her problems. She correctly attributed ComSysCA's falling sales to a lack of customer intimacy, but wrongly identified their systems as the root cause. ComSysCA's systems were a problem, and certainly did nothing to support or enhance customer intimacy, but replacing them could not possibly fix the problems ComSysCA faced. The problems were actually a result of organizational fragmentation and lack of external focus, the type of problems that cannot be solved by technology.

Jackie's misdiagnosis was heavily influenced by her previous positive experience with a CRM application in another company, but her basic makeup leaned toward oversimplification. Jackie did not understand that her previous company had been in an entrepreneurial stage of its lifecycle and had the benefit of growing with a system that empowered its existing corporate culture. ComSysCA was a decaying company from a different era that had become internally focused and inflexible, languishing in the laurels of yesterday. Jackie's mistaken diagnosis and her overconfidence in the ability of a system to solve the problem only served to further entrench ComSysCA's staff in their past behavior. Even if Jackie had not made obvious mistakes as a technology project sponsor, this project would have failed.

As did our project sponsors in Chapter 4, Jackie failed to understand and identify organizational maturity and related cultural issues that would have a dramatic impact on her project. Not only did technology not save ComSysCA, the system also further reinforced the notion among the sales staff that their existing systems and behaviors had always worked just fine and there was no reason to change. Among many other significant factors, this behavior led to ComSysCA's ultimate decline in the market. This was and continues to be a hard lesson for many executives: Technology, in and of itself, never solves the types of problems that ComSysCA faced.

Deadlines, Deadlines, Deadlines

Is this another tired reminder of the need to avoid arbitrary deadlines? Yes and no. Jackie's subjective determination of three months to complete the project had no basis in analysis or experience as it relates to a system implementation; it was therefore very foolish. It was, however, based on a legitimate business constraint. This constraint would have caused an execu-

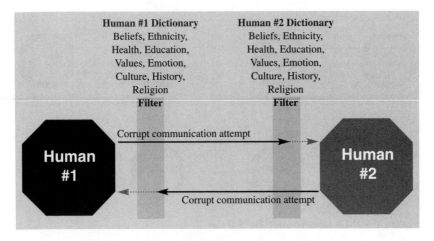

Figure 7.1   Communication Difficulties

tive more experienced with technology to limit system functionality and get a first release in place before the busy season. Instead, as many do, Jackie ignored the facts and nearly killed her team to get the system working. Projects executed in this manner are never successful. It didn't work for Jackie, and it won't work for you.

COMMUNICATION, COMPLEX SYSTEMS, AND MIRACLES

Do you believe in miracles? If you don't, take a moment to consider the dynamics of a typical communication attempt between cross-functional team members. In an ideal world, we would all conform to a perfect mode of communication that does not carry with it emotional baggage, ethnic background, social status, and so forth. We would talk and everyone would understand exactly what we meant by what we said. Unfortunately, that world does not exist, and it definitely did not exist in Jackie's project. As Figure 7.1 illustrates, even in the best and simplest of circumstances, communication is a difficult matter.

This diagram makes clear that each person's dictionary and filter cause a degree of corruption at every point of interaction. Now imagine the quality of communication on Jackie's project. The only team members who were 100 percent dedicated to this project were from Coviat: outsiders. Team members from accounting, MIS, sales, and marketing were told what they would do with the system rather than being asked how they would or could use the CRM system to improve customer service capabilities.

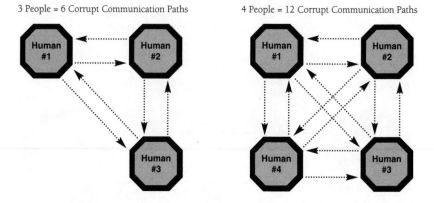

Figure 7.2   Communication Path Growth

Beyond the fact that all human communications are corrupt at some level, the situation gets even worse. As illustrated in Figure 7.2, between any two people there are two communication paths. Add more people to the team, and the growth in the number of communication paths is rapid and, to those who have never thought through this dynamic, very surprising.

The key effect here is that the nonlinear growth of communication paths, coupled with basic corruption in communication, results in a compounding effect that is extremely difficult to overcome. Figure 7.3 clearly shows the dramatic difference between the growth in the number of team members and the growth in the number of communication paths. While additional team members grow at a linear rate, the number of communication paths grows at an almost exponential rate, requiring more and more energy and skill to align the efforts of the people involved. The law of diminishing returns applies here and quickly limits the practical size of project teams.

The amazing thing about this is how counterintuitive it is. If you were to ask just about anyone to estimate the increase in communication complexity as team size grows and not allow that person to do more than a quick calculation, he or she would almost always significantly underestimate the impact of growth.

There are two key ways to mitigate these communication problems. First, you can try to eliminate miscommunication through a perpetual feedback mechanism that asks, "What did you just hear me say?" The message of the speaker is then adjusted to the dictionary of the listener until the listener reflects back with acceptable accuracy what the speaker

Figure 7.3   Growth in Number of Communication Paths Versus Growth in Number of Team Members

is trying to say. Some people practice a form of this by, for example, sending an e-mail that summarizes a phone conversation. Many software development processes and techniques help to mitigate this problem through formal documentation and sign-offs. Unfortunately, this process is usually unacceptable to executives such as Jackie because they think they don't have the time.

The other way to mitigate the problem is to limit the number of communication paths, either by limiting team size or through a hierarchical team structure. Limiting team size is a great approach because it requires that project scope be limited, which is usually a good thing for many other reasons. There are, however, situations in which the team must grow to a size that becomes unwieldy. In such situations, the team must be organized in a hierarchical fashion. Modern organizational thinkers find this objectionable, primarily because it seems to reduce cross-functional communication, but it is this very fact that makes it a viable way to keep communications problems in check. Some vital communication will no doubt be lost in the process, but organizing the players into a hierarchical structure can mean the difference between success and failure on large projects.

So, what does all this mean? It is extremely difficult and counterintuitive to grasp the true complexity behind any technology project, let alone one that cuts across so many different functions in an organization. In Jackie's case, as in the case of most project sponsors, she was totally unprepared to deal with this complexity. Her "just do it" mentality simply

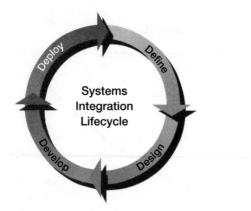

Figure 7.4 Systems Development Process

did not and does not work beyond very small project efforts. Communication between consenting humans is at best difficult; in the case of a large-scale project shoved down the throats of so many people, successful communication requires divine intervention.

I Want It All, and I Want It Now!

Jackie wanted everything, and she wanted it now. Certainly there were sound business drivers for her recommendations regarding ComSysCA's need for a CRM system. However, even if her approach had been more human friendly, ComSysCA would not have been able to absorb the amount of change she brought in the timeframe she dictated. Let's face it, software alone is extremely complex, but when people are added to the mix, it is almost impossible to complete a project within cost, time, and feature constraints.

These compounding complexities point to the need for extremely short-cycle, incremental development of complex systems. This gives the project manager, project team members, stakeholders, and all others affected by the project the ability to get their arms around how the software affects them and how it can and should be used to their benefit.

So how does this work in practical terms? Figure 7.4 illustrates the systems development process discussed in Chapter 6 (see page 85). We won't rehash what was discussed there, but we will add another dimension that is most clearly applicable to this story or any other strategic systems effort.

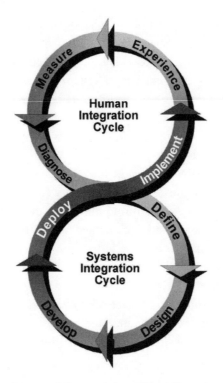

Figure 7.5 Technology and Human Integration Lifecycles

Technology is a tool used by people, so it would be foolhardy to devise a process for software development that didn't take into account the role that people play in the process. The upper portion of Figure 7.5 illustrates a dimension that is rarely given more than cursory treatment in most discussions about software development but is, as was demonstrated in our discussion about communication (see page 103), even more critical to the success of technology projects than the quality of the technology itself. In our opinion, a systems development or integration lifecycle that does not represent these components is incomplete and ineffective regardless of project size, quality of the software, or the experience of the team members.

The diagram expands on Figure 7.4 by showing the way in which people interact with technology. The "implement" phase is a period of human integration of the organizational, process, and technology components of the system. During this phase, people put the software and its features to use in the day-to-day context of business, often using only the most obvious and simplest of system features. Management expectations during this period must be realistically low. The "experience" phase is a period of growth and learning stemming from system use, as well as process and behavioral change. During this phase, users become more confident and explore and begin to use less obvious and more complex system features. Management expectations rise, and it is at this point that frustration with system limitations sets in.

The "measure" phase involves the formal tracking of system use and its positive and negative impacts on productivity and whether the intended outcomes are occurring. It is during this phase that the shortcomings of the system are measured and documented. All of these phases culminate in the "diagnose" phase, where we formally document our measurements and experiences and make recommendations for the next incremental change to the software.

Using a formal approach to system/human integration will result in a dramatic increase in user acceptance and sustainable change, all resulting in the organization achieving its original goals for the project.

AND DON'T FORGET . . .

As we have outlined, implementing large systems within a company is much more than a matter of technology. It also affects the business processes and the roles and responsibilities of people within the company. Let's briefly examine these three components of any organization, and how change in one requires change in the others:

- *Systems:* This area encompasses not only integration into existing corporate systems but also the deployment of the technology to the desktop of the individuals who will be using the technology. It also involves training on specific features and functions of the new system.
- *Process:* This often ignored but critical area is concerned with how existing business processes, policies, and procedures must change and adapt to the new technological environment. In Jackie's case, no thought was given to how the new system would integrate with or change ComSysCA's basic processes relating to customer interaction.

- *People:* The final area is ignored more than the other two. Just as technological change requires process change, process change requires organizational change. Roles change, new roles are created, and existing roles become obsolete. Responsibility shifts from one part of the organization to another. All of this must be recognized and dealt with, often requiring extensive reorganization and staff reassignments. Jackie never considered any of this.

CONCLUSION

However talented Jackie may have been, in this case she tackled a project that could be likened to the design and erection of a high-rise building without experience beyond the construction of a dollhouse. Jackie's experience with managing technology did not go beyond the effective use of her PC. Why then did she feel so comfortable driving this project? She had the same disease we see throughout this book: oversimplification with respect to the true complexity behind the strategic leveraging of technology. Table 7.1 summarizes what we've learned.

A recent study of technology projects revealed a powerful truth that must be understood if these types of projects are to be a success.[1] The study covered sixty technology projects and attempted to determine why projects fail or succeed. The results of the study were shocking. There was no statistically significant relationship between project "success" and the quality of technical execution. Did you hear that? Are you sure? Put another way, you can have perfect technical execution on a project and have the outcome be rejected and deemed a failure! Jim Dickie, a leading authority on CRM, writes that, "A critical pitfall to avoid is focusing too much on process and technology, and not enough on the people who design the system. You can design the best process in the world, and back it with the latest and greatest technology, but if your people don't buy into the project, it won't work."[2]

So, what's the bottom line? Simple: It's about people. Good technology is necessary, but not sufficient, for success. If you also take care of people, then your project will have a high likelihood of success.

Table 7.1 Do's and Don'ts of Software and Human Integration

Never	Always
Never assume that technology alone will solve any problem. Technology in and of itself will not and cannot save us. Technology at its core is simply process automation and information delivery. Far more is required to bring core corporate change than software and hardware. Technology is not a magic cure.	Always approach technology implementations with a holistic view of what is required to solve core problems you are attempting to address with a new system. Without this circumspect approach you might end up writing off 100% of your investment.
Never set deadlines in a vacuum. In business today there is no foolishness more often repeated than setting arbitrary deadlines. DON'T DO IT.	Always rely on a balance between project tradeoffs (schedule, cost, quality, and features) and corporate constraints (market forces, seasonality, cash flow, and so on) to determine project scheduling. Setting deadlines without a balanced consideration of both areas is just plain stupid.
Never assume that change involving humans will be easy, and never underestimate the effort required for effective communication! Humans are just plain hard to deal with. Change involving humans requires extreme efforts regarding communication, interaction, and coordination. Herding cats is way easier.	Always assign one person on a large project team to focus on communication and involvement by everyone impacted by the project. Do this along with an incremental approach, and you will find not only compliance, but acceptance and acceleration of the change and the desired outcomes.
Never bite off more than you and your team can chew. Once again, this probably sounds like tired advice, but it is fatal to bring about more change than your organization can absorb.	Always design, build, and deliver functionality incrementally. Give your staff time to absorb the change and extract the greatest possible benefit from each investment you make.
Never assume that it's only about software. Humans manage and use systems, not software. If the humans are out of sync, the software investment is lost.	Always build new functionality only after you have implemented, measured, experienced, and diagnosed existing organizational, process, and technology issues. Simple advice, but easy to forget.

CHAPTER 8

Out of Sync,
Down the Drain

Tell me what you think about this insanity. Suppose a company that manufactures portable mini-disk players decides to launch a new model along with a huge marketing campaign, one that the company hopes will double or even triple its sales. Suppose further that management waits until a week before the marketing blitz kicks off to tell engineering and manufacturing about its plans. What do you think: Stupid? Impossible?

You're right. You would surely think that no executive in his or her right mind would do something so foolish—but think again. Something very much like this is happening on a regular basis in corporations large and small. Otherwise exceptional executives are developing marketing and product strategies that will use the Web as a marketing medium or as a vehicle to support customer relations, sales, and even fulfillment, all without involving anyone who knows anything about the technical aspects of Web development. Pretty crazy? Well, it's an easier mistake to make than you might think. Read on.

XSOptics was rapidly losing market share to aggressive competition and thus experiencing dismal sales. Hall Kennett, the new vice president of marketing, had been brought in to resuscitate the ailing division and

---

The Story

Company Name	XSOptics, division of a leading optical products corporation
Industry	Optical products
Products	Consumer eyewear, particularly sunglasses
Size	Tens of millions in annual revenue, 300+ employees
Issues	Declining market share, inability to capture younger demographic groups
Key Players	Hall Kennett, new VP of marketing for XSOptics
	Carter Bain, CEO of XSOptics
	Dawn Martindale, independent marketing consultant
	Dave Emerson, account manager for KRK consulting
	Neena Bhatt, Internet architect for KRK

---

get it back on track. Hall's assignment from the CEO, Carter Bain, was to "think out of the box—we've got to get sales out of the ditch." The catch was, Hall only had six months to do it or the division and product line would be in danger of being shut down. Hall's first move was to bring in Dawn Martindale, a heavy hitter from a marketing firm he had worked with in his last company.

Dawn stood at the front of the room in the glow of her laptop and projector. "This two-season strategy will allow you to tailor your message to your two primary segments, the summer and winter sports enthusiasts. Although we will treat these as two separate segments, there is in fact a significant overlap between the two. Mountain bikers typically ski or snowboard, snowmobilers often have motorcycles, and so forth. Our research with existing customers clearly shows that people exhibit crossover behaviors depending on the season, but in the same general direction of their recreational patterns." Dawn glanced at Hall, seated near the head of the conference table. He smiled.

Hall and Dawn had worked hard for the past month, analyzing market research and formulating the two-season strategy. XSOptics (XS) traditionally had organized its product lines around age-differentiated segments, but Dawn had come up with convincing data showing that the company needed to focus on two season-differentiated segments. This wasn't exactly "out of the box" for the industry, but it was for XS, exactly the type of thing Hall needed. Winter was only months away, so he had to move quickly to implement the winter phase strategy.

Hall suddenly realized he hadn't been listening. "Comparing the demographics of the two segments yields a number of common characteristics, but one that is extremely important to us is computer and Internet use. The two segments are almost identical in their use of the Internet, with over 85 percent falling into the 'frequent user' category. Of these, more than 75 percent say they regularly make purchases over the Web, a figure that far exceeds that of the general populace. For this reason, e-commerce is a given as one of the central elements in your strategy. We propose a full-featured e-commerce site that can be easily adapted to the season and that will specifically target seasonal themes and behaviors. We'll bring it up in November as a winter sports site, then next spring we can 'put some summer clothes on it,' so to speak, to appeal to the summer sporting crowd. With your product line, you essentially have two major marketing opportunities each year, and you can target each with the same presence and basic technology investment."

Hall nodded. XS had a basic Web site, but it was simply a brochureware site; it didn't allow the customer to purchase sunglasses online. This puzzled him when he first arrived at XS, but after a while he realized that although the corporation was a leader in optical technology, it was far behind in the use of computer technology. Hall was convinced that this was his one and only shot at resurrecting XS and getting it back on track. He made a mental note that he needed to follow up with Dave Emerson, an account manager with KRK Consulting, before the end of the week. Hall had met Dave about a month earlier through a networking acquaintance. Hall told Dave of the plan to have an e-commerce site up by mid-November, in time for the winter season. Dave offered to bring in one of KRK's information architects to help with planning, but Hall declined, saying, "We need to get our marketing strategy in place before we start thinking about technology."

After the presentation, Hall and Dawn stood in the hallway outside Hall's office. "Great job, Dawn," said Dave. "Carter loved it. For the first time, I think he understands why we have to do this. As you were finishing up your presentation he leaned over and told me that we can expect budget approval. Let's take advantage of our momentum and get the media campaign rolling. I have already called manufacturing to bump up production on the winter line. Lock down the ad space in the winter sports rags, major market papers, and the banner ads in the skiing and snowboarding Web sites. In the meantime, I'll call Dave Emerson of KRK and get him in here to talk about the site."

As it turned out, it was over a week before Dave and Hall could schedule time to talk. The conversation went well, with Hall doing most of the talking and Dave taking notes. As Dave was leaving he said, "I'm not a techie, so I'm going to have to get with our technical folks and have them do the estimates. They'll probably want to talk to you directly, to clear up some questions that I don't even know to ask. I'll talk to them and get back to you."

Neena Bhatt, KRK's best Internet architect, listened quietly while Dave went over his notes. She asked a couple of questions, but didn't interrupt. Finally, Dave finished and said, "So what do you think?" Neena shook her head. "It can't be done," she said emphatically. "Forty-five days is not enough time to complete a project of this size, especially when they don't even have an existing online catalog or inventory system in place. We might be able to complete it by mid-January, but even that would be difficult with the holidays. Please do not tell the customer that this can happen in such a short period of time."

Dave knew that Neena was seldom wrong, but there was a lot of revenue at stake. KRK's relationship with this customer was important. Dave ignored her plea. "Look, I know that it will be difficult, but we have to try. How about you and I go see Hall and talk through this. You may be able to see some way to cut some corners and get something up by mid-November. He might even be able to slip the deadline a few weeks. I haven't talked to him about that."

A week later, Dave and Neena visited Hall. Hall was taken aback when Neena told him that it wouldn't be possible to get a full-featured e-commerce site up by mid-November. "I don't understand," he said. "Our current site only took three weeks to build. I know that the new one will be more complicated, but surely not that much more. Look, the Web site is the centerpiece of our marketing campaign, so we don't really have a choice. We've already made huge commitments for advertising space and the marketing collateral is almost all done, so it's too late to back out. If you guys can't do it, I'll just have to find someone who can." "Hall, we want to work with you on this," said Dave. "Let's not give up yet. How about Neena and I work on this a bit more and then we will schedule a longer meeting with you and Dawn and see if we can come up with a way to get this done."

In the car on the way back to KRK, Neena turned to Dave and said, "I don't understand. You know that we can't deliver what they need by their deadline, so why didn't you just say so? There's no need to go back and talk to them again—there's nothing to talk about. It simply can't be done." "Neena," said Dave, "there's a lot of revenue potential there. We can figure out a way to make this work. We just have to be creative." Neena stared at him but said nothing.

Two days later, Hall, Dawn, Dave, and Neena met in an XS conference room. They spent three grueling hours going over the details of the proposed site, looking for ways to cut back and compress the schedule. Repeatedly, Neena pointed out that the e-commerce and back-end functionality was on the critical path and that there wasn't much that could be eliminated from it, and she reiterated how removing other features wouldn't change the completion date much, if any. Finally Hall lost patience. "You guys, don't take this personally, but I'm going to see if I can find some other company who can do this. Thank you for your time. Maybe we can work together at some time in the future, but not now." With that he stood—the meeting was obviously over.

Hall cleared his schedule and spent the next week visiting with several other consulting firms. All were eager to land the contract until they heard the deadline, at which time they started backtracking. None was willing to commit to providing the required features by mid-November.

Finally, Hall gave up. He dreaded the idea of explaining this to Carter. It was apparent that he wouldn't have the site up in time, so the only thing to do was to slip the marketing campaign. He called Dawn in and asked her to cancel as much of the advertising as possible and to revise ads and other marketing materials to exclude mention of the e-commerce capability. "You've got to be kidding! We already have hundreds of thousands committed!" She calmed down quickly and said, "I'll see what I can do, but I don't know how much I can stop at this point."

Dawn was able to kill some of the ads, but it was too late to stop those in several winter sports magazines and a significant number of national newspapers. Hall called Dave, who supplied a Web programmer to quickly build an "under construction" page that apologized for the unavailability of the e-commerce site, asking the viewer to "return after January 1" and giving a number to call for questions or orders. At the same time, Hall asked Dave to provide him with cost and schedule estimates for building the site.

Hall then turned to his most unpleasant task, explaining to Carter what had happened and informing him that his winter sales forecast was being revised downward by more than 40 percent. "Hall, what were you thinking? Why in hell did you wait so late to start building the Web site?" Hall tried to explain that it wouldn't have been wise to get Web geeks involved while they were still trying to develop their marketing strategy, but Carter cut him off. "I'll tell you what, Hall. Right now, I have more confidence in the engineers than I do in you. I don't know of any way to explain this to the board other than to just come clean and tell them that you screwed up. I'll think about it and get back to you, but right now I don't hold out much hope. However you slice it, it's not going to be pretty."

Hall went back to his office and sat staring out the window at the mountains for a while. He then turned to his PC and pulled up the latest version of his resume. He never thought he'd be looking for another job so soon.

ANALYSIS AND CONCLUSIONS

Now, does this story seem simple to dissect and analyze? You're probably thinking, "The marketing guy screwed up and didn't involve the technical guy," right? We only wish it were that simple. The issue here is not simply that the marketing guy screwed up, but why he screwed up. The type of thinking he and other key players displayed is at the root of many failed technology and technology-dependent projects and worth serious, focused consideration. Before we dive in, however, it is important to note that at the strategy level, Hall had it right. The XS product line was ripe for the Web and the demographic groups XS identified. Its seasonal marketing approach was right on, and the ideas about using a core technology base and then adjusting to these seasons was a perfect example of how to leverage Web technologies to create new distribution channels for products. The core problem was a misalignment between the company's marketing strategy and how it would execute operationally, specifically regarding technology. This is a classic and all-too-common example of executives and senior managers who focus on the competitive domain without proper consideration of the impact on the operational domain.

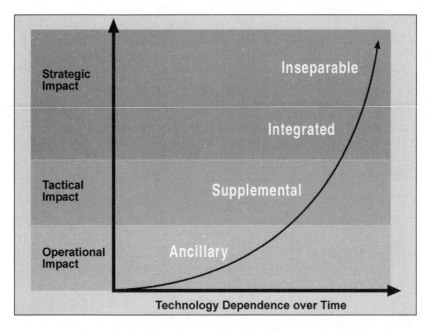

Figure 8.1   Historical View of Corporate Technology Dependence

No Need for Geeks

The statement that clearly revealed Hall's most critical error in thinking was, "We need to get our marketing strategy in place before we start thinking about technology." Hall is not alone in this thought process. Financial analysts, operations specialists, product planners, and others have been around corporations forever and are thus typically integrated into corporate strategic and planning processes. On the other hand, the people who develop software systems are, even today, relatively new on the executive landscape and rarely enjoy the same status as their peers in established disciplines. This is especially true in companies, such as XSOptics's parent corporation, that have had "back office" data processing and manufacturing systems for many years. These systems typically had little direct impact on sales or service; they were primarily aimed at enhancing the operational efficiency of internal business processes. Consequently, it would naturally seem unnecessary to get the people responsible for these systems involved in strategic marketing planning. Hall shared this dated view of technology and its role at the corporate strategy level, a view that proved fatal.

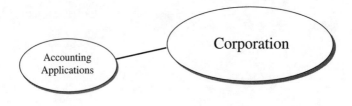

Figure 8.2 Ancillary Stage

Things have changed. Systems such as the one planned by XS directly touch customers, driving sales, fulfilling orders, and providing customer support. These capabilities were core to XS's survival and thus core to its strategy. Figure 8.1 begins to shed some light on where Hall was coming from and the problems with his core assumptions.

Hall's career growth occurred primarily in the 1970s. During this period, technology was still primarily in the "ancillary" stage of supporting organizational needs. As Figure 8.2 illustrates, during this time corporate technology was typically limited to accounting or even more basic systems that supported but were not core to corporate performance. Corporations at this stage could easily fall back on a manual workaround if one of these systems failed. This stage was primarily characterized by technology being used as a tool for achieving isolated operational efficiencies.

The next stage of technology dependence was what we call "supplemental." In this stage, corporate use of technology further developed through pockets of specialized applications that provided operational efficiencies but also began to increase corporate awareness of the value of technology for information management. At this stage, technology began to be a management or tactical level concern, and cross-functional applications began to appear. Networks began to emerge during this phase but were not yet pervasive or stable enough for an organization to consider them a foundational technology. Corporations at this phase experienced pain when systems failed but were still able to fall back on aging manual processes (see Figure 8.3).

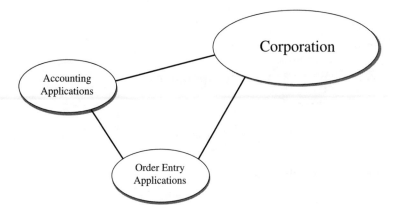

Figure 8.3   Supplemental Stage

The "integrated" phase (see Figure 8.4) slammed into organizations like a sudden summer storm and was characterized by explosive growth and chaos. At this point the computing revolution grew to affect almost every person at every organizational level. Many executives, asleep at the wheel, still believed technology to be ancillary or supplemental, but their organizations were rapidly growing dependent on technology for everyday corporate communications and functions. Interdepartmental and later enterprisewide networking, improved system stability, and wider application of technology as a tool to be employed by just about all workers marked this period. At this point, technology dependence was high and manual workarounds became extremely difficult, if not impossible, when systems failed. Corporate communications, efficiency, and effectiveness were all dramatically affected by systems failures. Technology began to have an impact on an organization's ability to identify and exploit market opportunities. At this stage, most old-world executives were forced by sheer necessity to wake up and raise their sights to a more strategic view of technology, and technology managers were often elevated to executive status (e.g., CIO, vice president of technology).

The "inseparable" phase (see Figure 8.5) represents another radical and important shift in the integration of technology into the corporation. In this phase, the technology of an organization and the organization itself are indistinguishable. Many corporations spawned in the last few years would not even exist, and could not now survive, without technology. Good examples of this can be found in the "pure dot-com" companies:

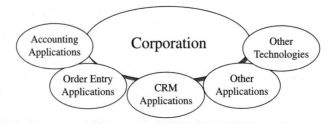

Figure 8.4   Integrated Stage

Figure 8.5   Inseparable Stage

Cut the cable to the Internet and the company shuts down. Technology is so much a part of the fabric of these organizations that without it they would not be able to meet market needs, would not be able to operate, or would simply not exist. In these organizations, manual workarounds have never even been an option. If technology is poorly managed or executed by a company at this stage, severe losses or even corporate death are likely.

It is important to note that although this progression generally represents corporate dependence over the last forty or so years, it also may represent a particular organization's maturation in its exploitation of and dependence on technology. Corporations today are scattered across this spectrum, but most are moving toward the "integrated" or "inseparable" stages. Figure 8.6 provides another view of how each of these stages progresses up to the strategy level in any organization.

Hall, with his new marketing strategy, unknowingly found himself at the very top end of this graph. After accepting the idea that XSOptics's

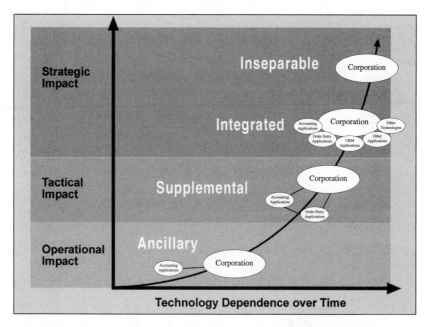

Figure 8.6   Historical View of Corporate Technology Dependence, Expanded

turnaround strategy would be fundamentally based on Web marketing, sales, order entry, fulfillment, and customer support, Hall was in a position of total technology dependence. Unfortunately, Hall and Dawn's view of technology was at least several major waves behind. They treated the Web as supplemental to their turnaround strategy, but in fact it was truly core and inseparable. They treated it as a tactical or operational issue and thus determined they could deal with it after formulating their strategy.

Setting corporate strategy without involving the experts who understand not only the technology but also its practical application is foolhardy and invites disaster. We understand that the "geeks" sometimes seem to act as if corporations exist for their play and pleasure, but if you must rely on technology, you'd better involve them early and often.

BEWARE OF CONSULTING SALES

Quality technical professionals are just that because their basic makeup is task-centric: They relate well to inanimate objects, for example computers.

In contrast, consulting services salespeople who successfully bridge the communication gap between consulting firm and corporate customer are at the other end of the spectrum: They relate well to humans. Therefore, we have the necessary involvement of people like Dave (a salesperson) and Neena (a technologist) on almost every outsourced technical project. The problem is that the mismatch between the two personalities and skill sets often causes serious communication gaps and misperceptions. This regularly results in the situation Hall faced. To Dave's credit, he did bring technical expertise to bear immediately, but he didn't like what he heard, so he stuck his head in the sand and ignored the problems. Neena, on the other hand, quickly identified what she considered high-risk madness and simply refused to budge. For salespeople and technologists to successfully work together requires mutual respect and willingness to compromise by both parties.

An unfair characterization of the two would call one an optimist and the other a pessimist. Neither characterization is truly accurate. Both are just trying to do their jobs, to sell and build software. Another factor that further aggravates this problem is that technologists and salespeople within consulting organizations are often compensated in ways that only serve to widen the gap. Salespeople are typically compensated on the basis of revenue, whereas senior consultants are often compensated on the basis of project-level profit margin. One is driven toward volume, the other toward quality. Neither is bad—in the right measure—but if one gains the upper hand, problems are certain to arise, and the customers are always the ones who pay the price. For executives to survive, they must understand that these factors exist and mitigate them by ensuring that there is balance between these issues. Because Hall failed to understand this, he wasn't even aware of the two positions, much less able to manage them.

It Can't Be That Hard!

We covered this in detail in Chapter 2, but it bears repeating: Don't blindly assume that Web software development is simpler, faster, or cheaper than traditional development. In a recent interview with the authors, Carl Fitch, co-founder and CEO of one of the nation's largest privately held technology-consulting firms, stated that after twenty years and thousands of clients and engagements,

> the challenges facing our industry are the same. Technology project sponsors have always expected technology to do more for them than it could, faster than it could, and for less personal and financial investment than was actually required. Now, with the advent of the Internet, the perception to reality gap has widened even further. To build enterprise systems to be deployed on the Internet, you must piece together very complex components, often from disparate vendors. So what you have is basically a flawed view of technology to begin with, compounded by all the recent hype and misperception surrounding how "easy" Internet technology is to build.

Hall was simply another in a long line of victims who have fallen prey to the erroneous conclusion that because the Web is free and easy to use, it must be cheap and simple to build a Web presence. Simple brochure-ware sites are indeed simple, but any Web site that has to transact business is going to be complex, will take a long time to develop, and will be costly. Don't be fooled: It can and will be difficult!

CONCLUSION

Hall's ignorance caused him to misunderstand how to effectively pursue a technology-based marketing strategy. There are several things he could have done to quell the storm he unwittingly sailed into (see Table 8.1).

It is essential that executives recognize the degree of their organization's dependence on technology and the implications of that dependence. Without this awareness it is easy to fall into traps, as Hall did. He was a talented and dedicated executive who launched himself into a storm of ones and zeros without being in any way prepared for survival. Don't be fooled by the pundits: Web technology is software, and software is difficult. The very nature of strategically driven technology initiatives ensures that these projects will be difficult to manage and implement. If they were easy they would not be strategic or mission critical. Be aware, get informed, acquire sound and timely counsel, and your project just might succeed.

Table 8.1   Do's and Don'ts for Integrating Technology and Business
Strategy

Never	Always
Never assume that your software project is easy and can be done quickly. Some software projects are easy and can be done quickly. If you are dealing with static content delivery over the Web, your project might be one of these. However, these projects are the exception rather than the rule.	Always engage a development professional to review your project at the conceptual stage rather than waiting until you have enough momentum to take you and your idea off a cliff. Always define effort, duration, cost, and resource requirements based on what you are specifically trying to accomplish. Don't make uninformed assumptions, particularly if you plan to bet your company on them.
Never wait until after your strategy is set in stone to bring your technology team to the table. If your strategy in any way depends on technology, technology should take nothing less than a strategic position in strategy formulation. To treat technology as ancillary or supplemental when it is core is to invite disaster.	Always engage technology experts early and often when basing corporate strategy on technology execution. Technology today is rarely non-core to strategy formulation and execution. Technologists must not only be brought to the strategy table, but must have a permanent seat.
Never engage in serious discussions regarding technology projects with a salesperson alone. Salespeople are necessary and beneficial to your relationship with your consulting firm, but they will rarely be involved hands-on with your project and thus cannot effectively make detailed and accurate representations of project parameters on their own.	Always demand that the technology lead who is likely to be part of your project be present when discussing the details of your project. This is especially true when talking about risk, effort, duration, cost, and resource requirements.

CHAPTER 9

Shark Fishing in a Rowboat

When architects and engineers make mistakes, buildings collapse, bridges give way, and sometimes people die. Businesses that necessarily rest the weight of their empires on technological foundations are just as dependent on sound architecture and engineering, but they rarely understand the truly precarious positions they are in, until it is too late. Driven by time and budget pressures, entrepreneurs frequently try to save time and conserve capital by building a simple first-version Web site or technology platform, planning to enhance it and make it more robust once revenue starts rolling in. This seems logical—a formula used by entrepreneurs for centuries—but the world of the Web is different.

In the "real" bricks and mortar world, you can build a store that proves too small and survive. On opening day, you end up with a full parking lot and customers standing in line. A few leave, but all in all you have a great showing; the results are seldom fatal. Traffic, parking, and human nature are working in your favor, providing natural limits to the number of potential customers that will appear at your door. The Web entrepreneur is faced with a very different situation. We have perfected Internet technology to the point that there are few if any natural constraints on customer demand. At literally any given moment, millions of prospects may appear at your door and enter your business, leaving you with a system that is at best functioning very slowly and more likely not functioning at all. Business rolls right over you; your simple first-version site just isn't up to the

---

The Story

Company Name	Great Homes Supply
Industry	Home improvement and light construction
Products	Building supplies
Size	$5 billion in annual revenue, 26,000 employees
Issues	Want to quickly add e-commerce capabilities
Key Players	Chuck Phillips, executive, new development
	John Romanowski, executive, market expansion

---

task, and there's no time to "stop and do it right." It's like going shark fishing in a rowboat: You'd better hope you don't catch a big one!

Chuck Phillips and John Romanowski had joined Great Homes, a national home supply company, fresh out of college and hungry for action, and they found it at Great Homes. The company had just been bought by ComPex Holdings with plans for aggressive growth, the perfect climate for Chuck and John. They had quickly proven themselves, and within a year had been picked to lead a "quick launch team," charged with rapidly opening a series of new stores across the United States. It had been fun at first, but by the end of the second year, Chuck and John were tired of the twenty-four-by-seven grind and ready for a change.

One evening they stopped at a local bar for a beer and burger. While talking about the latest grand opening, John had commented about how dedicated the home handyman had to be to endure the traffic and crowds on Saturday morning just to pick up some supplies needed for a weekend project. "It sure would be nice if we could make it easier on them, a way to buy home supplies without having to fight your way into and out of a superstore," John said.

Chuck set his beer on the bar and stared at John for a moment. "Damn, John. That's it! There's no reason why people have to fight traffic and crowds to go to a store anymore. Hell, people are buying TVs and cars over the Internet every day. If I need ten sacks of cement and a dozen two-by-fours, why can't I just order them online and have them delivered to my front door? I don't think there's anyplace on the Web where I can buy building and home supplies and have them delivered. You've heard the term 'click and mortar,' right? You order stuff from a Web site and a local business delivers it. Well, Great Homes will soon be in every major market in the United States. We could put up a Web site where people could order from the Great Homes catalog and the nearest store would deliver it. Mr. Handyman would arrive home on Friday afternoon and there would be a shrink-wrapped pallet sitting in his driveway."

Returning to the hotel, they talked and worked until the early morning hours. By the time they collapsed into bed, Chuck's laptop computer held the kernel of a business plan and financial model. The plan overview had all the standard components: marketing strategy, sales and revenue projections, staffing, and so forth. They weren't sure how to project the cost of developing the Web site, but after a bit of research they made a stab at it by including rough estimates of consulting costs, hardware, software, hosting, domain registration, and ongoing site maintenance costs.

The following week they presented the idea to their boss, Dee Grant, director of expansion and acquisitions. Dee immediately grasped the concept and pledged her support. She suggested that the best approach would be for ComPex to fund a separate company to operate the Web venture as an alternative sales channel, with a formal order fulfillment contract and service agreement with Great Homes. By the end of the following month, Dee had gained approval and a promise of seed funding from the board that would cover the first six months of operation. The funding did not include marketing and fulfillment integration costs because the board also committed internal Great Homes's teams to support the effort. John and Chuck were on their way to dot-com fame and fortune.

"That's the good news," said Dee. "Now the bad news. You know how they give you guys six months to bring up a new store? Well, they figure that since you don't have to build a building or stock the shelves, you should be able to bring up a Web store in half that time at a fraction of the cost. They're giving you ninety days to have it up and running. In addition, they said that you have to justify your funding draws one at a time. I convinced them that they should give you $200,000 to get moving, and that the clock shouldn't start until you're through with your current assignment, so you've got money and a little time to start planning and setting some things in motion."

The next three weeks were the longest of their lives, as they hired and trained their replacements for the new store. They worked with ComPex attorneys to complete the documents required to set the new company in motion. On the recommendation of the director of Great Homes's IT department, they convinced Jill Christensen, a senior project manager for Great Homes IT, to join their new venture as director of technology. Working by phone with Jill, they constructed a rough plan and schedule for building and launching the site.

Soon their newly designed logo was placed at the entry into their office space and BackyardSupply.com was truly in business. Chuck, John, and Jill wrote a short "Request For Proposal" (RFP) document covering the goal of the project, types of products and services to be delivered, a basic description of how they thought the site should look and operate, and a summary of the core business rules the site would have to adhere to. In the RFP, they emphasized the fact that the project had to be completed in three months and that costs had to be constrained. They asked three local consulting companies to submit a proposal, complete with cost and schedule estimates, by the end of the week.

Two of the companies responded. Their price estimates were similar, but only WebStrategists was in the ballpark on delivery timing. Even though it didn't appear that WebStrategists had ever handled a site with as much functionality and potential traffic, because timing was the most critical decision criterion, Chuck and John decided to engage the company on a time and materials contract to build the site. Work began immediately.

While WebStrategists worked on the Web site, Jill worked with a Great Homes technical team, making design changes to Great Homes's inventory database that would permit it to be used as a catalog source for the new Web site. Chuck and John worked with both teams, offering suggestions on site functionality along with expert guidance on content, product catalog, and other Great Homes-related issues.

They also worked with Great Homes's marketing team to prepare a marketing campaign. Great Homes depended on inserts placed in local papers every Wednesday to advertise its weekend specials. These newspaper inserts would be the primary advertising medium for BackyardSupply.com. For several weeks, each insert would devote half of the front page to an announcement of BackyardSupply.com, with instructions on how it worked. In addition, Great Homes would hang banners at the entrance and exit of every store announcing the site, inviting customers to take a flyer home with them. Chuck and John were satisfied that they would reach a significant portion of their target market, the home-owning handyman.

More important, they would advertise Web-only special pricing that they were certain would bring in business. For an introductory period, Web orders would receive a 20 percent discount, even on sale items. Some of the lost margin would be made up by the increased efficiency of Web sales, but the real purpose was to draw visitors to the site.

Two weeks before the site was supposed to go live, the two teams integrated their work. Chuck and John flipped a coin, and Chuck became the first "user" of BackyardSupply.com. Navigating swiftly through the site, he filled his shopping cart with "10 sacks of cement and a dozen two-by-fours" to be delivered to his house by Saturday morning. Completing the order, he grinned at John and clicked "Submit"—and the system promptly crashed.

The problem was simple and easy to repair, after which testing began in earnest. Chuck, John, and Jill, along with volunteers from Jill's technical team, placed order after order with every combination of stock items they could think of. They found several problems in the first few days, even crashing the site a couple of times, but WebStrategists responded quickly to each problem as it was uncovered and, as the go-live date approached, the site became rock solid.

Chuck and John beamed like new parents as the chairman of ComPex's board placed the first "official" order, a picnic table to be delivered to his lakeside summer home. Luckily, the site performed perfectly and within a minute an e-mail arrived confirming that the order had been received and would be delivered the next day by the Great Homes store nearby. Chuck and John treated the development teams to a blowout Happy Hour that evening, lasting until almost midnight. The project had been tough, but they reveled in their success.

Two days later, newspapers hit doorsteps and driveways, and Backyard-Supply.com came to life. Just like the well-known TV commercial, first one order came in, then five, then twenty, and so forth. Twenty-four hours later more than 750 orders had been placed. The system continued to perform perfectly, and WebStrategists stood down from their full-time system watch. A few calls came in from customers, but most were simply questions about stock items or requests to change or cancel orders or to change delivery instructions.

A week later, it became apparent that the advertising was a continued success. Site usage and order volume had been slowly increasing, and with the second newspaper insert, it surged. Jill received a call from the hosting company saying that the Web server was peaking at over 70 percent utilization, an indication that capacity should be increased. Jill called WebStrategists, who told Jill that, as planned, they would simply add an additional Web server to carry the load. It worked. After the installation of a second server, peak utilization dropped to around 40 percent on each server, a satisfactory figure for even the most conservative system administrator.

Over the next several days the load increased steadily, but the two servers handled it nicely. Jill was beginning to relax when she received a call from the hosting company. "Your database server is occasionally maxing-out," began the voice. After getting more information, Jill hung up and called WebStrategists again, informing them of the new problem. They promised to get back to her before close of business. Jill was anxious because she knew that this would cause serious performance problems, which could drive customers away.

Mike, the WebStrategists team lead, called the next morning. "We can't understand what's going on. The database server should easily handle the number of users hitting your site. Something funny is happening. We need to come down there to evaluate the problem." Jill agreed.

As she waited, Jill decided to examine the actual site statistics against projections to understand what was going on. She quickly determined that the number of visitors to the site was higher than projected, but by less than a factor of two. On the other hand, the number of items being ordered exceeded projections by a factor of eight! When Mike and his team arrived, they began examining orders as they were submitted, looking for anything suspicious.

It didn't take long. One of the team members soon said, "Hey. This order is from a contractor, and it's a pretty big one—over a hundred items." Soon thereafter another team member made a similar announcement, and it wasn't long before Jill watched an order for sixty-seven items come in from a contractor.

Jill asked WebStrategists' database administrator (DBA) to do a database query that counted the number of orders of one to five items, six to ten items, and so forth. About thirty minutes later, the DBA laid the report in front of Jill. "Check this out," he said. Jill felt a chill as she scanned the report. Over half of the orders were for forty items or more! They had expected the number of items per order to average less than ten, a critical estimate used in the design of the site. This meant that the customer profile they designed the site for was significantly different from the profile of the customers who were actually buying from the site. Exactly why, or what it meant to the system wasn't clear, but she knew that she had to get Chuck and John involved immediately.

"Damn, why didn't we think of this!?" John stared at the report as Chuck continued. "Offer a 20 percent discount and who do you attract? Small to mid-sized contractors, that's who! We designed the site for home handymen, not contractors. Why didn't we think of this?"

"So, Jill, what does this mean to the site?" asked John. Jill took a deep breath and exhaled slowly. "Well, the load on our Web servers is higher than expected but that's not a problem; we can fix that by simply adding more servers. Our real problem is that we're getting about eight times the number of database accesses we anticipated and the database server just can't handle the load."

"So can't you just add more database servers?" Chuck asked. "It's not that simple," Jill replied, shaking her head. "The approach WebStrategists took was the simplest and quickest way to get the site up. The architecture of the site allows multiple front-end Web servers, but only a single database server. Having multiple front-end servers accessing multiple database servers gets complicated, taking more time and money than we had available. All of our projections indicated that one database server would handle the load for at least the first six months. That would give us the time and money to re-architect the site to support multiple database servers. As it turns out, our projections were way off. The idea that contractors would be major customers at the site simply didn't occur to any of us, so we're just not prepared."

During the next several days, Jill and her team worked long hours trying to tune the database server to handle the load. They were able to improve its performance, but not enough to solve the problem. Chuck and John made the decision to kill the introductory 20 percent discount, but were too late to stop the offer from hitting the week's paper.

As the load continued to increase, the site began to operate ever more slowly. Frustrated customers began abandoning orders and calling Great Homes's customer service number, complaining about the problem. Because of the volume of complaints, Great Homes's management quickly realized that they had a public relations disaster brewing and put pressure on Chuck and John to solve the problem. Chuck and John in turn pressured Jill to come up with an answer, but could tell from the look on her face that there would be no answer: They had a problem that wasn't going to be fixed anytime soon. The WebStrategists team was working long hours to change the architecture to support multiple database servers, but the new system was at least two months away. Finally, in desperation, Chuck and John had WebStrategists put in a quick fix that limited the number of items per order to twenty. This had the desired effect of reducing the load on the database server, but the number of customer complaints soared as a result.

Two days later, ComPex learned of the problem. Two of the board members appeared unexpectedly at BackyardSupply's offices, with Great Homes's president and two vice presidents in tow. The meeting that followed was ugly; Chuck and John would either fix the problem by the end of the week or the site would be shut down and the entire concept reevaluated.

Over the next two days, Chuck and John worked almost around the clock with Jill and WebStrategists to come up with a solution, but to no avail. Everything they thought of required changes to the basic architecture of the site, a task similar to changing the architecture of an existing building. There simply was no quick solution, and because of the volume of bad press, at week's end the site was temporarily shut down and an emergency meeting of ComPex's board was held. The board decided to bring the site back up under an emergency team of Great Homes's IT department, with Jill remaining as project manager. The board also determined to dissolve BackyardSupply.com and bring the operation under a more comfortable management structure within Great Homes. With their positions eliminated, Chuck and John were told that they could either apply for open positions within Great Homes or resign. Knowing that their careers at Great Homes were irreparably damaged, both chose to leave.

ANALYSIS AND CONCLUSIONS

The fallen heroes in our story weren't fools. The business concept was sound, the market was obviously there, and competition was nonexistent.

Chuck and John were hard working and experienced in the home supply business. Jill was equally hard working and experienced in technology, and the WebStrategists and Great Homes technology teams were competent and exceptionally responsive and supportive. With the deck stacked so decidedly in their favor, how could they possibly have crashed this hard?

Easily. With technology, it only takes a single critical oversight to cause failure, and the players in our story committed several, each avoidable if they had known to watch for them. Their sin wasn't stupidity or laziness or anything of the sort; it was instead the most dangerous mix possible: ignorance and overconfidence, a combination that guarantees disaster. Let's examine their mistakes and learn from them.

ARBITRARY DEADLINES

Who in his or her right mind would approach a homebuilder and demand that it cut the build time of a new home in half, just because someone happens to think it could be done that fast? Ridiculous, right? Then why would any executive or project sponsor think that he or she could arbitrarily set the duration of a complex software development process?

Here's the answer. There is a generation of lemming managers who actually believe that telling people to "Just do it!" is the right way to manage because that's what they've read in a book or magazine. To be fair, many managers are under extreme pressure to get things done, either by market forces or by sponsors who do not understand the complexities of technology projects, but even that doesn't justify the imposition of arbitrary deadlines. The ComPex board had gotten into the habit of forcing employees to cut corners to meet arbitrary deadlines, an approach that usually worked in the physical world of managing stores but that proved fatal in the world of software construction.

There are four core constraints that must be aggressively managed on any development project: features, quality,[1] schedule, and budget.[2] If an external entity constrains a project by imposing a deadline, the project team must be allowed to adjust some combination of features, budget, and quality. The most practical way to implement and enforce this type of thinking is through the use of the constraint tradeoff matrix. At the beginning of each major release, the project manager must sit down with the

Table 9.1   Constraint Tradeoff Matrix

Goal	Features	Quality	Time	Cost
Optimize	✓			
Constrain		✓		✓
Negotiate			✓	

project sponsor and document the tradeoff decisions represented in Table 9.1. The rule is that you can optimize one thing, constrain one or two things, and negotiate the remainder (at least one).

Table 9.1 depicts a scenario in which the customer wants as many features as possible implemented, at no more than some fixed cost, with a fixed minimum level of quality, and is willing to negotiate the delivery schedule. The exact meaning of optimize, constrain, and negotiate are shown in Table 9.2. Consistent use of the constraint tradeoff matrix forces the team to face and make the tough decisions required for success and ensures that all participants understand the same project realities.

Because of their inexperience with technology projects, Chuck and John simply accepted the deadline, along with the unstated expectation that the site would be full-featured, selling all products and services that Great Homes provided. From day one, Chuck and John were in way over their heads. If they had understood even the basic principles of the constraint tradeoff matrix, they would have been able to effectively resist and even educate the ComPex board to make a better decision about these issues. As it was, they didn't even know that they were in trouble. The bottom line here is that without the knowledge and tools to effectively negotiate the basic makeup of a project, the project manager is way out on a weak limb.

On the other hand, corporate executives have the right to set deadlines based on what they see as strategic opportunities and risks to the company. In this case, the deadline may have been totally legitimate. If we assume this to be true, then the blame must fall upon Jill, the project manager. She should simply have uttered the magic phrase that executives love to hear: "We could if . . . " When asked to do the impossible by management who refuse to take "No" for an answer, the smart employee always answers, "We could if . . . ," stating the conditions that will turn the

Table 9.2   Constraint Tradeoff Guide

Goal	Features	Quality	Time	Cost
Optimize	As many as possible	Highest quality possible	As soon as possible	As inexpensively as possible
Constrain	At least some required set	Meet set quality requirements	No later than some date	No more than a certain cost
Negotiate	Features are negotiable	Quality is negotiable	Schedule is negotiable	Cost is negotiable

impossible into the possible. The "We could if . . ." in this case would have been to do an initial site release to a limited audience with limited features and functionality, but based on a robust and scalable architecture, a site that could have then been expanded without having to redesign the basic architecture while in flight.

FLAWED CUSTOMER AND TRANSACTION PROFILING

Chuck and John failed to accurately define who their customers would be and what their buying behavior would be. They were so focused on the home handyman that they didn't even consider other buying behaviors. This critical oversight led to a simplistic site architecture that couldn't support the behavior of the actual customer population, the small to mid-sized contractor. Although it is simple to change the external features of a site such as graphics, text, or even functionality, changing the core architecture is difficult, time consuming, and expensive.

When defining your market, you must consider all potential market segments and related buying behaviors, not just your target segment. If a tire dealer decides to have a sale on tires, he must consider the possibility that he may attract a fleet operator, leaving him with nothing to sell to his target customer, the now irate individual car owner. Chuck and John focused exclusively on the home handyman, completely ignoring the seemingly obvious fact that there are other purchasers of home supplies. Had they sought the help of a professional marketing strategy and research firm, the outcome would most likely have been different.

FOOLHARDY MARKETING CAMPAIGN

Chuck and John's decision to offer a 20 percent discount on all items purchased through the Web site was one of the nails in their coffin. The discount proved to be an excellent way to quickly build traffic—but the wrong kind. Had the offer been limited, say, to only the first ten or so items, or to some dollar amount, the desired effect might have been achieved. As designed, the discount's greatest appeal was to an unintended audience.

Even professionals in the marketing field make mistakes. For an amateur to make marketing decisions in this context is like playing Russian roulette. Chuck and John should have engaged a marketing professional with extensive experience in retail trade to develop the marketing campaign and buyer profiles. A marketing pro would have recognized that a mass marketing campaign, such as inserts in local newspapers, reaches not only the intended audience but others as well, and would have been more likely to anticipate and mitigate the unintended result. Although Great Homes did provide peripheral marketing and advertising support, a real marketing professional would have been a powerful addition to the core project team.

FAILURE TO TEST MARKET AND PILOT THE SITE

The ComPex board's speed-to-market pressure, coupled with Chuck and John's confidence in what appeared to be a rock-solid Web site, blinded the team to a simple, universal fact: The only way to be sure of something is to try it! Test marketing and pilot operations would have exposed their miscalculations in time to make critical changes. As it was, the impact of national marketing and operations left them without options. They ended up with a "Great White" in their boat.

Always perform pilot operations and test marketing. Always! Limit your test marketing and operations to a well-delineated geographic or demographic market segment or a "friends and family" group. Failing in small, relatively isolated markets is embarrassing but rarely fatal. Consider it an experiment, one to learn from, and carefully study the results. Perform projections onto your full market and confirm that the projections agree with your expectations. Only then should you consider a mass marketing campaign.

A TECHNOLOGY TEAM WITHOUT A TECHNOLOGY COACH

The selection of Jill for this project was wise, but there still was a huge hole in the team. Many managers mistakenly believe a strong technical project manager can single-handedly pilot an outsourced project to success. Chuck and John had complete confidence in Jill and believed that she would successfully manage WebStrategists during the design and construction of the site. They were wrong. Although Jill was an excellent project manager and technologist, she knew almost nothing about systems architecture and thus had to depend entirely on Web-Strategists. This left WebStrategists facing conflicting priorities, and the easy winner is always the one that generates the most revenue for the least effort.

The "ilities" (see Glossary) are primarily a result of good architecture and system design. In this case, the critical missing "ility" was scalability: The site simply could not be readily scaled up to meet demand. If Chuck and John had engaged a strong architect or systems designer to work with WebStragetists, the outcome would almost certainly have been different, even given the unanticipated buying behavior. They needed an architect with a clear understanding of Great Homes products, services, systems, and customers, someone who would have naturally surfaced the Web-Strategists design oversights. Not having an architect to direct a technology team is like not having a coach for a football team: No matter how good the players are, without someone designing the plays, the team is not likely to win.

A business manager should never outsource a mission critical technology project without having a systems architect, chief engineer, chief technical officer, systems design expert, or someone of similar skills and abilities who can guide the design of the system to meet requirements. Simply put, someone on the customer side of the equation who intimately knows the customer's business needs to own the "ilities" that define critical system attributes. Without an "ilities" architect and owner, there will be no "ilities" in the resulting system.

CONSULTANT MALPRACTICE

The WebStrategists team was clearly negligent for failing to communicate to its customer the potential consequences of an architecture that was not robust and scalable. Although the team did not anticipate the transaction profile problem, there were obvious limitations to the design it proposed. This is much the same as a doctor not informing a patient of the potential side effects of a surgical procedure so that the patient can determine if the risk is worth the potential reward. In this case, the patient died!

To summarize, most managers are ill equipped when it comes to hiring and successfully managing consulting firms. The sad irony here is that as discussed in Chapter 8, more and more managers like Chuck and John are being thrust into roles as technology project sponsors. On top of that, the unfortunate chaotic and immature state of the consulting industry promises to further increase the probability of project failure when the Chucks and Johns of the world are at the helm. Table 9.3 shows a few key items that would have saved Chuck and John a boatload of pain and personal career-crushing consequences on this project.

Table 9.3   Do's and Don'ts for Technology Project Management

Never	Always
Never allow deadlines to be set in a vacuum. If features, budget, and quality are fixed, deadlines must be flexible. If a deadline must be fixed, features, budget, or quality must be negotiable. To make these decisions, executives and the project team must work together to determine the cost and value of proposed features. Reducing the decision to quantifiable trade-off parameters helps to eliminate emotion and personal opinion, resulting in better decision making.	Always constructively and thoughtfully resist the imposition of arbitrary deadlines. In particular, if time, features, budget, and quality are all fixed, the project team has a responsibility to inform management that failure is imminent. The value of setting a deadline must be objectively examined: If we do (or don't) make the deadline, what will be the benefit (or cost)? This must then be weighed against the risk imposed by an excessively aggressive deadline. If the risk is acceptable, the deadline sticks, if not, it should be adjusted, or some combination of features, budget, and quality should be adjusted.
Never embark on a national or even regional technology-based product/service launch without the involvement of mar-	Always profile target and potential buyer/user behavior when designing systems and Web sites. People use things for

(Continues)

(Continued)

keting professionals. As with many Web projects, shortcuts are the norm, and Great Homes paid the price for applying insufficient resources to this team in many forms. Web and software ventures are businesses and should be treated with the same thoughtfulness and investment that any traditional business venture would require for success.

Never attempt to fully outsource mission critical systems to consultants and assume that an in-house project manager will solve all your problems. The bottom line is that this never works. You must have the core expertise reside in your in-house team, especially if the project is mission critical.

Never hire a consulting firm to build mission critical software unless it has a verifiable track record of building similar applications in similar industry verticals. As we've said before, the consulting industry is full of wannabes who will look you in the eye and assure you that they are capable and experienced. Always get references and always review previous work both from a process and product standpoint when dealing with mission critical projects.

Never launch a product/service without testing it first. The marketing pro would not do this, but the Web has somehow put the minds of many good people to sleep.

purposes designers never dream of. Consumers use B2B sites and businesses use B2C sites. Such use must be anticipated and accommodated in the design. "Understanding your market" means more than just "understanding your target market." You must also examine secondary markets and ensure that their potential impact, both in volume and transaction type, is accommodated in the design.

Always engage an internal technical architect to work with your project manager and the systems integrators on mission critical projects. You need someone on your side who understands and has your interests at heart, both technically and financially.

Always seek out integrators that understand and have worked in your industry before with industry-specific applications. Had Chuck and John investigated further, they would have found that this was the first significant-scale e-commerce project WebStrategists had ever worked on. Their incomplete user profiling and their failure to clearly communicate the potential shortcomings of their chosen architecture were both evidence of their inexperience.

Always select a small test market and/or user group to test your product or service before national or international release. It is better to fail small and learn than go out in a mushroom cloud (read "Superbowl ads") that everyone can see.

Finally, and this is the central truth of this chapter, "Be prepared to succeed!" In addition to being diligent in market research, sales projections, and other business metrics, a little paranoia is helpful. Ask yourself what would happen if your projections were off by a factor of two, five, or ten. Would you survive? Then design and build accordingly. If you're going after big fish, you'd better be in a big boat.

CHAPTER 10

Intra-*What?*

Knowledge is power, and much of the Internet wave was and is about the sharing of knowledge. It is about information flow, conversations that would not have otherwise happened, and ready access to information formerly inaccessible or even unknown. That boundless power of information flow can also be unleashed within organizations, resulting in dramatic improvements and benefits to corporate efficiency and effectiveness. Much of this has happened under the banner of the corporate intranet, an internal Web built using Internet technology. However, if corporations fail to understand how to successfully facilitate these conversations through technology, they are more likely to cause damage than to experience benefits. Most progressive organizations have attempted to leverage the power of information flow, but very few have succeeded.

Aside from the scientific and medical communities, there are very few entities in which knowledge is more important than in a consulting company. The collective knowledge in the heads of a consulting company's employees is core to what that company has to offer, its most valuable asset. The unfortunate reality is that consulting companies rarely fully leverage this most valuable of assets. Let's take a look at such an organization and learn from its mistakes.

The Story

Company Name	Gallagher & Hines Consulting
Industry	Professional services
Products	Management consulting
Size	$80 million annual revenue, 500 employees
Issues	Corporate knowledge is not being managed
Key Players	Andy Barta, principal consultant
	Gerald Wray, senior consultant
	Roy Gallagher, CEO
	Peter Lennon, CIO

Andy looked out the window at the setting sun. He had arrived at work before sunrise, coming in early to prepare for a meeting with his client, and now he was ending the day writing a status update. Andy was a rising star in G&H, something that he and everybody else who mattered knew, but here he sat, under the gun to finish a fixed-fee consulting engagement that wasn't going well. The engagement involved a complete assessment and re-design of the human resources (HR) function for a major corporation. Andy had never managed this type of engagement before, and although he had two HR experts on his team, they had never consulted to a HR organization before. The worst part was that he and his team were having to invent most of their processes, tools, and templates for the engagement on the fly, resulting in schedule slips and higher than expected costs. The way things were going it was unlikely the team would hit the deadline, and the profit margin for the engagement wasn't going to meet the company's expectations. Andy's perfect record with G&H, as well as his pride, were at risk.

Andy's cell phone rang. It was a friend and fellow G&H consultant. They visited for a few moments and then Andy began talking about the problems he was having on the project. He was just getting wound up when his friend interrupted, saying, "You know, you oughta talk to Gerald Wray. He's done a half-dozen HR projects." "You're kidding," said Andy. "I didn't know that, although, it makes sense. The old coot has done just about everything else you can think of. I'll call him." Hanging up the phone, Andy mentally kicked himself. Why hadn't he thought of Gerald? If he had talked to Gerald at the start of the project, he would probably have saved tons of time and money by now.

Gerald Wray had been around "forever," at least in G&H terms. Joining the company almost fifteen years earlier as employee number five, he quickly became respected for his abilities. Roy Gallagher, G&H's CEO and one of its founders, had once said, "If Gerald doesn't know it, it's not worth knowing." The high regard of the CEO and other leaders in the company made Gerald an obvious choice for a management position in G&H, but he chose to remain in the consultant ranks. He liked the excitement of client consulting and had no desire to become burdened with administrative chores and office politics.

The next morning Andy called Gerald and told him his problems with the engagement. Gerald listened, asking a few questions and offering a few observations. Finishing, Andy asked, "So, since you've done several engagements similar to this one, I'm hoping that you can give us some pointers on our processes, and that perhaps you might have some templates and stuff we could use. Any chance?" "Sure," replied Gerald. "I can't give you much of my time, but I have a set of templates and documentation, what I call my 'HR library,' that you can have. Everything you'll need should be in there, and if not, you can call me. I'll send it to you." Andy hung up the phone feeling much better. About five minutes later his computer chimed—an e-mail had arrived. Attached to the e-mail was a "zipped" library of templates, documentation, and sample deliverables. Andy felt a swell of relief as he scanned the files. Here was just about everything he needed.

Five weeks later, thanks in large part to Gerald's "library," Andy delivered his final presentation to his client; the engagement was over, and a major success to boot. He was relieved and excited about finishing the engagement, but this excitement was overshadowed by his excitement about an idea that had been bugging him since his conversation with Gerald.

Andy had used the term "intellectual capital" before, but it really hadn't meant much to him until the day he opened Gerald's "library." It occurred to him that G&H didn't "own" the intellectual capital that Gerald and other G&H consultants carried around in their heads and on the hard drives of their laptops; in fact, G&H didn't even know that most of it existed. An enormously valuable company asset was totally unmanaged and underutilized. If the information could be collected, classified, and stored in a central computer repository within the company, it would then be available to anyone needing it. Andy was excited. Here was something that would not only be good for the company but would also help Andy become known as a leader within G&H. Andy prepared a presentation and scheduled a meeting with Roy Gallagher, G&H's CEO. He was confident that Roy would see the value of the concept.

He was right. In fact, Roy liked the idea so much that he called Peter Lennon, G&H's CIO, into the meeting. Peter listened without expression while Andy again explained his concept. When Andy finished, Peter started to speak but was cut off by Roy. "I think this is a great idea," he said. "Pete, how about assigning one of your guys to work with Andy to flesh this thing out—you know, costs and schedules and such—and let me know the results. We can save a lot of money with a system like this, so I'm willing to invest some money in making it happen." Although he didn't share his boss's enthusiasm, Peter nodded and agreed. His staff was already stretched too thin, but he chose his battles carefully, and with Roy so excited about the idea, he knew that this was one he didn't want to fight.

Two weeks later, Andy delivered the cost and schedule estimates to Roy and Peter. Roy visibly winced when he heard the cost figure but held true to his commitment and agreed that it would be worth it. At the end of the meeting, Roy approved the budget and directed Peter to assign the necessary people to the project team. Peter, again thinking of his overworked staff, reluctantly agreed.

Andy immersed himself in the project. Working with what turned out to be a part-time project team, he defined the features of the system, worked out the user interface, and defined the rules governing content: who could store things in the system, how they were managed, and who could access them. The design progressed rapidly, and at the three-week point, Andy and the team presented the design to Roy and Peter. Roy obviously liked what he was hearing, commenting frequently and asking a few questions. Everything went well until they got to content management.

Andy's idea was for content to be managed by the users with little administrative control or interference. He believed that the secret to success for systems like this was in ease of use and accessibility. He had hardly begun to present the content management part of the design when Peter interrupted. "Andy, I like everything you've said up to this point, but I've got a real problem here. This isn't a toy for the users to play with; this is a mission critical business system, one that requires the same degree of security and management control as our accounting system. The system is going to contain a lot of valuable proprietary and client-sensitive information, information that has to be protected. I understand where you're coming from, wanting to make the system friendly and easy to use, but I don't think that putting a few management controls in place will have much of a negative effect. In fact, it will result in better, more dependable content, which will increase user confidence and make it more likely people will use the system." Andy wanted to disagree but could sense that Peter wasn't likely to change his position on the matter, so he nodded agreement and said, "Okay. We can easily put in more access controls and work out some procedures for submission and approval of content. I'll get that done and run it past you within a couple of days." Peter smiled and nodded.

Over the next week, Andy met with Peter several times, working out the details of security and control for the system. Peter was insistent that the system be "locked down," allowing only authorized employees to access it, and limiting access for every individual to those areas and functions that were essential in the performance of his or her job. He was adamant about content management, insisting that all content be submitted to the "Knowledge Central editor," a position to be created within the IT organization. The editor would determine whether the content was appropriate for inclusion in the system; audit it to ensure that nothing confidential or otherwise unsuitable was contained in the submission; edit it for spelling, grammar, and style; and then submit it to the appropriate executive for final approval. The executive would approve or disapprove the submission and, if approved, specify which classes of users would be allowed to view it. Only then would it be loaded into the system. Andy tried a few times to get Peter to relax the restrictions but failed.

With the design complete, Andy turned the system over to the development team and focused his attention on an internal campaign to advertise Knowledge Central to the consulting staff. He began with a series of e-mails, followed by a twenty-minute presentation at the company's quarterly meeting. Finally, as the projected "go live" date approached, Andy held a series of short training sessions, using a live prototype of the system to demonstrate its functions. He emphasized the value of the system as a document library that would enable consultants to avoid "reinventing the wheel" on every assignment. Andy was happy to see interest among the consultants build. He was confident that the system would be widely accepted and used.

Because most of the development team members had other assigned duties, they worked only part-time, slowing progress. Even with that, the system was ready for user acceptance testing (UAT) only two weeks after the projected date. Peter insisted that since G&H's executives and senior managers would control the system, they should be the ones to do the UAT. The next Saturday morning Andy presented a two-hour training session, after which the system was brought online and testing began. All execs and managers had been given "administrator" privileges, allowing them to access the entire system and to "publish" information at will. Testing went well, and shortly after lunch, Roy declared the system operational. He sent a company-wide e-mail announcing the availability of the system and encouraging everyone to sign on and try it. He finished the e-mail with, "In closing, I'd like to thank Andy Barta for all the hard work he's put into this. This is going to have a direct impact on our bottom line, and we have Andy to thank for it." Andy smiled to himself when he read the e-mail. Knowledge Central was going to be his ticket to a management position in G&H.

Shortly after lunch on Monday, Andy got a call from the lead developer of Knowledge Central. "We've already had visits by almost half of our consultants," he said. "This thing is taking off!" Andy called Roy and conveyed the news. "Great!" he replied. "Andy, I can't thank you enough for this. Great work." Andy began to relax; the system was a success.

Andy started a new consulting contract the next week, helping a precision tools manufacturer refine its supply chain processes. A few days into the contract he decided to check Knowledge Central to see if anyone had submitted anything that he might use. He knew that G&H had completed several similar engagements in the past that he could draw from. To his surprise, the system was empty—not a single document to be found, no news items, and nothing on the company calendar. He called the Knowledge Central editor and asked if he had received anything. "Yeah. I've received five documents. I rejected two because they contained proprietary information that I felt was too sensitive to publish. I've sent the other three to the appropriate executives for approval but haven't heard anything from them. It will probably take them a week or so to turn the docs around and get them back to me." Andy hung up the phone feeling a twinge of worry. Without content, he knew that the system would be worthless. He decided to call Gerald Wray and see if he was planning to submit anything.

"Well, I was going to, but haven't," said Gerald. "Most of my stuff is kind of old, plus it was developed by-me for-me, so it needs to be cleaned up before I'd submit it, and I just haven't had time. There *were* a couple of things that I thought might be useful as they are, but when I went out on the system to submit them I discovered that I had to fill out a long submission form, so I didn't submit them. Maybe I can get to it this weekend. Frankly, I was looking forward to using the system, but it has turned out to be so hard to use that I'm not sure anymore." Andy hung up the phone feeling even more uneasy.

Two weeks later, the system still contained only a few items. Peter pointed this out to Roy, who sent another company-wide e-mail encouraging people to "submit anything that might be of interest to anyone else in the company." Even with this, only a few submissions were made. Without content, there was no reason for people to visit the site, so usage fell and the initial interest and excitement disappeared. Finally Roy, in desperation, sent another e-mail to the company mandating the use of Knowledge Central. "Knowledge Central is potentially the most important thing that has happened in G&H in a long time, but that potential isn't being realized. We need content! By close of business next Friday, I want every consultant to examine his or her files for documents, templates, or anything else that might be of use to other employees, and to submit those files to the editor. We have the greatest group of consultants in the industry, and your collective knowledge is our company's largest asset. We need to capture all that knowledge and put it in a place where it can be shared. That place is Knowledge Central."

As Friday approached, there was a small surge in submissions. Over the next two weeks, the editor and executives rejected much of it for a variety of reasons. The remainder was posted, but usage of the system remained low. Roy consulted with Andy, asking for ideas on how to get people to use the system. "We've invested a lot of money in a system that people aren't using, a system that was your idea. I was hoping you might have some ideas."

Andy shook his head; he had none. Roy looked at Andy as if he had been betrayed, then said, "Oh. I guess I was expecting more from you." Andy's heart sank. His promising career suddenly didn't look so promising.

ANALYSIS AND CONCLUSIONS

The Knowledge Central system is still functional at G&H today, but it is neglected and little used. G&H is surviving, although finding it difficult to compete with its competitor's pricing while maintaining a decent profit margin. Andy is still a consultant, his chances of rising in the company shattered by the failure of his brainchild. Roy's confidence in technology has been shaken, and he recently stated that, "It will be a cold day in hell before I spend that kind of money on another system." A pretty dismal ending to our story. So, what happened?

Millions of dollars are tossed down the drain each year on intranet and knowledge management projects like these. The most amazing thing about this story, and a fact that drives the problem home, is that this is a professional services firm. They are in the business of advising clients about issues surrounding knowledge and human capital management. Now if a world-class consulting firm struggles with an implementation like this, what is the likelihood the rest of us will see the return on our investment? Let's crack this one open and find out how G&H could have better survived this mess.

TECHNOLOGY ALONE NEVER SOLVES PROBLEMS (AGAIN!)

G&H had no formal business processes for the capture and management of intellectual capital. Because it had a strong IT services team, the company easily jumped over that hurdle, but without the necessary processes and people structures in place, the technology just sat out there in never-never land quickly aging and becoming irrelevant. Figure 10.1 illustrates the three key components within the organizational domain of any company. Regardless of what an organization is attempting to implement, if the change is of any significance, all three of these elements must be addressed and brought into balance for the change to be truly sustainable and effective.

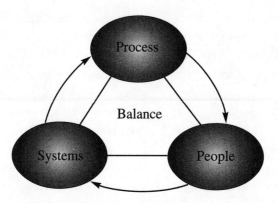

Figure 10.1   Executive Thought Framework

If we dissect this model and each component we begin to see where G&H's project and many like efforts go wrong, resulting in loss of corporate benefit and investment:

- *Systems:* To begin on a positive note, G&H got this one right. It was a firm with solid internal technology talent. Andy correctly determined that G&H could greatly benefit from such a system, and he valiantly sold it to his management team. The problem, as is common with even the brightest of consultants, managers, and the like, is that Andy had tunnel vision with respect to the technology. He radically underestimated the organizational framework required to effectively integrate this technology solution into the organization. Yes, he did do a good job trying to sell the tool, involving stakeholders and potential users, but he did not understand the powerful nuances of the ecosystem of his organization and how his new animal could flourish in a world that was not in any way built for its survival. In the case of G&H, not only was the core investment a loss, but the company now had one more system to maintain. Even worse, the project that was to save the company millions and dramatically increase the value of its services ended up costing far more than the hardware and software alone after all the distractions and problems with trying to get the corporation's buy-in to use the system. Technology alone, no matter how well designed or implemented, never solves problems.

- *Process:* The next essential component in the success of this or any project is process: how the work gets done. This was a huge area of failure with G&H. It happens over and over: No matter how experienced or competent the manager, when it comes to a technology solution, most subscribe to the "implement it and they will come" fallacy. Consequently, even the highest-quality software rarely sees the level of use it could, and organizations suffer as a result. To make matters worse, when they do implement process, it is usually for the purposes of controlling information rather than to meet the goal of timely and secure delivery of information. This was the case at G&H. Instead of pursuing process design and implementation that would encourage system use, G&H, by making it hard to get information into the system, virtually guaranteed the opposite, and in doing so guaranteed that it would lose more than its investment in software and hardware.

One of the central messages of a recent work on the subject of the New Economy, *The Cluetrain Manifesto,*[1] is that when organizations try to control the flow of information they essentially stop the flow of information. G&H's CIO had an old-world mentality when it came to information management. He saw his job as protector of corporate data from the "dummies out there" instead of seeing his job as a facilitator of information use. The rigid processes put in place to "control" the information were not only foolish but guaranteed that not even the best intentions of the best consultants would break down the barriers required to effectively leverage this system.

The key questions related to process on this project should have been:

What would be the easiest way for people to use the system?
How can we make it painful for people when they avoid using the system?

Information management processes must be facilitative, rather than prohibitive or controlling, if they are to encourage widespread use of the system. When corporate requirements are in conflict (e.g., security versus accessibility), the organization must weigh the outcomes of emphasis on each side and determine the appropriate balance. In this case, the scale tipped toward security and sealed the coffin on this project without even a hint of discussion about the balance between security and valuable information flow.

- *People:* The final but most important component within an organization is people. What is amazing about this and many similar projects is that the factors that motivate people to use the system were discussed after it was essentially rejected. The problem with this timing is credibility. The law of first impressions works exactly the same with software as it does with people, and this is particularly true if there is a requirement for usage that demands changes in work behavior. In this case, management simply assumed that consultants would see the benefit and use the system. Let us be clear that one of the immutable laws of the software universe is that if the system does not directly and obviously benefit users, they will find a way to not use it, even under the threat of executive mandates.

The first questions about people issues should have been:

What would motivate people to use a knowledge-sharing system in this company?
What would demotivate people from using the system?

Following are a few more issues about system use incentives that should have been isolated, managed, and leveraged rather than ignored:

- *Incentive to contribute to the system:* The next key question would be for G&H to ask, "How important to the organization as a whole is the activity we are requesting of our employees?" The G&H team was extremely naive to think that any consultant would give up personal or family time without compensation to input all of his or her trade secrets into a corporate intranet. The only way G&H could reasonably have expected this to happen would have been through a strong incentive system that drove and reinforced the desired behavior.
- *Incentive to utilize the information in the system:* The key motivating factor for consultants to retrieve and use information from the system would be a reduction in effort and time required to complete their

work. However, if they are salaried or are compensated based on hours billed, they have no compensation-based incentive to drive behavior toward efficiency, or even quality! Only the most conscientious of consultants work without incentive, especially when the tradeoff has such huge personal impact. A widely used knowledge management system would have been of enormous benefit to G&H, but without proper incentives, the behavior required to make the system a success simply will never occur because submitting content to the libraries is just too time consuming. These factors may not be as prominent in other industries, but no matter what the situation, they will influence behavior regarding the acceptance or rejection of technology.

You Don't Know Me

There is another huge people-related hole that Andy and his team fell into related to people. As a management-consulting firm, many of G&H's services revolve around building teams and organizational development, which is founded on the idea of involvement. Why in this story did they spend so little time digging into the true needs of their consultants? This would have stirred up huge internal pre-launch buy-in for the system, particularly if a handful of the company's best and most influential employees had a hand in designing and then naturally selling the benefits to their peers. Instead, as with most large corporate initiatives, there was a flurry to just get it done so that the benefits could be derived sooner rather than later. However, taking shortcuts like this rarely if ever works when so much of the corporate ecosystem must change to reap the benefits. This is the exact same reason that so many large ERP and other like projects "fail." Corporations must build solutions around individuals who do the work. If you fail to consider the complete operational context (process, people, and systems), your new technology system will fail. Build it with, through, and around the individuals, not on top of or outside of them.

Go Pound Sand

If you place too many controls on the use of a system—particularly one designed to facilitate communication—you will annoy and alienate users, and they won't use the system. A wise approach is to use the "zero-base" approach: Start with no controls, then require that every proposed control be proven necessary. This approach often causes IT managers to develop ulcers, but the benefits of these controls must always be weighed against the cost of the loss of free flow of information. Without this type of analysis, and with internal technology managers typically pushing for lock-down or total risk elimination, you will find that you have built a playground (a great system) and then constructed a barbed-wire fence around it.

CONTROL, CONTROL, CONTROL

A final note worth repeating relates to the CIO's perspective in this case. Many companies today have rightly recognized the need to elevate technology management to the "C," or executive, level. However, this has exacerbated another common problem, the idea that internal IT departments know what the users and the business need better than the users and business unit owners themselves. This is often a subtle belief confined to back-room commentary about the "dummies" out there in the business, but it is a powerful and destructive inhibitor to the success of many organizations. Internal IT groups should always have as their first charter to be a service to the core business rather than a control center for information. These two positions are at radical extremes in approach and structure. Unfortunately and commonly, corporate users abuse and misuse corporate information, causing IT professionals to further entrench on the control side of the equation. However, the misuse by a small population rarely justifies a philosophy of control that inhibits the benefits that could be achieved through the free flow of information in any organization. Suffice it to say that if you are to truly leverage the power of technology in your organization, your IT department must take the stance of an enabler of business rather than a controller of information.

EXECUTIVE MANDATES

When Roy saw that he was not getting compliance from his employees he resorted to the mandate, "Use it or be punished." To be clear, Roy was no dummy. He had built a solid national consulting firm based on talent and wisdom in the consulting industry, but in this case he failed to manage the forces that would ultimately determine the success or failure of the system. Instead he issued a command for use that would hamper adoption by driving resentment against the system and management. Compliance may go up when these commands are issued, but what is gained will never even come close to what could be gained by voluntary compliance compelled by the perception of clear personal benefit. If you ever find yourself ready to issue a mandate, it is a solid sign that the implementation is already out of control and likely not to succeed. It's time to go back to the drawing board and ask yourself how you can leverage the higher motives of your employees toward system use and personal and corporate gain.

To be clear, we are not saying that every implementation must be extremely elaborate, complex, and difficult, or require compensations systems changes, organizational process changes, and the like. What we are saying is that if all these factors are not at least considered and managed, the likelihood that the desired outcomes will occur is almost nonexistent. Sustainable change and benefits from technology never ever come out of technology in and of itself. Table 10.1 is a list of do's and don'ts to remember.

It is worth noting that in this final chapter of Part 1 we have given you a brief glimpse into our Executive Thought Framework (Figure 10.1), which is covered extensively in Part 2. Suffice it to say that most of the mistakes made in all of these chapters revolve around decision making that lacked sufficient view of the larger picture. Most of the mistakes made in life and technology have this in common. Myopic zeal, the frantic pace of business, personal motivators for success—all of these elements drive and excuse extremely damaging personal and corporate behavior. Yes, we must compete at the pace of the market, and yes, we must move fast and be flexible, but if we cannot begin to be a bit more circumspect about our business practices, the chaos will only continue to grow at career, corporate, and industry peril. Our hope is that these stories have allowed you to play "fly on the wall" and gain some wisdom about how to avoid these mistakes. In Part 2 we hope to further deepen this wisdom by providing you with a model that forces thought outside of the technology box into the realms that truly determine success in technology execution.

Table 10.1 Do's and Don'ts for Technology and Change Leadership

Never	Always
Never assume that technology alone can or will solve any of your problems. Without a holistic view of the factors that drive people to use the systems you are implementing, you will rarely reap the intended benefits of the system.	Always assume that you must diligently and purposefully address people and process for any significant technology-based project to be successful. Without this assumption you will find yourself with an engine but no vehicle to take you where you want to go.
Never ignore motivators and de-motivators for system use. Even the best people will rarely choose to do something that does not directly benefit them. They will be especially likely to reject even a good system if it requires them to change familiar behavior.	Always consider compensation or reward structures to support significant system implementations. Without these structures, employees will rarely fully embrace system use, and often will try to find ways to continue to work the way they did before the system came into play.
Never allow technology to be at the center of any technology-based project. This may sound a bit contradictory, but these projects are never about technology, they are about solving business problems for individuals in the company. The hearts and minds of people must be captured and engaged if the technology investment is to be fully realized.	Always put individual users at the center of technology projects. If you want to solve real problems and experience real buy-in, then people, humans, individuals must be what your projects are about.
Never allow your internal IT organization to position itself as "controlling" information. IT entities exist to manage and facilitate the free and safe flow of information, not to control it. Lip service is common but will not do here. If you want to find out and measure the success of your IT organization at enabling your company's information flow, survey the individual users. Be prepared for a shock. Many in-house IT shops are a significant hindrance to corporate efficiency and effectiveness because they position themselves as control rather than service entities.	Always err on the side of flow rather than control. There are times when information must be secured and difficult to get to, but these times are rare and typically follow very specific and isolated needs. The more good information people have about their jobs, their companies, and their customers, the better decisions they will be able to make. The benefits are obvious and powerful.
Never resort to executive or management mandate to gain employee compliance. If you find yourself doing so, your project has already failed. You need to go back to the drawing board and figure out how to resurrect and re-implement your original ideas but with greater emphasis on people and process issues.	Always seek to leverage the power of influence rather than the influence of power. Employees convinced and driven by positive benefits become believers and evangelists instead of passive-aggressive resistors and detractors.

Part TWO

Decelerating

the

Stupidity

CHAPTER 11

The Roots of Stupidity

LOOKING BACK, LOOKING FORWARD

It's time now to move from stupidity to sanity. It's time to pull it all together; to review the common threads that ran through all the technology-related business failures in Part 1 and to reveal the uncommon but simple thinking used by those who have experienced success. Building on the experiences you gained through our case story chapters, we help you reach a new perspective from which you will see and think far more clearly about technology and business. We present specific insights and tools that you can use to survive. Following is a brief summary of the mile markers along your journey to clear thinking and powerfully effective execution:

- This chapter provides a look at the accelerating chaos that, unless we can slow it, threatens to overwhelm us and cause huge damage to our economy, our businesses, and our personal lives. It reveals the key destructive threads running through all of the case story chapters: the mistaken beliefs, common myths, and faulty thinking that lie at the heart of the problem. It also provides a brief glimpse of the answers to our problems, answers that will break the threads of stupidity forever.
- Chapter 12, "The Executive Thought Framework," introduces a powerful tool for executive thinking. Here we explain and illustrate

the power of this model and tie it back to the problems, principles, and tools in the preceding chapters. This model will help you avoid all those hundreds of other problems we didn't have paper, ink, and time to write about.

- Chapter 13, "Preparing for Battle," outlines a practical but powerful process, based on the Executive Thought Framework, which will ensure that your use of technology is appropriate and targeted to truly meet your business needs and objectives.

By the time you are finished, you will be armed with the knowledge, tools, and wisdom you need to not only survive but thrive in the world of technology madness.

INCREASING DEPENDENCE, INCREASING DANGER

The influence of technology on our world is so pervasive that in most cases our social and business institutions are totally dependent on technology to function on a day-to-day basis (see Figure 11.1). This, along with the other factors outlined in the remainder of this chapter, promise that the dramatic pace of technology adoption will act as a force to accelerate the "stupidity" and damage in the marketplace. If left unchecked, this trend will result in huge financial, productivity, and personal losses. Even worse, our confidence in the good of technology will inevitably be threatened. The result is an industry and potential societal backlash against technology and corporate irresponsibility that could cause an irrecoverable cynicism to settle in and degrade the quality of corporate and personal life.[1] The opposite is also possible. We could decide to self-regulate, self-correct, and take the higher road to corporate profitability and the pursuit of wise commerce. Not likely, but possible.

THE MYTHS

The key missteps of the executives, sponsors, and project managers in all of our stories revolve around a few "big myths" about technology cur-

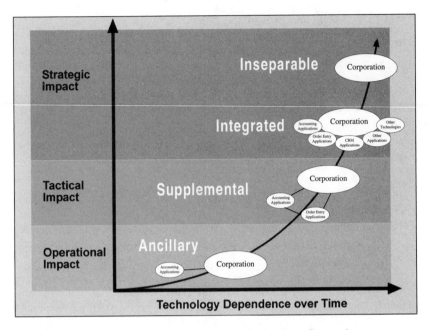

Figure 11.1   Historical View of Corporate Technology Dependence

rently making the rounds. These myths have been responsible for corporate losses totaling in the billions of dollars and promise to continue to trap even the most able among us if we cannot fight through the hype and find the truth. The myths and the facts are contrasted in Table 11.1.

So, why would otherwise intelligent and usually skeptical professionals fall for these myths? Is there some magical power about these myths that draws them to their death, like moths to a flame? No, but there is an explanation. There is a common belief that makes business professionals far more vulnerable in our current environment. This belief is that the Internet is free and simple to use.[2] You can spend the evening surfing the Web and not pay a penny, and it's simple: If you can use a mouse, you can surf the Web. So, from a usage standpoint, it *is* free and simple. The problem is that many people, including executives experienced in technology, subconsciously conclude that because the Web is free and simple to use, then Web software must also be cheap and easy to produce; in fact, they extend this belief to all software, Web or otherwise. This erroneous chain of beliefs sets them up, making it easy to accept any myth that agrees with their

Table 11.1   Myth Versus Fact about the New Rules and Technology

The Myths	The Facts
There are "new rules" for business success in this "new" economy (e.g., market share is more important than profitability, build it and they will come, and so on).	There are no new rules, as recent economic developments prove. You have to make and effectively manage cash to stay in business.
Technology solves problems.	If you still think so, you're doomed. People, using technology to execute business processes, solve problems.
Technology is easy, or easier now than ever before.	Only in our dreams. It's difficult, and not likely to get much easier anytime soon.
The Web is a revolutionary medium or technology for transactional business.	It's not. It is a revolutionary way to deliver content, but it does little to simplify the building of software to facilitate business transactions.
It is easier to develop Web applications than to develop software using more traditional means.	Not a chance. The tools get better every year, but this is not a function of the Web or a result of the Web, it's simply the march of progress.
Brilliant technologists make brilliant business leaders.	Rarely. Any business leader lacking business experience is a disaster waiting to happen.
Technologists do not belong at the strategy table.	Big mistake. They shouldn't drive strategy, but technology is such an integral part of most businesses that it is stupid not to consider it when setting strategy.

beliefs. With the "free and simple" misconception as a backdrop, executives, entrepreneurs, and investors swallow the hype about the latest technology or the fad techniques of the latest gurus, leaping into technology execution expecting quick, easy, and cheap solutions to critical problems and market opportunities.

Ah, if only it were so, but as we saw in the preceding chapters, Web software, and in fact quality software in general, is neither cheap nor easy to build or to implement. Someone once said that the software designer's job is to "engineer the illusion of simplicity," something the designers of most Web-based software excel at, but "illusion" is the key word. The simplest appearing solutions are often the most complex, with much of the complexity directed at producing the illusion of simplicity. "Cheap and easy" software solutions exist for only the most trivial of problems. If you understand and believe that, it is unlikely you will ever fall for one of the myths or suffer the corresponding consequences. Your best insurance is a realistic belief system, one that recognizes that nothing comes free, and that if it sounds too good to be true, it almost certainly is.

One of the common threads running through our case stories has been mistaken belief and faith put into one or more of these myths. Now let's examine another common thread. There are a few specific business entities and personality types that crop up repeatedly, often driving victim companies to an untimely demise. Let's look at them.

Problematic Agents and Painful Personalities

Agents of stupidity are those business entities that have profited from and continue to propagate the myths driving our technology-centric economy into the digital ditch. Many survive and flourish on the fruits of greed. On the other hand, others have a sincere desire to bring real value to their clients. Unfortunately, even this group is often an unsuspecting carrier of the disease. Let's take a brief look at the troublesome trio causing most of the chaos for unwary executives, entrepreneurs, and investors.

Agents of Stupidity

Creative Agencies. Creative agencies have taken the Internet industry by storm. Their influence has grown and will continue to grow at a rapid pace as they bring skills to the table heretofore unknown to the software development world. Only a few years ago it would have been unheard of to include animation in a software product. Now, with the advent of Flash, DHTML, and other graphical Web tools, most of the hottest corporate sites and much of the popular software on the market today have some form of animation woven into their user interface. These tools, applied in concert with the core strengths of these agencies, have resulted in dramatic advances in the quality of the user experience in all types of software applications and especially on the Web.

The bad side of this picture runs parallel to the issues outlined in the previous section. Developers currently surfacing out of creative agencies, no matter how talented, simply do not have the gray hair gained by those who have wrestled the software monster to the ground for so many years. They typically[3] do not understand sound systems design and architecture and rarely have the faintest idea of how to build mission critical "ilities" into their software. However, they often will far outperform traditional developers and engineers in connecting with and gaining the confidence of customers and individual users. Consequently, they are often called upon to "own" technology projects for which they are totally unequipped, with predictably unsuccessful results.

In the recent past, industry visionaries like Don Tapscott[4] forecasted a time in the near future when we would move from the "artisan" or "craft" phase of software construction into the solid "engineering" phase. In the "engineering" era (which was supposed to be dawning about now), they predicted dramatic leaps in productivity and quality in software development. This is in fact happening in isolated corners of the industry, but in the core of the industry, and especially on the Web front, the engineering era is becoming a dream that is every day moving farther into the distant future. Because of the dramatic market demand for software and the influx of amateur "professionals" and creative agencies, engineering productivity and quality in the software industry have, for a time, been shelved. These factors have caused a huge wave of project failures due to "ilities" problems. The industry is simultaneously making isolated leaps ahead while stumbling, fumbling, and relearning the tried and true rules of the game.

Technology and Professional Services Firms. "We put the welfare of our customers first." Yeah, sure. Just so long as it doesn't get in the way of making a buck. Let's face it; the sole purpose of any business, including a consulting company, is to return maximum value to its investors. If doing that means you have to be nice to customers, you will, but let's be honest about the motivation. For many, it's all about making money, nothing more, nothing less.

Most consulting firms in the computer industry, whether called a "consulting company," "professional services firm," "systems integrator," or whatever, have a simple business model. Hire people with the essential skills needed by your clients, pay them the least amount possible, and bill the client at the highest rate possible for their time. There are variations on this theme, but under the covers, it always boils down to buying an hour of someone's life and selling it to someone else at a profit. (Does this model sound familiar?)

So, does this mean that all consulting companies are wolf packs, preying on their innocent customers and employees? Not only "No," but "Hell, no!" We have spent many years of our professional careers as consultants and plan to continue doing so. Consulting can be a noble profession (as long as greed is not the primary driver), a profession essential in the business world.

Consulting companies have boomed and are continuing to boom. There are occasional downturns in response to market fluctuations, but the simple fact is that the industry is being driven by the huge financial incentives for both the founder-owners and the employees of these firms. Consulting firms typically pay more for technology talent, they treat their employees well, and they are motivated to train their employees so that they can charge higher rates. The individual consultants not only like the pay but find that they are usually treated as "experts" when they enter client companies. Most like the regular change of scenery and the challenge of doing several "gigs" every year.

The result of all of this is that consulting companies have cornered a large share of the talent in their respective industries. This is in no way intended to belittle the talent within other businesses, but rather to point out that the talent pool within consulting companies has become an essential resource their clients are typically forced to depend on. The resulting demand invites greed. Every consulting firm in the country is faced with the temptation to push rates higher while holding wages down, often resulting in both unhappy customers and employees. Assuming a healthy economy, employees can solve the problem by going down the street to the next company, usually with a significant increase in pay, but the poor customer has nowhere to go to escape the rising prices and declining quality. The very thing that makes the consulting industry successful, its ability to attract quality employees, is also its Achilles' heel. Greed and opportunism threaten the industry.

The other important fact we must recognize is that consulting companies are largely sales organizations, not service delivery organizations. Who in our industry has not heard someone say something like, "If you can sell it, we'll figure out how to deliver it"? Having more business than you know how to deliver on is seen as a good problem to have. It means that demand is high and business is good. The focus is on selling, not on delivery.

But you aren't going to stay in business long if you don't deliver the goods. This means that you need high-quality, risk-managed delivery, which in turn requires talented people, facilities, tools, processes, methodologies, training, and a lot of other very expensive items. Unfortunately, the leaders of sales-oriented organizations are genetically predisposed against investing the money required to build a top-drawer delivery organization. The best in the industry know that they need to invest in their delivery organizations but rarely can convince themselves to do it. This internal conflict is a daily fact of life in most consulting firms.

Without the investment in building a quality delivery organization, most consulting companies rely on a hero-centric culture, their survival depending on the "hero of the day" to rise to the occasion and slay the dragon. Oh sure, most have some fancy delivery methodology with a trademarked name that they prominently display in their marketing materials, but the fact is that the delivery organizations in most consulting companies are little more than pools of very talented and hard-working individual heroes. This can and does work some of the time, but often it fails. All the talent in the world can't make up for the absence of robust, effective development processes and associated standards. This means that failures will occur, and the customer will be the loser. The name of the game here is, again, *caveat emptor.*

Hardware and Software Vendors. Even those of us who have been participants in the technology revolution of the past thirty years or so find the pace of change incomprehensible. The power of a palmtop computer today far exceeds the wildest dreams of the mainframe designers of the late 1960s. We now move a 1970-year's worth of data in seconds, practically free. The industry has transported us from the green-screen text interface to almost movie-like animated graphics and sound. Encyclopedias of information can be stored on a single disk and accessed almost instantly. Never in history has so much change and resulting chaos happened to so many people in such a short time.

We owe this advance to the creative genius of hardware and software professionals. They have managed to keep pace with the predictions of Moore's Law,[5] at least doubling the speed and capacity of computers every two years or less. This means that today's computer chips are about 200,000 times as powerful as those of 1965. If the trend continues, in the year 2025 this multiplier will rise to over 1 billion. Life is better, longer, and more pleasurable because of these advances, and the future promises to be even brighter because of technology.

That's the bright side. Now let's consider the rest of the story. What spurred this unbelievably rapid march of progress? Well, as you might guess, it's that old five-letter word, "money." Most hardware and software companies are good corporate citizens and are peopled by some of the most brilliant and hard-working individuals in the world, but the pursuit of money is the primary driver behind the change. Now there's nothing wrong with making money, but things start to get ugly when short-term greed takes over, and this is what has happened and is happening in much of the computing market.

When the hardware vendor comes out with a new processor that doubles the speed of yesterday's fastest, there are probably a few people who actually need the extra speed, but let's face it: Most of us can't tell the difference. So, is the vendor likely to admit this, to tell you or me that we really can't use and thus don't need the extra speed? Hell, no! We're made to feel like we're going to be losers if our computer runs at only half the speed of someone else's. The result is millions of perfectly capable computers headed for closets and dumps every year. And what of our software-vendor friends? Ditto. You're made to feel that you have to upgrade to the latest version of whatever office software suite you use. Why? Well, that's beside the point. Just trust us, you do. And by the way, if you don't upgrade your software, your support will expire in just a few versions (read months or years). Another interesting catch in an industry that has, in some sectors, lost its soul.

So how does this relate to the central topic of this book? Because it's easy to make stupid mistakes by believing that the latest-greatest hardware or software will make a difference, when only occasionally is this true. Let's face it: The Web site you built using previous-generation hardware and software is going to continue to operate just fine; there's no reason to mess with it. Likewise, last year's office software, CRM system, or whatever worked last year and will continue to work this year. (Even with over fifty years of combined experience, we have rarely witnessed a full-featured off-the-shelf business infrastructure application being used to anywhere near full benefit by a business.) Eventually, increasing maintenance costs and the need for more capability will demand the upgrade, but until then, "If it ain't broke, don't fix it" is usually good advice.

PAINFUL PREDISPOSITIONS AND PERSONALITIES

Although your behavior is based on your beliefs, your personality is the engine that drives it. If you're a "type A," you'll act like one. That means that your approach to a particular situation is somewhat predictable, with predictable outcomes. Now, we're not going to delve into the realm of psychology; instead, we want to look at a few common predispositions and propensities found in the lead characters of our stories. Perhaps you'll recognize yourself and can thus anticipate situations that may lead to trouble for you. These categories are not perfectly delineated; they are merely descriptions of tendencies that seem to pop up over and over behind the wheel of chaos.

The Pure Type "A." "We don't have time to do it right—just do it!" You've probably heard some variation of that yourself. First of all, let's admit that sometimes it's true: There simply isn't time to aim before firing, and you have to depend on your experience and a healthy dose of luck, and hope for the best.

Okay, now let's move on to the other 99.5 percent of the business situations you are likely to run into, situations in which there is time to do it right. If you have time to do it right, and assuming you know how to do it right, is would seem obvious that you'll do it right. Well, we hope that is true of you, but we all know people who simply don't have the patience to slow down and spend the time and energy required to do things right the first time. Even in the most relaxed of situations, they generate an emergency and force decisions to be made and actions to be taken, quickly moving on to something else. The result is usually disaster.

Luckily, most of these people are also brilliant. Their brilliance manifests itself as "an intuitive talent": They seem to almost always do the right thing. "Almost," but what happens when they find themselves making decisions about things about which they have no knowledge or experience? What happens when they have to make a critical decision about technology, for example, and don't have the technological background on which to base the decision? If they're smart, as well as brilliant, they will recognize their limitations and seek help. Unfortunately, many of these people aren't so smart, and they end up making technology decisions with tragic results.

Even worse, there is a subset of this personality type bright enough to understand terminology and basic concepts about technology who then assume they know far more than they actually do. These people truly "know enough to be dangerous," and they *are* dangerous. Why? Because they aren't aware of all they don't know and just assume that what they know is sufficient to make sound decisions. Left to themselves, they are no less than a disaster waiting to happen.

The Naïve Executive or Entrepreneur. An even more serious problem, covered extensively in our case studies (for example, page 117), is the growing number of executives who are sponsoring, driving, buying, and deploying technology. Growing up and maturing in their own disciplines has made many successful in their space (e.g., manufacturing, accounting, marketing). Now, because of strategic and competitive pressures, they are forced to employ technology to gain or maintain satisfactory operational efficiencies and competitive edge. They *must* leverage the benefits of technology, or they will be replaced by someone who will. This poses a serious problem for many of these executives. Without a sound understanding of how to successfully use or manage technology, they will continue to cause damage to their organizations through their well-intended misapplication and misuse of technology.

The Naïve Technology Zealot. Some people just love technology. They always have the latest gadget or gizmo, and if you ever show the slightest interest, you find yourself spending the next half hour listening to them babble enthusiastically while you make occasional intelligent comments like, "Uh huh," and "Really?" and "Hmmm . . ." We've always had such people around, but they really came out of the woodwork when the Web hit town. Suddenly they could not only play with the latest gee-whiz hardware and software, they could make money at it, too! You can almost hear them saying, "Wow, you mean I can get paid to do this?" Next thing you know, they were starting companies and gaining stature as industry leaders, often garnering the praise of the equally naïve, headline-hungry technology press.

Well, these power-users and technology nerds have been both bad and good news. The good news is that their energy and boldness have propelled the technology industry into the future at a rate that was unthinkable a few years ago. Emboldened by ignorance, they held out their hands and were flooded with cash from investors hungry to make their fortunes in the technology revolution. Although a great deal of this cash was squandered in incredibly extravagant and negligent ways, it nevertheless brought about a great deal of change, much of it positive, in the world of technology. That their enterprises have ended up on a long list of failures does not lessen their contribution to the extraordinarily rapid advance of technology.

The bad news is that when talented but inexperienced enthusiasts begin to build technology systems, then to start companies and to direct industries, they are doing so without the benefit of the many years of wisdom gathered through the blood, sweat, and tears of dedicated computer and business professionals. The increasing quality and usability of software tools have enabled overconfident amateurs to venture into the heretofore-taboo realm of the programmer-guru. The problem is that these tools absolutely cannot furnish the wisdom required to produce sound systems design and architecture. Anyone can pick up the tools of a master carpenter and use them. However, only the well-trained and experienced master carpenter can produce master works of the carpenter's art. Looked at another way, your child can effectively construct a playhouse out of a cardboard box, but would you want to work or live in a skyscraper that your child designed and built? This analogy is obviously ridiculous, but it is disturbingly accurate. The equivalent idiocy is being played out every day in companies around the world, as strategic technology initiatives are placed in the hands of bright and energetic but nonetheless ignorant amateurs.

From host-centric mainframe computing, up through distributed computing, and now back to something similar to host-centric computing,[6] there were millions of mistakes made and thousands of methods developed to combat these mistakes. Now, when myopic but determined technology aficionados dive out into the murky pool of ones and zeros, they often do so to their peril, the peril of their organization or investors, or the peril of the poor IT manager who ultimately will have to own and clean up the mess. Likewise, when the companies they found collapse under the weight of sheer stupidity, their investors, customers, and employees pick up the bill.

The Manager-Leader. Everyone knows the difference between leadership and management, right? Right, and I've got this great property in Florida I'd like to talk to you about. The simple fact is that most people who are in positions of leadership aren't leaders, they're managers. Leaders establish a vision and evangelize it, they light the path, they always have the "big picture" in mind, they cheer and encourage and occasionally kick a few butts. Managers manage. Ten people working for a leader have the choice to be leaders themselves or to be managers. The same ten people working for a manager have no choice but to be workers. There is no opportunity to take a leadership role or even to manage; their manager-boss makes the decisions and it's their job to carry them out. "I'm in charge. Just do what I tell you," is the managers' attitude.

So, why is this personality type a problem in our world of technology? There are two major reasons. First, they destroy the creativity and initiative in those who work for them. Some of these employees move on; the remainder become discouraged and demotivated dullards. Great software is the result of creativity and passion. Dullards have not, cannot, and will never produce great software systems.

Second, many of these flawed managers are arrogant and noncollaborative. They don't want to hear other ideas or opinions; they already have all the answers. This means that they make a lot of arbitrary decisions, many of which will cause problems. Of course, when a problem arises, the manager blames it on the poor sucker who left the last fingerprints on it. A great example of this popped up more than once in the preceding chapters, when arrogant fools set arbitrary deadlines that resulted in pressures that resulted in shortcuts that resulted in disaster (for example, page 133).

The bottom line is that every technology project, in fact every business initiative, needs a leader, someone with vision, someone with enthusiasm, someone to cheerlead and encourage and maybe kick butts. Managers can't do it, and managers produce lousy systems.

The Righteous Right. In Chapter 5 we encountered a project manager named Lynn, whose personality and engineering background combined to produce a person who only knew one way to get things done—her way—the *right* way. In the story, her orderly approach gained the client's confidence and brought her into favor, but that same approach ended up smothering the creative team, leading to failure. This really happened and does happen, to real people.

Rigorous processes and standards have made the incredibly complex NASA space program amazingly safe. When human lives are at stake, or when the existence of the enterprise is on the line, you'd better be sure that things are being done right. But when the stakes are lower, and when the impact of failure is less, you have to start a balancing act. Rigorous process and standards are costly, so much so that their financial impact may make a project infeasible. You have to balance cost and benefit of process carefully to achieve the optimum results.

So what happens when an excessively risk-averse personality ends up at the helm of a technology project? Well, if the purpose of the project is to put people on Mars, good things happen, but if the project's purpose is to produce a small Web site or to build a limited internal operational support system, you will at best spend too much time and money on the project and at worst spend a lot of time and money and end up without a system. Beware of the person who knows the *only* right way to get something done, and who is unwilling to compromise, because it will be you who will lose.

The Over-Eager Believer. Here's a goofball we all know, the naïve moron who thinks that because something worked somewhere else, it will work here. The "something that worked" could be almost anything, but we'll restrict our discussion to "somethings" that relate to technology, usually a software product, bought or built, that "worked great!" The "somewhere else" is likely to be a company that person read about in an article, a place a friend told him or her about, or maybe some place he or she used to work. A good example is Jackie Wells in Chapter 7, who thought that the CRM system used by her former employer would be the cat's meow for her new company. It wasn't. If our goofball is the mail clerk, the only harm will be the annoyance of having to listen to him or her babble, but if the goofball happens to be an entrepreneur or executive empowered to make technology decisions, you're about to have a great "speed of stupid" experience. Hang on!

Here's a simple fact of life, one you should accept and remember: There is no such thing as "one size fits all" software. Even standard off-the-shelf software packages almost always require configuration and customization to work well. Every company is different, every customer is different, every situation is different—and every software solution has to accommodate those differences. The software-something that works for the company down the street won't work for yours. Maybe something similar will do—plagiarize the hell out of it—but don't believe that you can just transplant it and it will work. And don't believe the goofball who tells you it will, especially if that goofball is you.

And Others . . .   The personality-based predilections covered here are those that seem to cause the most problems, but there are certain to be others. The point is, although you probably can't change your natural propensities, by understanding them and the effect they have on your behavior you can learn to recognize situations in which they may cause a problem, then compensate. You're the highest life form on the planet, so act like it!

So, What's the Answer?

A Partial Answer: Standards and Certification

Imagine getting settled in on an airliner and, just before takeoff, overhearing one of the flight attendants talking about the pilot. "From what I hear, he's a real whiz kid. He's only twenty-three, but he can do things with airplanes that are hard to believe. The amazing thing is, he's never had a lesson and doesn't have a license! Can you imagine?" No doubt, you would be white-knuckled during that flight.

The aviation industry recognized long ago that people would die if standards were not put in place and enforced. Sure, sometimes the regulations go a little too far, but at least when you step onto an airplane you can be assured that it was designed by licensed engineers and manufactured in a certified facility, that it is maintained daily by certified mechanics, flown by licensed pilots, and guided through the sky by people and systems that meet rigorous government standards. The result is the safest means of transportation ever, even safer than walking!

So, doesn't the same apply to technology? Given the lives, the careers, and the fortunes at stake, surely the same kinds of standards and licensure are in place in the computing industry, right? Wrong, dead wrong. The whiz kid pilot is replicated all over the world of technology. Without training, testing, or apprenticeship, brilliant young men and women are entering our field, often rising rapidly and gaining considerable stature among their peers because they appear to be able to "just do it." They appear to do the right things, building systems that look right, but when the systems are put under the stress of operation, they often fail, with devastating results. It's like building an airplane that looks good but is structurally unsound and impossible to operate and maintain.

This is stupid! That we are still without certification and licensing requirements in our industry is a disgrace. The plumber who comes to your office to unplug the toilet must be licensed and has to perform his work in compliance with a book of regulations, but not the designer of your mission critical corporate computing system or even the software that guides your laser surgery equipment. Is that insane, or what? The computer industry *must* begin to push toward training, testing, and licensing of computing professionals. Although certification and licensing requirements are not the entire answer to the problems that plague the industry, they would be a basic and important start.

YOUR ONLY REAL PROTECTION

Okay, so we all agree that it's a dangerous technology world out there. People at least as smart as you and I have made and are making really stupid mistakes that have disastrous consequences. There are forces at play that promise to accelerate the stupidity, and we can't expect the government or industry to step in and protect us anytime soon, if ever. So, what's the answer?

If you will allow us a personal note, we love this answer: The answer is between your ears. The most important thing is how you think about technology. In the previous chapters we exposed you to a variety of mistakes, and in the next two chapters we analyze those mistakes and extract some important conclusions from them, but we'll give you the punch line now: You will succeed in the employment of technology only if you understand it, its role, and its limitations, and only if you understand the motivations and limitations of the people you will deal with. You will succeed only if you *think* correctly, because only through correct thought can you see and avoid the land mines and booby traps that lie in wait. Your only protection in the technology jungle is *you!*

We did our best to write this book in an out-of-the-box, accessible manner, aimed at the executive who has little real experience in the effective deployment of technology. Through story and analysis, we attempt to provide a variety of tools, perspectives, principles, and mental models for you to use. You now know a lot of mistakes not to make, the important myths that lie in wait for you, and some of the personality-based behaviors that cause problems. So how do we pull this all together and make it useful? Is there a way to generalize everything we've come up with so that we can avoid all those *other* mistakes that weren't covered?

The answer is "Yes!" One of the major things that differentiate humans from the rest of the beasts on the planet is that we can observe and analyze a situation, then modify our behavior to avoid something similar happening to us. It is to this end that, in the next chapter, we introduce a model for human thought that functions as a framework to help us modify and constrain our native behavior. If you adopt and adhere to the model, you may just avoid becoming a character in our next book.

CHAPTER 12

The Executive Thought Framework

Okay, the fun's over. It's time to get serious about saving your bacon. Everything up to this point has been intended to convince you that smart people just like you make dumb mistakes every day when employing technology. If we've done our job right, you're at least a little concerned that you might someday suffer a similar fate. Now it's time to present a path through the technology jungle, a path that will allow you to gain the perspectives necessary to succeed.

A Crisis of Thought

If there is a common theme running through today's corporations, it is chaos. Businesses large and small share a common set of problems: disorganization, confusion, misalignment, lack of direction, conflicting agendas; we could go on, but you're probably living many of these challenges right now. Why? Why do intelligent people find it so difficult to successfully manage the complexities of day-to-day business? Thousands of books have been written on the subject, graduate schools across the nation teach it, and tens of thousands of consultants around the world make a living on it. So why does it remain such a huge problem?

It remains a problem because we inevitably focus on the wrong things, and when we do focus on the right things, we do so out of context. We focus on metrics or reengineering or technology, without a meaningful contextual framework. We view the world and make decisions from an extremely disjointed and myopic perspective. We spend our time and energy trying to identify and correct the *effect* rather than the *cause*. We learn how to predict an upcoming slump in sales and what to do about it, how to monitor production and what to do if it slows, how to identify organizational morale problems and what to do to correct them. The thing we don't learn is *why* these things happen. We don't seem to understand that the sales slump, the slowing of production, and the employee morale problem are probably related, with a common root cause. Our framework for thought is superficial: Identify a problem, fix it, and get on to the next one, fast! We live our corporate lives in reactive mode, rarely spending more than a few minutes of the day being proactive, getting out of the box to think. The result is as certain as death and taxes: Chaos reigns supreme.

The root of this problem lies in the very foundations of Western thought. Western thought, to its credit, has mastered taxonomy; we are masters at the systematic classification of things into hierarchical groups and discrete categories and then managing each category independently. The impact of this thought process is so ingrained that during every minute of every day there is a seasoned MBA somewhere who is proudly optimizing his or her business unit while wreaking havoc on other units that provide input to or receive outputs from his or her systems.

In contrast, the rise of systems thinking in the Western business world is a reflection of the influence of Eastern thought. Eastern thought seeks more to understand and manage the relationships between categories rather than the detail within the categories themselves. It seeks to understand how things interact, what effect one element has on another, an element's relationships in the larger context of the corporate ecosystem, and how all of this can be managed to produce predictable outcomes. Which of these patterns of thought is superior? The answer is neither. The best managers and leaders in the world understand and leverage the best of both.

Another historical basis for the poor mental models and thought processes of many managers is rooted in the Industrial Revolution. When we shifted from a primarily agrarian society to an industrial one, we slowly lost much of our natural and contextual understanding of complex systems, of cause and effect in the context of time and space. In complex systems, cause and effect are always distant in time, space, and uncertainty. In the supposedly simple world of agriculture, the farmer knows this as well as he knows his own name. He knows that to produce a yield that will sustain his family next year, he must take appropriate action now and over the next several months. There are no last-minute changes or rapid adjustments in farming; months or even years separate cause and effect, and uncertainty is an everyday fact of life. Well, whether you like it or not, the same is true in business. It is unusual to be able to effect significant change rapidly without experiencing unexpected results. The harder you push, the less certain the outcome and the more troublesome the side effects.

The Industrial Revolution began the process of erasing this natural understanding of complex systems from the Western mind, a mind that was already predisposed to disaggregated thought in spite of our agrarian roots. Now we have Internet shopping, fast food, microwaves, and pay per view television. Everything, it seems, is instantly available to us as consumers. Conditioned to expect instant gratification, we make decisions within the complex systems of our workplace and expect instant results. When we don't get them, we immediately make another change. An example of this is an executive acquaintance who, upon moving into a new office building, felt cold. What was his response? He shoved the thermostat lever to the right to get heat. A while later he felt hot so he slammed the lever toward cold. The amazing thing was that he became irritated and convinced that the system was defective. You get the point. He created extreme and uncomfortable variances in the office environment because he did not have the patience to make small adjustments, wait for feedback from the change, and then act again. The variance that he created in his environmental system is similar, in principle, to the chaos that managers generate every day through knee-jerk decisions that lack proper perspective.[1] In fact, this same executive was famous for constantly jerking his organization from one extreme to another until it could do nothing but fail. Remember, in complex systems cause and effect are always distant in time, space, and uncertainty.[2] We must slow down and think about the potential unintended consequences of our actions; we must think proactively. Without the benefit of this perspective, we will constantly introduce unintended variance in our own systems (business systems), and they *will* break down.

But, you protest, "Get real, I don't have *time* to be proactive—I don't even have time to think." To that we firmly reply, "You don't have time to not be proactive." In his landmark book, *Seven Habits of Highly Effective People*, Stephen Covey describes learning to focus on "doing the right things" rather than "doing things right."[3] He clearly points out that you *must* spend a significant portion of your day in "Quadrant II" activities, those that are important but not urgent, if you are to be effective rather than just efficient. You must spend time rising above the noise of day-to-day business and look at your organization, and at the business environment, from an elevated perspective. You must spend time understanding why things are such a mess and identifying and fixing the root causes rather than the symptoms. You must invest more brain-cycles in strategic thought and fewer in tactical and operational details so that when you *are* confronted with those details, your actions are deliberate, decisive, and sustainable.

Here's our claim: Without the model for thought that we present in the next section, or one similar to it, you will eventually find yourself living a story similar to one of those in Part 1 of this book. You will overlook causative factors and critical relationships within your business. Your aim will be off, and you will miss the target you are trying to hit. Your reactive decision making will cause unnecessary and potentially fatal variances that will sap the efficiency and effectiveness from your business systems. You will wonder about but never understand why it takes so much effort to make "simple" outcomes in "simple" systems more predictable.[4] You *will* fail. No "ifs" about it; it is only a matter of when, and how big.

Here's the practical reality: If you are to differentiate yourself from the chaotic "sky is falling!" herd of executives, you absolutely must *stop*. If just for a few moments each day, or for a few dedicated hours each week, you must stop and step out of the fray and think holistically: systemically. You must rise above the fray, gain perspective, recognize and understand the interdependencies of the systems you manage; only then will you begin to make good decisions, decisions far superior to those of your peers, and you might even begin sleeping again at night. In contrast, without a framework similar to the one we propose, your decisions will be at best suboptimal and at worst disastrous. Too many brilliant people have fallen into these traps. Intelligence or pability alone will not save you; perspective will; integrative thinking will; wisdom will.

Finally, you may still be skeptical and may have in mind a few recent cases in which "flying by the seat of the pants" worked. To that we reply, "Exceptions do not make a rule." For every fortunate company that survived decision making at the speed of stupid, hundreds failed, with resulting damage to tens of thousands of careers and billions of lost investment dollars. Brief periods of economic over-exuberance have no doubt catapulted a few fools to fame and fortune, but as John Dvorak observes, "in a hurricane, even pigs can fly."[5]

THE EXECUTIVE THOUGHT FRAMEWORK: A FOUNDATION FOR STRATEGIC THOUGHT

Many before us have concluded that defective thinking lies at the root of most of the problems we find in the business world today. Working from the assumption that this observation is true, the obvious question is: "What can I do to improve *my* thinking about business?" As you might guess, we have an answer, the Executive Thought Framework (ET Framework).

The ET Framework is a model that provides an integrated view of the key elements you must consider when making strategic or mission critical decisions. We're not going to drag you through an in-depth review of strategy or related organizational development methodologies. We will not present a pompous academic model that is difficult to understand and use. Rather, our aim is to present a deceptively simple yet powerful framework that will elevate executive thought, particularly concerning how to better and more effectively employ technology.

Before we move forward, it is important to note that this framework is not an exhaustive model for detailed action. There is no such thing. In recent times, complex methodologies and those who sold them gained a bad reputation for trying to create cookie-cutter approaches to solving all business and technology problems. They failed because they were too complex and inflexible and did not allow for the breadth and depth of complexity in the real world. In contrast, the ET Framework is just that, a *framework*, an outline, a guide that highlights key components that are common and applicable to almost every conceivable scenario rather than a limited few. To apply it requires brainpower, discretion, and determination, none of which can be mechanized into a canned process. In other words, don't expect the ET Framework to do your thinking for you, because it won't.

To be clear, there is nothing fundamentally wrong with the concept of methodologies, but few executives ever truly understand the strengths and weaknesses of these tools and how to leverage them to their greatest benefit. On the other hand, a framework like the one we provide (which is not a methodology) can be likened to a multidimensional, interrelated outline for strategic thought. It reveals and identifies each area requiring consideration and provides perspectives that will naturally reveal obvious courses of action.

THE FRAMEWORK: AN ANATOMY OF STRATEGIC THOUGHT

The ET Framework is a unifying theme behind the analysis and principles derived from the case stories in Part 1 of this book. This framework and other similar models have guided us and many successful executives in developing and deploying winning technology strategies in organizations. It is powerful, it is practical, and it is proven. Let's dive into the details.

As Figure 12.1 illustrates, two primary domains must be considered when developing sound technology strategies. The upper domain is the business environment, which we refer to as the "competitive domain," and the lower domain is that of the organization, which we call the "organizational domain." A more accurate drawing might place the organizational domain inside the competitive domain, but we find such a drawing to be confusing and less practical in actual use.

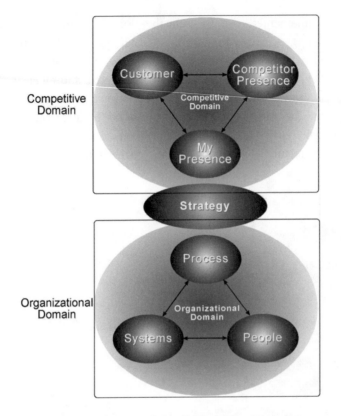

Figure 12.1   Competitive and Organizational Domains

The Competitive Domain: The Battle Space.   The competitive domain is where your company lives or dies. The focus in this domain is on customers and their needs, on competitors and their market presence,[6] and on your company's market presence. Your primary objective in this domain is competitive advantage, and the technological opportunities and challenges within this domain relate primarily to the development, marketing, sales, delivery, and support of products and services targeted at specific market needs. Most mission critical technology initiatives affect or are affected by this domain and should thus be shaped by the strategy formulated here.

The Organizational Domain: Friendly Forces and Weapons for War.   The organizational domain is where *you* live on a day-to-day basis. It's where your vision gets turned into reality and where all the good and bad decisions are made and implemented. The focus in this domain is on process (how things get done), people (who does them), and systems (the technology and tools they will use). Your primary objective in this domain is organizational excellence, to be both organizationally effective and efficient. The technology opportunities and challenges within this domain relate to providing systems that allow people to do their jobs better, faster, and cheaper. Technology failures in this domain relate primarily to a lack of understanding of the interrelationships among people, processes, and systems.

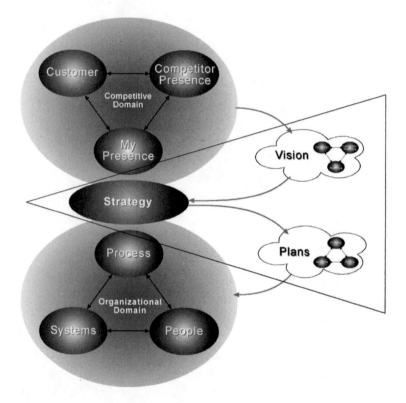

Figure 12.2 Vision, Strategy, and Plans

Vision, Strategy, and Plans: Your Battle Plan. Companies can execute perfectly at an organizational level while failing miserably in the marketplace. The opposite is also true: Companies can perfectly identify needs, products, and differentiators in the market but execute so poorly at the organizational level that in effect, they defeat themselves. It should be obvious that happenings in the competitive domain (opportunities and threats) influence what you do in the organizational domain, and likewise that your capabilities (strengths and weaknesses) in the organizational domain influence what you can do in the competitive domain.

The "strategy" component of the Framework maps between the two domains and is where every executive should spend much of his or her time (see Figure 12.2). It's where you assess the opportunities and threats in the competitive domain and the strengths and weaknesses in your organizational domain, then form your vision, strategy, and plans. It's the wheelhouse from which you steer your organization through competitive waters. If you aren't spending a considerable amount of your executive time and energy developing and refining your vision, strategy, and plans, your organization is a pilotless ship headed for disaster.

Winning companies of the future will be those run by executives who understand the competitive and organizational domains and interrelationships within and between, then develop the vision, strategy, and plans to turn this understanding into action. The winners will be those who are able to grasp these timeless truths and who can execute with the wisdom provided by those who have gone before, particularly those who failed. Study of their failure provides us with insight that only a fool would ignore.

The ET Framework captures the essence of this wisdom and makes it simple and practical to use. Let's now dive a level deeper and discuss how this framework for strategic thinking can provide a light to illuminate your path to success. To do this we dissect each of the components or sub-domains in the competitive and organizational arenas. Each section explains the basic elements of each sub-domain and then covers the most common errors found at the extremes (over- and under-emphasis) within these sub-domains.

THE COMPETITIVE DOMAIN:
A DEEPER LOOK AT KEY BATTLE SPACE CONSIDERATIONS

The competitive domain is the environment in which a business chooses to compete. In this domain, you will find customers, competitors, suppliers, market makers, regulators, and others. The three most common important entities in the domain, the ones that normally require most of the attention of embattled executives, are your customers (actual and potential), your competitor's presence, and your own presence.

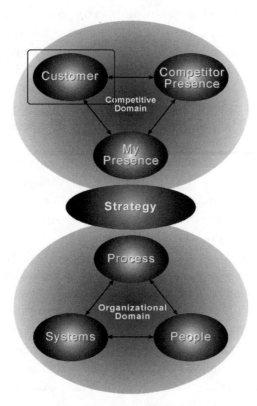

Figure 12.3 Competitive Domain – Customer

Customers: Who Are They, Where Are They, What Do They Want? Customers have what you and your competitors want: money. To get it you have to offer a value proposition that is perceived by the customer to satisfy a need better and/or cheaper than that of your competitors. To succeed, you must correctly identify market demand: the type, volume, and velocity of actual or potential customer need. In new and undefined markets, you must at least identify what you don't know and will have to learn as you venture into uncharted territories.[7] Fail at these basic points and you're dead. In the case story in Chapter 3 millions were spent under the spell of Internet fever to get a product to market that the market did not want and could not use even if it wanted it. The players in our study failed to gain a clear understanding of the market they were entering, despite the fact that there was ample information to work from. The unfortunate irony of this

Table 12.1 Customers: Errors at the Extremes

Too Little	Too Much
It is very common to see startups with little to no understanding of the customer confidently launch headlong into obscurity. While traditional methods may not always meet the needs of a startup, they are always a great place to start. Focus groups, traditional demographic profiles, and similar study methods can be extremely helpful in better positioning your organization for success. It is simply irresponsible and usually disastrous to launch into previously trodden territory without taking heed of past failures and successes. Just because you have a new twist to an old idea, such as a new medium or a unique distribution strategy, does not mean that people will react differently to your product or service. Do the research. Aim before you fire and you are likely to hit the target.	One of the negative characteristics of mature organizations is the need to mitigate all or most of the risk by aiming too much before firing. When launching a new venture into new markets, there is often little or no data to gather via traditional methods or through which to formulate a traditional plan. In these cases, the organization is wasting its time seeking more and better information (as in "Ready Aim, Aim, Aim"). It is time for calculated risk. At this point you should define what you must know in the future to be successful and seek that information and education through action and experience in the market. Experiment. State your hypotheses and test them, literally. Once you begin to gather data, formulate new hypotheses based on what you have learned. The key here is not to continue firing without clear targets regardless of how big or small they are. Have you hit or missed the target? Is it the right target? How did you adjust? Without the answers to these questions you are no better than a blind person flailing in the dark.

case is that the new-rule pundits stood on the sidelines of this disaster and cheered as our protagonists ran headlong off a cliff.

Traditional methods of determining product viability in the marketplace are still valid and can be relied upon to determine if your Web or technology product strategy is realistic. The mad rush to the Web, fueled by the investment community's gold-rush mentality, resulted in literally hundreds of startup companies pushing products and services that no one wanted. In a frenzy of mass stupidity, billions were spent without ever asking the people who had the money if they would be willing to pay for these products and services or even spending a moment to assess product viability in any way whatsoever. See Table 12.1.

Your Competitor's Presence: Who Is the Enemy, What Are They Doing? Current and future competitors will be pitting their product or service against yours,

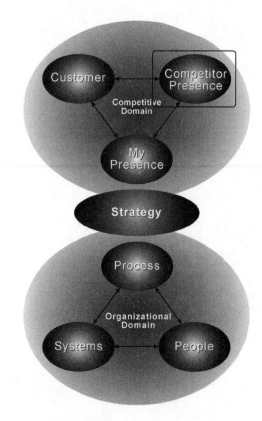

Figure 12.4   Competitive Domain – Competitor Presence

vying for the same customer dollar. One of the key factors that contributed to the dot-com carnage was a complete absence of competitive awareness, both in not accurately identifying competitors and in not moving with adequate speed to overcome or mitigate their emergence. Again, traditional but powerful tools like strengths, weaknesses, oportunities, and threats (SWOT) analysis are designed to facilitate clear thinking as you prepare your venture for battle in the marketplace. This stuff does not require an MBA to use. It just takes a few hours of dedicated time to take aim before firing. Without a basic framework and the perspectives they provide, launching a product, service, or a company is like expecting to catch a ride on a train by hurling your body in front of it: just plain stupid.

Your Presence: How Are You Positioned for Battle?   A long time ago some unknown genius first said, "Perception is reality." Nowhere is this truer than in the competitive arena. Your customers rarely have the opportunity to mea-

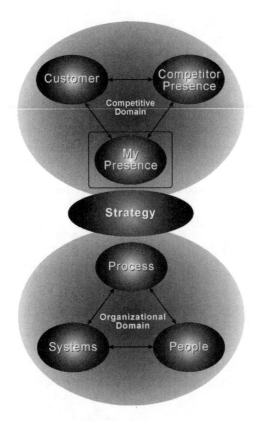

Figure 12.5   Competitive Domain – My Presence

sure, in any absolute sense, your product or your company's ability to deliver and support their needs. Their response to your value proposition is based almost entirely on their *perceptions:* their perception of their own need, their perception of you and your product, and their perception of your competitors and their product. Those who will thrive and win are acutely aware of this perception problem and constantly monitor and manage it.

Competitive Domain: Summary.   So, to succeed you have to understand the customer's perceived need, understand your competition's products and the market's perception of them, and then carefully craft your product and your message so that your potential customer becomes your actual customer. Simple? Apparently not. During the height of the dot-com madness, billions were invested in ventures that totally ignored these simple facts, and those same billions have now been mostly lost. Writing down this description of what it takes to succeed feels a bit condescending be-

Table 12.2 Competitors: Errors at the Extremes

Too Little	Too Much
Acting like the enemy does not exist allows them to establish a far better position from which to attack and destroy you. Studying and understanding the threat posed by your enemy and their strengths and weaknesses compared to yours can help you determine which strategies will work and which won't. Without this information you are likely to spend millions going after markets that will yield nothing, be surprised when competitors steal your customers because your offerings are inferior, or just stand by and watch while they simply walk away with the market. Lack of knowledge of your competitors at any stage of growth is a deadly trap waiting for you to fall into it.	Some companies become obsessed to the point that they are emotionally affected or controlled by their competitors. They read every press release and fret that a competitor lies in wait around every corner. As a result, they become paralyzed and only move in new and unique ways when they are sure a "big bad" competitor won't show up to challenge them. Big or small, fast or slow, your competitors can help you win if you watch them with proper perspective, then strategize and execute. When you watch too much and by doing so, stop moving, you know you are hanging out at the wrong end of the risk-reward continuum.

cause it is so simple. The problem is that it is rarely if ever followed by the inexperienced and ignorant disciples of the "new rules."

THE ORGANIZATIONAL DOMAIN: CARRYING YOUR STRATEGY INTO BATTLE

After performing your due diligence in the competitive domain, you come to the point where you believe you have something to offer. You've designed and packaged your product in a way that will appeal to the customer. You've compared your product or concept with the products of your competitors who will be competing for the same dollar from the same customers. You've talked with potential customers and pitched your product to test their responses. You have a killer marketing campaign planned. You're convinced that you have something that is significantly different from or better than your competitors, something that can compete in the market and make a profit, and you're ready to launch. Now is when it gets really hard—now you move into the land of execution, the organizational domain.

This domain is primarily concerned with the "how" of running a business. How do I execute? How do I develop and launch my new product or service, or how do I launch an existing product and service through a new

Table 12.3 My Presence: Errors at the Extremes

Too Little	Too Much
If you fail to build a dominant market presence, your competitors will simply dominate you. One of the easiest ways to let this happen is to believe the popular but incredibly stupid statement, "Build it and they will come." Maybe that works for a ball field in the middle of a magic corn patch, but don't bet your business on it. If you're a successful executive or entrepreneur, you've surely already learned that the greatest product or service in the world won't sell itself—it requires blood, sweat, and tears. Develop a marketing plan that will shape perceptions, execute it, then measure and refine it, and do it again. Don't stop—your competitors won't.	Jon Nordmark, president and CEO of eBags, recently commented, "Too much money makes people stupid." At no time in history has this been more apparent than during Superbowl XXXIV in January of 2000. Seventeen dot-com companies, apparently made stupid by their newfound "wealth," bought advertising spots, paying millions for airtime alone. Did they really think they could shape the public's perception of their company and its offerings in a cute (dumb?) thirty-second ad, viewed by millions of drunken football fans?* Come on, advertising on the back of milk cartons would have saved millions and worked better. Save some money for the payroll!

*At this writing, almost half of those companies are dead or dying.

distribution channel or to new markets? How do I build a business infrastructure that will sustain customer and general business demands? And how do I do all of these things in the most effective and efficient manner?

Believe it or not, this domain is where many Internet and new economy companies fail. The reason that this is not common knowledge is that the press is better able to understand and report on external rather than internal factors. For example, one recent and very public dot-com death was caused by incredibly poor technology choices (similar to our case story in Chapter 9) that led to the inability to scale to meet customer demand. Did the press report this? No, they never even touched on these issues, and the former president was not about to admit that the company failed due to poor execution. Exactly what percentage of the dot-com failures have been due to internal problems is unclear, but the number is certainly significant.

Before we plunge into further organizational sub-domain details, we need to clearly put something in perspective. In the organizational domain, we examine three entities and their relationships with one another: people, systems (or technology), and business processes. A stage production (e.g., a play or performance) is a great analogy for understanding these three entities and their relative importance to one another. In this analogy, technology is a prop gun and process is the script that says Character A is supposed to use the gun to shoot Character B, but it's the actors—the people—that make the play come to life.

It is exactly the same in the organizational domain. Technology by itself (the props) is of no use. With process (the script) to prescribe how technology will be used, its value can be seen, but only when people are added to "power" the processes can the real value of technology be realized. There are glimpses in Part 1 of what happens when too much focus is put on one entity of these three (particularly technology) to the exclusion of the others. A stage populated only by props is without meaning or value; technology alone is useless.

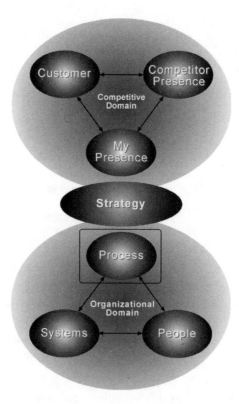

Figure 12.6   Organizational Domain – Process

Process: The "How" of Execution and Scalability.   Yes, we know that "process" has become a dirty word in the current "just do it" world, but you might as

Table 12.4   Process: Errors at the Extremes

Too Little	Too Much
Too little attention to process in an organization manifests itself in problems that are repeatedly patched but never truly repaired (e.g., excessive customer or internal pain, excessive costs for results realized, or just plain corporate chaos). It is unfortunate that so few executives understand the value of the deliberate design and implementation of process. This is particularly true of the visionary entrepreneur. Here's a solid bet you will always win: Ask an entrepreneur to tell you the number of steps involved in some business process within his or her organization. Then bet your house that there are at least twice as many steps. You will inevitably end up with a second home. Why? Because optimists always underestimate the amount of effort it takes to solve a problem, and thus rarely commit sufficient time and effort to do so. If you are one of these, when confronted by a process-related problem, triple the amount of dedicated effort and energy you think it will take to solve it. You just might succeed at solving the problem the first time.	Some organizations, particularly mature companies with a strong engineering component, are obsessed with process. They believe that every time an exception occurs they should have a new procedure or process to eliminate the exception. Their employee manuals are inches thick, things happen in slow motion, productivity sucks, and innovation and creativity are almost nonexistent. Remember this truth: The more procedures or defined processes you have, the more exceptions you will have. It's a fact. The reason that managers exist is to deal with exceptions. Processes should always be designed with the 80/20 rule in mind. Structure processes to orchestrate the 20% of the work that produces 80% of the value, then manage the rest by exception. Otherwise, process will become a substitute for thinking and your organization will be headed for the graveyard named "Bureaucracy."

well accept the fact that there is no gain without pain, there is no such thing as a free lunch, and denying the existence of gravity doesn't mean you can fly. Deny the need for business processes and you will become the victim of your own folly. Accept it: You need process!

"Process" is the answer to the question, "How can I ensure that my business will profitably grow?" The second law of thermodynamics states that all things naturally decay from order to disorder. This is not a debatable point. The forces of nature and the immutable laws of our universe tell us that unless we want chaos and entropy to degrade our organizations, we must bring order to bear and then continually work to maintain it. Well-managed business processes, supported by an appropriate organizational structure, are the only defense you have; your company's efficiency and effectiveness are almost solely dependent on them. Businesses without sound organizational processes will never be as successful as they could be. Sound process design provides a mechanism through which we bring the order necessary to predictably deliver on our promises. Process provides order; order provides manageability; manageability provides scalability. And scalability is a life or death matter in business.

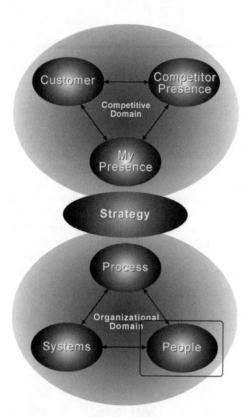

Figure 12.7   Organizational Domain – People

People: Engaging and Leveraging the Hearts and Minds of the Troops.   People are also subject to the law of entropy. Given sound structures and framework to operate within, people will usually produce beneficial outcomes for themselves and their companies. Given poorly designed processes and structures, people will yield unpredictable and undesirable outcomes. The Industrial Revolution sought to master the hands of people. That process

Table 12.5 People: Errors at the Extremes

Too Little	Too Much
Entrepreneurs who err on this side of the continuum are an interesting breed. They are usually introverted and are very analytical and task oriented. Turnover rarely bothers them, and their management mantra is usually something like "suck it up." What they typically fail to recognize is that even if you don't intuitively understand the damage on the human side, the math is obvious and problematic. Turnover is extremely expensive and costly to organizations. Burnout is the same. Engineering human pain and discontent out of an organization always results in lower costs and higher productivity. There is no more important factor in organizational management. People are the fuel, the engine, and the brain of every organization. Everything else is ancillary. Fall down here, and nothing else matters.	Too much emphasis on people usually comes through the attitudes and beliefs of the extrovert leader, the people lover who tries to avoid the pain arising from natural conflict resulting from growth and change in a developing organization. This emphasis builds pockets of dysfunctional behavior around personality. In fact, extrovert leaders typically design their businesses around people instead of around sound processes and structure. These organizations are easy to identify because there are always a handful of people who are deemed extremely valuable to the organization. These organizations will never scale up. They are dependent on heroes to solve problems, rather than on repeatable processes and sound structure and leadership, and the simple fact is, heroism doesn't scale.

worked then, but it doesn't work any more. In the Information Age, we must capture and empower people's hearts and minds, gaining their willing engagement, if our companies are to thrive. In several of the case stories an amazing irony surfaced: Managers attempted to employ people-enabling technologies while ignoring or treating poorly the very people they were seeking to empower. Sound organizational design provides organizational processes and organizational structures to work within that enable and empower people to achieve what they are asked to do.

Systems: Technology to Support the Troops. Today, this sub-domain is unfortunately where many organizations are attempting to begin their change efforts, an attempt that is absolutely, unequivocally wrong and will fail. The case story in Chapter 3 was a great example of this all-too-common techno-centric zeal. Even if the company had been able to perfectly execute on a technical level, the venture would still have failed. Information systems, whether a traditional filing cabinet or an ERP application,

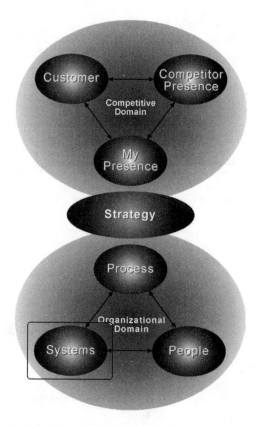

Figure 12.8   Organizational Domain – Systems

play a very limited role in organizational success. Why? Because, as we illustrated earlier, they are inanimate objects. They must be acted upon or triggered by a human to work. Through process and people, systems enable and empower an organization to achieve its goals. However, if systems are treated as a higher order actor in a corporate structure, the outcomes will mirror those in many of the case studies in Part 1. Systems are simply tools for getting the work done. There is no magic here, no glamour, nothing really special. Technology systems are the modern equivalent of typewriters and filing cabinets: tools for people to use in the conduct of business.

Organizational Domain: Summary.   The organizational domain is the native home of most people who have come up through the ranks. They

Table 12.6   Systems: Errors at the Extremes

Too Little	Too Much
Extremely risk-averse organizations often fall into the too-little category with technology. They overestimate existing productivity and underestimate the value of automation. In today's economy, the leaders of this side of the continuum are usually from an older era of computing (see Chapter 8 for a more complete treatment of technology dependence) or just completely ignorant of the power of technology to empower employees and reach customers. Frankly, they are a dying breed, and rightly so. There is no chance of having a successful, growing, market-impacting company in this environment without substantial investment in enabling technologies. Rip Van Winkles who think otherwise will wake up to find that their market no longer exists, or that their competitors have ripped it from their sleeping hands.	Those at this extreme see technology as magic, as a tool requiring little effort to achieve results of monumental proportions. Because of market conditions, these people are in the majority and thus the primary focus of this book. They see a technology solution for every problem. They are typically impatient with attempts to solve problems manually (read "simply") and are always ready to invest in more technology. They are also usually disappointed in the outcomes of their projects and the people who manage them. Why? Because in their eyes the systems should always cost less and do more, and it's obviously the fault of the IT staff, or the project manager, or some other poor schmuck who happens to be in the line of fire. They are champions of technology, but end up defaming the very thing they champion.

have an advantage over "dot-com wonders" who have never occupied a managerial role, but even these battle-hardened veterans often overlook the fundamental fact that a business is a complex system, with interdependencies and interactions that must be understood and accommodated in management processes. Remember, you have to address process, people, and systems—together. You can't change one without affecting the others, and only when they are aligned and mutually supportive will you succeed.

VISION, STRATEGY, AND PLANS: THE HIGHEST ORDER OF THOUGHT FOR STRATEGIC ADVANTAGE

Unless you've spent the majority of your professional life on the dark side of the moon, you're probably sick to death of people preaching the religion of vision, strategy, and planning. Millions of pages have been written on these topics, so it's unlikely we will say anything you haven't heard before. Despite this widespread exposure, many haven't gotten the message. Maybe you're special and you understand and apply the principles of this hallowed threesome, but most of your peers don't. We believe that a primary reason for this is that most discussion of this topic is esoteric and impractical. We have chosen a much more accessible and practical approach, one that you can actually remember and use.

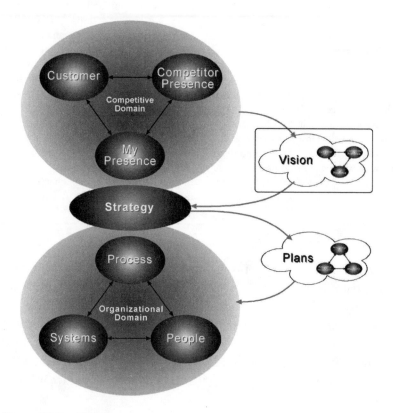

Figure 12.9 Vision

Vision: Who and What You Aspire to Be. Vision, in simple terms, is what your company aspires to be and achieve. In the business world, your vision will usually be stated in terms we used in describing the competitive domain: customers, competitors, and your presence. Vision takes little notice of current organizational constraints and is in fact often unattainable by the organization in its current state.

Table 12.7   Vision: Errors at the Extremes

Too Little	Too Much
Many executives dismiss vision as unnecessary—they know what their organization has to do, and don't have time to spend dreaming or communicating to others. They stick with "reality" because they're comfortable with the concrete and uncomfortable with the abstract. They believe it to be unnecessary and thus a waste of their time. However, as a wise man once said, "A task without a vision is drudgery." People have a natural need and desire to be a part of something bigger than themselves, something tangible and worth pursuing. A corporation is merely a bunch of individuals organized to achieve things that any one of them could not have achieved alone. Consequently, the biblical injunctive is true: "Without vision, the people perish." Managers who fail to establish a clear vision will find that people in their organizations will never achieve coherence and harmony and will require constant supervision and correction. A clear, well-communicated vision allows an entrepreneur to exert his or her influence on the organization beyond the scope of direct control. Never underestimate the power of a vision and the destructive impact of the absence of one.	Here's the complete quote: "A task without a vision is drudgery, and a vision without task is but a dream."* Too much vision usually manifests itself in too much talk and too little action. Such visions are typically esoteric and not quantifiable. If you are clueless when asked how you are going to achieve your vision, then your vision is useless. Vision must have an impact on the hearts, minds, and hands of the people doing the work to be effective. If it doesn't, then it's a worthless exercise, a waste of money. Vision must be practical, yet beyond the reach of the near-term state of the organization. It must be something you can say that people understand in the current context of your organization, even though it can't be attained today. It must be convertible into solid plans and actions that each person can own, internalize, and execute on. If your vision does not meet these tests, throw it away and start over.

*Inscription on a church in Sussex, England, circa 1730

Vision serves two major purposes. First, it gives you and your team a target to shoot at, something that is always within sight but beyond reach, something that will guide you in the development of your organization. Without vision, you have no destination in mind. You will wander aimlessly, attempting little and achieving less. Second, a well-articulated vision should inspire your employees, impress your customers, and frighten your competitors. It provides a rallying point around which to develop the momentum to carry your company to success. Vision can be powerful, so believe in it.

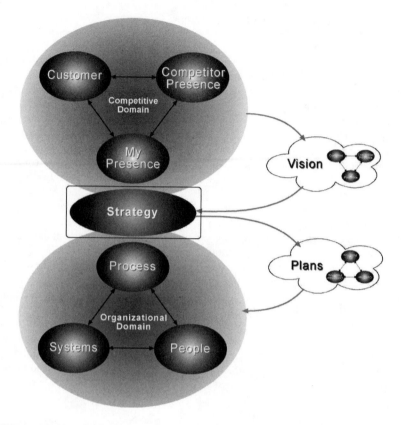

Figure 12.10   Strategy

Strategy: Defining and Controlling the Battle Space.   In keeping with our "we're at war" theme, we use a military definition of strategy: "Strategy is about defining and controlling the battle space." This means that your strategy must first define the space you've chosen to compete in (within the competitive domain), then specify how you will exercise dominant control over that space by the force of your organizational domain. Note that the important point is that there are two parts to strategy: defining where and when you will compete, then defining how you will control and dominate that competitive space. Good strategy is just that simple. It is the component that ties the competitive and organizational domains together and determines how you intend to push forward in your plans for world domination.

Table 12.8 Strategy: Errors at the Extremes

Too Little	Too Much
Strategy is the basis for planning. By defining where and when you will compete, and how you will gain dominance in that space, strategy sets in place a sound foundation from which to create operational plans. Without strategy, planning becomes haphazard, based on hunches and guided by instinct. This approach runs rampant in young companies, particularly those moving at Internet speed. There is no strategy and little planning, only execution. The result is misguided execution, ineffective at best and destructive at worst. Young companies don't need to spend huge amounts of time and energy on strategy—to do so is wasteful and paralyzing—but it is just as dangerous to spend no time on strategy. Strive for balance.	To be honest, it is rare that a company places too much emphasis on strategy. Most corporate executives wouldn't know strategy if it bit them on the ankle, so it's unlikely they will err to this extreme. Nonetheless, there are situations where even a moderate amount of time spent on strategy is too much. Sometimes you don't have time to carefully measure before cutting—you have to cut and run! Large bureaucratic organizations tend to always insist on doing everything according to the book, and if the book mandates the development of a strategy for every situation that arises, the organization is bound to do so. The result is ponderously slow reaction time and an inability to deliver real time responses. Don't go overboard: There is no such thing as "one size fits all" in the world of business. Be prepared to throw the book away when the situation demands it.

Plans: Converting Vision and Strategy into Reality.   Plans are how you will execute within the framework of your strategy to achieve your vision. Plans are usually stated in the terms we used in describing the organizational domain: people, process, and systems. True, the objective of the plans may be focused on the competitive domain, but the actions that will be taken are based within the organization. They are organizationally oriented, aimed at producing specific results effectively and efficiently and with a high degree of certainty. These plans usually deal with two facets: organizational preparation and organizational execution.

The preparation part of planning addresses the ways in which the three organizational components—people, processes, and systems—must change to prepare your organization to execute the plan. The execution part of the plan defines the systematic process the organization will follow to achieve your strategic objectives. The key point is that *both* parts of planning must be performed to be effective. In particular, you can't over-

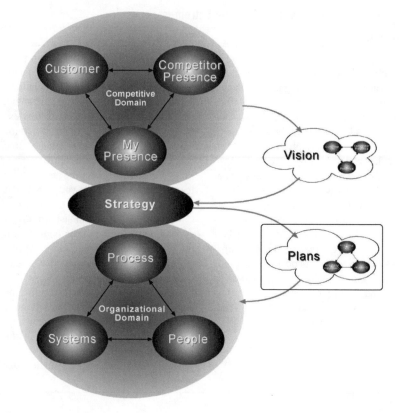

Figure 12.11   Plans

look the preparation part of planning with impunity. If you do, you will find yourself flogging an unprepared organization that has little chance of reaching your goals.

Vision, Strategy, and Plans: Summary.   This is one of the most important parts of this book. We hope you've been bored because you already knew and were doing all of these things; if so, congratulations. On the other hand, if we've made you feel a little uncomfortable, listen to your discomfort and do something about it. It's not so hard. Just remember:

- *Vision* is directed toward the competitive domain and addresses opportunities and threats.

Table 12.9   Plans: Errors at the Extremes

Too Little	Too Much
If you have reached this point without being convinced that you always need to do some level of planning, then you should stop right now, return to the first chapter, and start over—you must have been asleep. Lack of planning manifests itself in the ugliest of ways: lack of direction, confusion, inefficiency, ineffectiveness, mistakes, conflicts, unintended results, pain, low morale, and eventual failure. Now, where would we find a company like that? You can probably answer that question for yourself. Planning, based on strategy and aimed by vision, will eliminate these woes and make you successful. Plan!	Clarity! The purpose of planning is simple. If you remember this you will always do well. The core purpose of planning is communication and alignment of your entire organization along a course of action. It is not, as those who err on this side of the extreme might believe, to mitigate all risk and to ensure that all steps are defined and documented before they are taken. Here's a test: If you find that your planning efforts excessively cut into the time needed for execution, you're doing too much. By the time you are finished with your planning, the market will have passed you by. In addition, the goal of a planning exercise and the corresponding documentation is communication: Everyone hears and understands, and, as a consequence, is aligned; everyone is working toward the same goal. If your planning efforts do not have this result, you have failed. Do it right! Plan, document, communicate, execute, monitor, refine—it's simple!

- *Plans* are directed toward the organizational domain and address strengths and weaknesses.
- *Strategy* is the bridge between the two.

Simple, huh? Hang on to it. Use it: avoid the extremes. You will be amazed at the incredible clarity in perspective and direction you will gain.

A Very Important Note.   We have seen many failed attempts at strategic thought and planning. The issue, contrary to popular opinion, is not the methods, the frameworks, or the difficulty of finding the time, it is making the personal commitment to change the way we work. When all is said and done, failure to pursue strategic thought and action simply reflects a lack of commitment. The reality is that once these disciplines are mastered and practiced, it literally takes only minutes to use these tools and gain the benefits they provide. Do yourself a favor: Use the ET Framework to create a vision, define a strategy, and develop and execute plans.

But How Do I Actually Do It?

This framework will not cure all that ails your business, but it is a fact that if the key players in every one of our case scenarios had used it, they would have made far better decisions and would have been far more likely to succeed than fail. The question for you is, "How do I use it?" The framework we provided is surely much too basic to apply, right? Wrong. The key word is *framework*. The ET Framework is not intended to be specific or to cover every detail. It's like the tools in your physical tool box in your garage or utility room. The tools themselves don't solve problems; if and how you use them creates the real value. With that in mind, following are a few suggestions on how to use the framework:

1. Whenever you are facing a decision or discussion of strategic proportions, draw or at least visualize the ET Framework. Ask yourself how each of the domains and sub-domains is involved in or affected by your decision. Consider the relationships between the components and what effect changing one will have on the others. Consider your organization's strengths and weaknesses and the opportunities and threats present in the competitive domain. In this manner, you are much more likely to recognize mistakes and oversights before they occur.

2. Before you do anything else, it is essential for you to understand where your organization is in its maturation process. Every organization is somewhere between the cradle and the rocking chair and, as illustrated in Chapter 4, failure to understand *where* your organization is in its lifecycle or *what* its level of maturity means can be fatal. Works by Ichak Adizes[8] provide understanding and guidance in assessing your organization's level of maturity and provide a context for decision making that recognizes your organization's ability to implement and benefit from your decisions.

3. Now ask the following extremely basic questions relating to your proposed decision.[9] When they are answered against the backdrop

of your organization's culture and maturity, these questions provide invaluable guidance to the decision maker:

A. *Why?* What is the purpose of what you are considering? Will it support your strategic objectives? Will it be supportive or in conflict with your current business initiatives? Is it important enough to warrant your limited time and attention? Should you be spending your time and money on more important things?

B. *What?* What do you want to do, and what will you have to do to implement it? Are the answers to these questions in harmony with what you currently do?

C. *How?* How will you implement your decision? What will the business processes to support it be like? Will they be complex or simple? In particular, will they be too complex or rigorous for your organization to implement? Will the benefit be worth the potential cost?

D. *Who?* Who, both inside and outside your organization, will be involved in or affected by the decision or implementation of the decision? Will it require more people or longer work hours, or have a negative impact on current processes? Will training be required? Will roles and responsibilities change? Will your current organizational structure support the changes, or will you have to restructure?

E. *When?* What are the time dimensions that you must consider? Is there a deadline? Can you reasonably make it? Once implemented, what will be the time-related impacts of your decision? Will they be cyclical? Will the timing affect other processes? Will there be time dependencies between the change and existing processes?

F. *Where?* Where will the decision be implemented and executed? Will geographical considerations be a factor? Will distance, which often equates to time, be a factor?

G. *With what?* What systems, data, equipment, and facilities must be available to implement and execute your decision? Are they in place, or will they have to be developed or acquired? What will they cost, and do you have the time, money, and organizational bandwidth to secure them?

4. A key consideration in all of this is that, in a complex system, cause and effect are separated by time, distance, and uncertainty. This means that in a complex system, there are a few things you can control, but most you only influence. A good example can be found along the path to the bottom line: You can control costs, but you can only influence revenue. That's why in times of financial stress most executives, particularly those with a quantitative or financial background, focus on the cost side of the equation. They are comfortable there because they can directly control costs, whereas generating additional revenue in the short term usually evades them. You have to consider whether the potential distance between cause and effect, particularly along the time dimension, makes your idea unworkable or unproductive. Also, if you don't have direct control (meaning you cannot immediately effect change with perfect certainty), you have to be prepared for less than perfect outcomes.

5. On a final note about practical implementation, it is important to recognize that if you have limited experience using strategic planning or other similar tools, you are likely to quickly become overwhelmed. The simple fact is that if you try to use any framework or methodology in a rigorous fashion, especially without practice, you will quickly become frustrated and reject the tool. To avoid this trap, you must use the framework in the most natural setting possible and only to the degree that you are comfortable with. Don't get caught in the same trap as many have with respect to overly rigorous application of methodologies. Use the framework as far as it obviously and naturally benefits you, no farther. Each time you face the need for strategic thought, bring the framework out and use it again. Each time your analysis will be more complete and your decision making improved.

SUMMARY

Antoine de Saint-Exupéry, author and philosopher, once said, "You know you've achieved perfection in design, not when you have nothing more to add, but when you have nothing more to take away."[10] There are certainly frameworks and methodologies more complex than ours available to executives, but complexity can be your worst enemy because it saps your energy and leaves you confused and discouraged. The ET Framework is simple but complete, practical but powerful, and can easily be embraced and applied. Use it! You will find yourself making decisions that are of a far higher quality, with fewer unintended consequences, and with results that are far more beneficial. Its power lies in its simplicity.

CHAPTER 13

Preparing for Battle

Now that you understand the roots of the problems you face and have the ET Framework to guide you, it's time to get ready for battle. We need weapons that will allow us to slay the technology dragon. The weapons we have for you are in the form of tools that will help your projects to succeed. Venturing into any significant project without these or similarly focused tools is foolish and irresponsible. Many of these tools were briefly introduced in one or more of the case story chapters. In this chapter we review and elaborate on them, instructing you on when and how each should be used.

A warning is in order. In Chapters 11 and 12 we operate at the strategic level. This chapter is noticeably different, because the topics covered here are at the detailed operational level. Although of a lower level, we assure you that the material is nonetheless important: It's the kind of information that can mean the difference between success and failure, so hang in there!

WEAPONS AND TACTICS FOR SLAYING THE TECHNOLOGY DRAGON

Okay, maybe technology isn't a dragon, but it made a good title. The fact is, though, that if you are ever faced with the responsibility of rescuing a failing technology project, you may find yourself wishing for a simple old-fashioned dragon. Avoiding problems with technology projects, or solving them when they occur, makes dragon-slaying look easy. To help you in the battle, we've assembled an arsenal of weapons and a collection of tactics for you to use.

RISK MANAGEMENT

Just so there's no misunderstanding, we'll begin by stating unequivocally that if you embark on any technology initiative without doing early and regular risk analysis and mitigation planning, you're stupid and part of the problem. Ouch! Painful, but true. In fact, in our opinion, if you're only going to do one thing right, make it risk management, because if you constantly assess and manage risk, chances are it will force you to do most other things right. Do it!

Risk management starts before the project begins. Assessing the market, competitive, business, and environmental risks provides an initial "box" around the project, telling you such things as critical time to market dates, investment constraints, competitive differentiation requirements, and possible legal or regulatory constraints. The only way for you, as project sponsor, to accurately assess the degree of management and process rigor necessary on a project is through a pre-launch risk assessment. In the case stories we see several examples where project teams exercised either too much or too little process rigor; in all cases, the degree of rigor applied was arbitrary and fatal.

Another way to fail while doing risk management is to limit your attention to only one domain (see Figure 13.1). Mistakes at this level fall at two extremes. Project managers and technologists tend to only identify and manage risks that are specifically related to technology, to project scheduling and staffing, or to completeness and correctness of features and functionality. They usually disregard risks associated with failure to meet time to market requirements, user acceptance, or other business- and market-related risks. Project sponsors, on the other hand, typically only see risks in the business and market domains, with risks relating to time to market and product feature at the top of the list. For any project to be successful, risks from each domain must be assessed, combined, prioritized, and managed through specific mitigation strategies and plans.

Figure 13.1   Risk in Context

A final warning is that risk management must be an ongoing activity to be effective. Risks come and go and change almost daily. The ones that were unimportant during the formative stages of the project may later become critical, threatening the very life of the project. You should make risk identification, assessment, and mitigation planning part of your everyday, or at least every-week, routine. It's the only tool we know of that offers anything close to a guarantee of keeping your projects on track.

So you're convinced and willing to try it. How? Well, it's simple to do, but also simple to do poorly. One of the major problems you face is that your subjective judgment of the importance of a risk is practically certain to lead you astray. Take our word for it, you'll suck at risk management if you do it by the seat of your pants. You'll naturally prioritize risks by one or more of the following characteristics:

- *Probability:* You'll select as most important those risks with the highest probability of becoming a reality.
- *Impact:* You'll focus on the risks that would have the worst impact if they actually became a reality.
- *Immediacy:* You'll perceive the most immediate risks to be most important.

More often than not, risks with one or more of these characteristics will, in fact, be the ones you should spend the most time and money avoiding,

Table 13.1 Calculating Risk Exposure

Risk	Probability (percent)	Impact (1-10)	Exposure	Immediacy (S, M, L Term)	Mitigation Plan
Investment money not available	20	10	2.0	S	Hold line on costs, reduce features, con-strain quality
Competitor provides more features	40	5	2.0	M	Focus on and emphasize high-value differen-tiating features
Competitor beats us to market	30	6	1.8	M	Get to market fast with minimal feature set

but to focus on any one of these to the exclusion of the others will result in mis-prioritization. To properly rank risks, you need to do so by exposure and immediacy. A simple spreadsheet (see Table 13.1) that calculates exposure (impact times probability)[1] will allow you to rank risks. If two or more risks are of approximately equal exposure, they should be ranked by immediacy. Simple, huh?

Let's briefly discuss risk mitigation. The purpose of a mitigation plan is to minimize total exposure. We reduce exposure by reducing probability and/or impact. Following are the common mitigation themes and how they might be applied to address the first risk in Table 13.1, "Investment money not available":

- *Eliminate the risk:* Use personal funds instead of external funding.
- *Reduce the probability:* Engage a professional to assist in obtaining funding.
- *Eliminate the impact:* Arrange a backup line of credit.
- *Reduce the impact:* Plan an alternative first release of the system that can be completed using funds on hand.
- *Transfer the impact:* Purchase an insurance policy.

As these examples indicate, there are many ways to mitigate risk, and it's not difficult to do. It just takes a little time, organization, and brainpower.

So now you know how to do risk management, but aren't convinced. "I don't have time to do anything this complex," you say. Not so! Risk management, as with all the tools we discuss here, is surprisingly simple. Its seeming complexity is more a perception than a reality. An in-depth risk analysis for even a large project can take as little as an hour to complete, and we guarantee that it will be the most valuable hour you spend on your project. Unmanaged risk is truly a dragon poised to devour you and your technology endeavor.

CONSTRAINT MANAGEMENT

Having done a risk assessment for your project, you now have a solid foundation from which to make some of the most difficult decisions a project sponsor will face. Every project will be constrained by one or more limitations, and managing the project within the context of these constraints requires planning and discipline. You must decide which things are most important, requiring optimization, and which are less important. You might as well face it now: You're going to have to accept compromise and tradeoffs. You can't have your cake and eat it too.

The constraint tradeoff decisions you're going to have to make relate to schedule, budget, features, and quality. The most common and often fatal mistake here is to attempt the impossible, to attempt to optimize all four. In your dreams! This mistake is very common. It is amazing how often it is repeated among project sponsors, and for some reason it is rarely identified and addressed. It seems as if the tendency to make this mistake is somehow woven into the typical executive's or entrepreneur's psyche; he or she wants it right (the most features and highest quality possible), fast (delivered yesterday), and cheap (for the smallest amount possible). If you're guilty of this kind of thinking, you need to unravel that diseased thought from your brain and bring reality to bear on project constraint management. As a good friend of ours is fond of saying, "Emphasis on everything is emphasis on nothing."[2] Every project is going to have limitations placed on it, and failure to identify and manage within those limitations is just plain stupid. Stop it!

Furthermore, you don't get to make the constraint tradeoff decisions at the beginning of the project and then conveniently forget them. The tradeoff decisions you make become the baseline for the project, the

Table 13.2   Constraint Tradeoff Matrix

Goal	Features	Quality	Time	Cost
Optimize	✓			
Constrain		✓		✓
Negotiate			✓	

foundation upon which every subsequent decision will be based. You can't arbitrarily make decisions in conflict with your tradeoff decisions without paying a price. If you want to later add a feature, you need to revisit your tradeoff decisions. To get the extra feature, you have to add time or budget or give up some quality. Likewise, demanding that the product be delivered ahead of the original schedule means that one or more of the other three constraints will have to change. Recognizing this and implementing a formal change control process ensures that decisions regarding project changes are made in the light of their cost and impact, thus ensuring that the outcome of the project is what *you* decide it should be. Yes, such a formal process is restrictive and painful if you're a control freak who wants everything your way. But do yourself a favor: Apply the maxims "For every action there is an equal and opposite reaction" and "There's no such thing as a free lunch" to you and your project—behave!

We presented the constraint tradeoff matrix (see Table 13.2) in Chapter 9. It is a great tool for making all parties on a project honest and keeping them that way. It forces you to make decisions early in the project and to stick with them. It's also a great tool for ensuring that the impacts of changes on project scope, timeline, or budget are considered before the changes are approved.

The tool is strikingly simple to use. The fundamental rule is that you can have only one checkmark in the "Optimize" row, no more than two in the "Constrain" row, and no more than two, but at least one, in the "Negotiate" row. Obviously, you should also only have one checkmark in each column. For a more detailed discussion of this tool, see Chapter 9. The important thing is to use it. Fill it out, hang an enlarged copy on the wall, and refer to it whenever you have to make decisions about any of the constrained items. It will keep you on track.

PROJECT TEAM ROLES AND STRUCTURE

A software development project is a witch's brew of confounding complexity that places conflicting demands on the project members. Without well-defined roles and responsibilities, even the most conscientious of team members will eventually give in to pressure and do that which is easiest, or fastest, or which relieves the most pain. To succeed, you have to define roles and responsibilities, then ensure that they are adhered to.

Many software development processes come with associated project team models, usually a list of roles with a description of the responsibilities associated with each role. On a large team, you usually will have one or more persons occupying each role; on a small team, a single person may fill more than one role. There is a lot of theory about which roles may be assigned to a single person and which must be assigned to different people. We won't try to go into such detail; it is sufficient here to simply discuss the general idea of the roles and responsibilities. The fact is that most problems result from failure to define roles rather than from details associated with the assignments or how roles relate to one another on the project team. A representative set of roles is summarized in Table 13.3. You may need more or fewer, depending on the size and nature of your project. Consider this a guide only.

PROJECT COMMUNICATIONS

In Chapter 7 we presented a clear demonstration of the challenge of interpersonal communication between project members. The nonlinear increase in complexity can be dramatic and deadly for a large project. For this reason, it is imperative that clear and open communication be established from the outset of the project. This will not happen by chance; if you assume it will, you will fail. The only way to ensure that communication will occur is to formally define communication paths. You have to ask yourself a series of questions such as the following:

- What critical information must be communicated?
- Who has the information that has to be communicated?
- Who needs the information?

Table 13.3 Representative Team Roles

Role	Responsibilities
Project Sponsor	The project sponsor has primary responsibility for customer satisfaction, ensuring that end-user needs are communicated to the project team, and that the product produced by the team meets those needs. The product sponsor is also responsible for ensuring that the end-user business units are prepared to integrate the system into their processes and organizational structure. Note that the project sponsor is often also the customer. The project sponsor controls the constraint tradeoff decisions.
Project Manager	The project manager ensures that the project sponsor's constraint tradeoff decisions establishing the desired balance among schedule, budget, features, and quality are adhered to, and that any changes to these decisions are approved by the project sponsor with full understanding of the impact of the change. The project manager controls all decisions regarding project staff, task assignments, and other factors impacting constraint tradeoffs, particularly schedule and budget. It is reasonably accurate to observe that the project sponsor "owns" decisions that affect features and quality, whereas the project manager "owns" decisions that affect schedule and budget.
Development Members	The development members of the team are responsible for building a product that meets the customer's requirements. The developers control decisions regarding technical design and development. It must be noted that there are several subroles within development, including architects, designers, programmers, and database experts.
Usability Members	The usability members of the team are responsible for ensuring that the product meets end-user usability requirements and for ensuring that the users are trained and supported as the product enters use. They control all decisions regarding user interface, education, and support.
Testing Members	The testing members of the team are responsible for ensuring that all shortcomings of the product are discovered and communicated. They control all decisions regarding testing and quality validation.
Logistics Members	The logistics members of the team are responsible for ensuring the smooth deployment and implementation of the product. They control decisions regarding operational readiness, deployment, system management, and support.

Table 13.4   Communication Plan for Development Phase of Mid-Sized Project

Information	From	To	When
Project status	Project manager	Project sponsor	Weekly or on significant change
Project risk	Project manager	Project sponsor	When risk changes
Scope change	Project manager	Project team members	When scope changes
Task assignment	Project manager	Team member	On assignment or change
Task status	Project team members	Project manager	When status changes

- What is the best way to convey the information?
- Does the information change often enough to require periodic recurring communication?

Your answers to these questions will help you construct a formal communication plan. You must also recognize that communication needs change as the project progresses, so you have to continually revisit the questions and revise your plan. The partial example in Table 13.4 is typical for the development phase of a mid-sized project.

On very large or cross-functional projects, it is advisable to designate a single individual to "own" and facilitate communications. This role is in addition to those outlined in the previous section and is best assigned to a nontechnical person with excellent interpersonal and communication skills.

SOFTWARE DEVELOPMENT PROCESS FRAMEWORK

There are many software development processes around, and they've been around for a long time. Just about every developer eventually goes through a stage where he or she realizes that there must be a better way of doing things and so invents a new process. Luckily, most processes fall into one of two broad categories: "waterfall," in which things happen in strict sequence from beginning to end of the project, and "iterative," in which multiple short development cycles are executed in sequence. Waterfall processes are shunned today, so we'll focus on a representative iterative approach we call the "4D Process Framework." We make no claims of originality or uniqueness for this framework; it's very similar to several others you will find in use today.[3]

Whether it's 4D or something else, every successful software development process has certain key characteristics:

- *Predictability:* We can reliably produce an outcome that satisfies our constraint tradeoff decisions.[4]
- *Repeatability:* Very little happens by chance.
- *Controllability:* The project sponsor controls changes to baselined constraint tradeoff decisions.
- *Manageability:* The process can be continually monitored and managed.
- *Adaptability:* The process can be adapted to meet varying needs for process rigor depending on project risk.
- *Continuous improvement:* The process can be improved through feedback and refinement.

It would seem that using a sound software development process would always yield obvious benefits, and it does, to a point. However, as we demonstrated in Chapter 6 and Chapter 5, the misuse of process is a natural and common occurrence. "We don't have time" and "We *always* adhere to our process" seem to be the most common mindsets that cause this misuse. Organizations typically either see process as a panacea and blindly check their brains at the door when using it, or they see process as an annoying and unnecessary damper on their desire to "just get it done." Both perspectives are defective, but unfortunately most organizations tend to be closer to one of the extremes rather than the middle ground.

The progression of thought to this point is extremely critical and provides the basis for striking the proper balance between extreme process rigor and no process at all. The process begins with risk analysis and mitigation planning and is followed by constraint analysis and tradeoff decisions. These two activities provide the basis for answering the question,

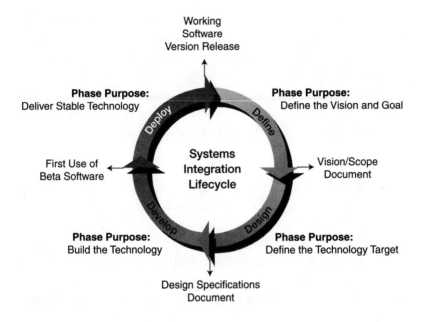

Figure 13.2   4D Software Development Process

"How rigorously should we use process?" If project risk is high, then the rigor with which process and other management techniques are applied must be increased; it's just that simple. If risk is high, you may spend weeks or even months in each phase; if risk is low it is possible to iterate through an entire lifecycle in a few hours. Similarly, if quality requirements are extreme (e.g., human life is at stake), then complete and correct process must be rigorously followed. Every initiative, regardless of the risk and quality constraints, should follow some basic series of steps to allow for clear goal setting and controlled outcomes, but no more than required. Applying rigor without specific requirements in mind is simply irresponsible and destructive.

Figure 13.2 is a breakdown of the basic 4D software development process, along with corresponding relationships to risk mitigation.

As you can see, there are four phases: "define," "design," "develop," and "deploy," thus the name "4D." A number of iterative software development processes in use today have four similar, albeit differently named, phases. We would also like to point out that the exact details of each phase are somewhat subjective and may vary from one implementation to another. The important thing is that all such processes share four similar phases and certain key activities that must be completed. Let's examine each phase in detail.

Define Phase. The purpose of the "define" phase is to define the goal and desired outcomes of the effort. Some of the topics addressed during this phase are:

- *Vision:* What would we do if we had unlimited budget and time?
- *Risks:* What are the risks, and how can we mitigate them?
- *Constraints:* What are the constraints (features, budget, time, and quality), and how will we balance them?
- *Scope:* Based on the risks and constraint tradeoff decisions, what are the actual goals of the project?
- *Project organization:* What people, processes, and systems will make up the project?

The primary deliverable marking completion of this phase is the vision/scope document, which outlines each of these components to the degree required to successfully move into the "design" phase. It is important to note that at this point this document does not fully define the system or project details. These will be established during the "design" phase.

Design Phase. The purpose of the "design" phase is to fully specify the desired outcomes of the effort. In particular, detailed specifications of the system and a comprehensive project plan must be completed. Some of the topics addressed during this phase are:

- *System specifications:* What will the system look like, and how will it work? This specification will be very comprehensive, addressing every possible detail of the system.
- *Schedule:* How long will it take to complete the system? More specifically, what are the measurable milestones, what activities must be completed to reach them, who will complete these activities, how long will each take, and what dependencies exist between them?
- *Budget:* How much will it cost to complete the system?

The primary deliverables marking completion of this phase are the design specification document and the project plan. It is important to note that both are living documents and will almost certainly be refined during development. It is also important to note that this phase does not require months to complete or reams of paper to document. All of this may conceivably be completed in a two-page document, depending on the scope of the project. Our recommendation is to get through each iteration of these four phases as quickly as possible.

Develop Phase. The purpose of the "develop" phase is to build the system defined in the design specification. All programming must be completed, and each module of the system must be separately tested. Some of the topics addressed during this phase are:

- *Coding:* The programs and other components that make up the system will be created and tested.
- *Test planning:* How will the system be tested? Plans for testing, initiated during design, will be completed.
- *Final design specification:* What features are included in the system, and what features originally "in scope" are not in the final system?

The primary deliverables marking completion of this phase are the final design specification, the test plan, and the system source code and executables.

Deploy Phase. The purpose of the "deploy" phase is to test and refine the system and supporting elements, bringing everything to a state where the system and its environment are ready to be placed in service. Some of the topics addressed during this phase are:

- *System stabilization:* The system must be tested and any significant faults corrected. This testing will usually include both "integration testing," which is performed by the project staff, and "user acceptance testing," which is performed by actual end-users.
- *Environmental readiness:* The environment must be prepared for the system. This will include things such as installing and testing servers and network equipment, establishing connectivity to the Internet,

defining operational procedures, hiring and training operational staff, and so forth.

- *User preparation:* Users must be trained and their work environment and processes prepared for the system.
- *Implementation planning:* A plan must be established for launching the system, including cut over from any existing system. A fallback plan, to be executed in case the new system fails, must be created and communicated.

HUMAN INTEGRATION PROCESS FRAMEWORK

This topic is worthy of an entire book by itself. Many project failures lie at the feet of those who ignore the issues here. People are the most important aspect of any project, of any company, of any effort to achieve anything of substance in life. Why then is there so much debate about how to motivate them, move them, inspire them, and involve them? We don't have time to rehash Theory X and Y and discuss organizational development and personnel management theory. Let's just be very clear: In Chapter 7 we outline what we call the human integration component of a systems integration project lifecycle (see page 107). If these types of factors are not taken into account in *any* sizable software investment, you are an absolute fool to think that your efforts will yield any return on investment.

The primary deliverables marking completion of the "deploy" phase are a functioning system and happy users. However, the happy users part is where most projects fail, not in the technology arena. Because all development methods are and have been designed by software developers, far too little attention is paid to user acceptance and integration. The ironic thing is that this is the most important part. Several years ago the Project Management Institute released a study on sixty-two technology projects, concluding that there was no statistical correlation between perfect technical execution and user satisfaction.[5] The implications are obvious. The project has only just begun once the first release of the software is deployed. Figure 13.3 illustrates key components to human integration success along with their relationship to the ET Framework. Our addition of these four components to a more traditional lifecycle is intended to deal with the three key components in the organizational domain: process, people, and systems.

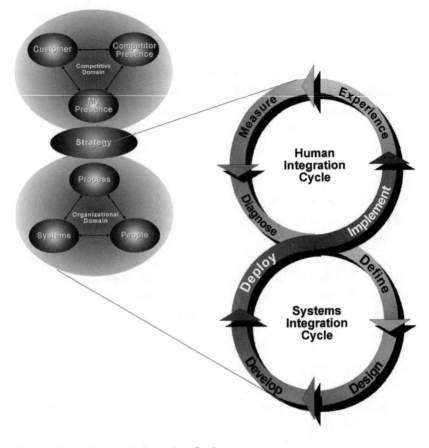

Figure 13.3   Human Integration Cycle

Implement Phase.   The purpose of this phase is to begin using the software in a true production environment. What is often ignored in a traditional "deploy" phase is the work of integrating the use of the software within the day-to-day context of business. Ignoring or not giving equal weight to these factors is like building a perfect engine for a race car, rolling it up to the car, and then expecting it somehow to put itself in and work. The problems experienced in these areas are particularly endemic to CRM software implementations, as illustrated in the case story in Chapter 7. Following are questions to be addressed during the "implement" phase that are critical to getting the engine into the car and working to maximum benefit:

- What are the changes required in business processes now that we have the new system in place?
- How will those processes be accommodated by the new system?[6]
- What work behaviors must change to experience the maximum benefits of the new system?
- What reward and/or compensation structures must be in place to encourage use of the new system?

Experience Phase. The "experience" phase can be likened to the period after you first learned to ride a bike. Now that you have the basics down, you begin to experiment with speed, turning more aggressively, and all the other detailed skills. In this phase, people make the system part of their daily routine. They begin to discover things they did not know they could do, benefits they did not know existed, and problems they did not anticipate. Retraining is typically necessary in this phase for the late or hesitant adopters, and the power-users begin to surface lists of issues that are hindering their progress.

Measure Phase. The "measure" phase begins to move the implementation into a new period of change and improvement. From the natural momentum in the "experience" phase, the "measure" phase begins to quantify the impact of the last systems release and prepare the users for improvements and upgrades. This phase specifically asks two key questions:

- Where and how much is the system enhancing productivity, and how can we leverage the enhancing functionality toward even greater improvements?
- Where and how much is the system inhibiting productivity, and how can we mitigate this problem in the next release?

Diagnose Phase. This is the final phase in the human integration cycle. It involves interpretation of the experience and the measures in a way that provides a list of priorities for the next release of the software. It determines the true cause of systems problems and whether they are software, business process, or people related. Often, problems attributed to software are really people issues and training is in order. In other cases, people try to use the software in ways it was not designed for, which may call for process and/or systems modifications. Finally, some problems with the software may only require minor configuration changes that can be made as discovered; others may require complex changes that are best left for the next release. The completion of this phase is marked by stakeholder consensus on a prioritized list of proposed enhancements and changes for the next release of the software.

MICRO-RELEASE CYCLES

As we pointed out more than once in Part 1, it is usually advantageous to do multiple releases of a system, with each release incrementally more functional than the previous one, rather than finishing the system and dumping the whole thing on the users at once. The incremental approach reduces the risk of developing the wrong system features, providing more opportunities for end-user feedback to fine-tune the system to the users' actual needs; in addition, it keeps "Type A" executives pacified because they're seeing real progress rather than just hearing about it.

The Micro-Release Cycle is simply a variation of the 4D Process Framework we presented on page 90, with the emphasis being placed on rapidly and repetitively releasing incremental enhancements to the system being produced. Each cycle through the process framework is done in a manner that optimizes schedule and constrains budget and quality, while features are flexibly negotiated. The result is a quick development cycle (usually measured in days), constrained to a specific expenditure limit (usually expressed as staff-hours), with limited and negotiable features and functionality improvements. It works: Try it.

SUMMARY

These are only a few of the tools that exist to help keep projects on track, but we believe them to be the most important. If you want to know more, you will find that many project management and software books have been written covering these and other tools in excruciating detail.[7]

Conclusion

CONGRATULATIONS!

You've hung in there and we're almost home. It's been quite a journey, experiencing the pain of smart people making dumb mistakes, then examining the root causes and discussing ways to avoid making similar mistakes yourself. You've seen the development of our central theme, that defective thinking lies at the root of almost all business failures. If we've succeeded at all, your perspective on business decision making, particularly regarding the employment of technology, should have changed forever. You are now, more than ever, positioned to succeed with your next technology venture. Just to be certain, we're going to devote a few paragraphs to driving home some of the key points of our central theme and to encouraging continued study and thought about these critical topics.

CRITICAL WISDOM TO TAKE WITH YOU

There are a handful of concepts that form the basis for successful executive thought. Following are those we consider most important:

- *Get out of your box.* Your little corner of the world may be important, but it's not all that is important. To emphasize one thing (e.g., technology) while you slight another (e.g., people) guarantees you will look stupid. "Balance" is the name of the game.

- *Recognize the complexity.* Recognize that your business, and the competitive domain in which it lives, is an incredibly complex system. In a complex system, things are rarely as simple as they seem. This is primarily due to the interdependencies between things: You can't change one element of a complex system without affecting others, often in unanticipated ways with unanticipated consequences. There's also the fact that in a complex system, cause and effect are separated by time, distance, and uncertainty. That simply means that there aren't many things you can directly and specifically control; most you only influence.[1]

- *Resist the hype.* This doesn't mean that you should *ignore* the hype, especially since you usually don't know that something is hype until it's too late. Listen to everything, but be suspicious of things that sound too good to be true or that go against conventional wisdom. Don't assume that just because the person saying something is smart or successful or powerful, it is true; for example, some of the greatest tragedies of the dot-com debacle were fueled by brilliant and successful venture capitalists who were themselves both victims and purveyors of hype.

- *Caveat emptor.* Anyone who wants your money should be considered a liar until proven otherwise. *Caveat emptor* isn't just a catchy Latin phrase—it literally means "buyer beware!" Vendors, consultants, and service providers are mostly honorable people with honorable intentions, but there are enough bad apples in the barrel to demand caution. Check references, monitor performance, and don't be bashful about confronting problems. The good ones will appreciate your diligence; the bad ones will reveal themselves under scrutiny.

- *Use the tools.* We've presented a number of tools, in particular the ET Framework. We've harped on the need for process, risk analysis and management, and many of other things. If you've never used any formal methods or processes, you're probably feeling a little intimidated by them all. Don't be. Go back to Chapter 12 and re-read the "But How Do I Really Do It?" section (page 204). If you're facing a project and are going to have to get involved in the details, the tools presented in Chapter 13 should be of interest to you. None of this is very complex, and the 80/20 rule applies: You should get 80 percent of the benefit even if you only apply 20 percent of the tools we've covered. Do it!

TOPICS FOR ADDITIONAL STUDY AND THOUGHT

- *Self-mastery:* Without self-awareness and self-mastery, we are doomed to repeat the mistakes of the past. With it, there is little we cannot overcome and accomplish. Steven Covey's *Seven Habits of Successful People* is required reading. Peter Senge's *The Fifth Discipline* is a profound source for thought about self-mastery and will lead you to more resources that can assist you in this area. Finally, both *The Oz Principle* by Roger Connors, Tom Smith, Craig R. Hickman, and Thomas Smith and *Personal Accountability* by John Miller provide guidance in taking charge of your life by accepting responsibility for events around you.[2]
- *Leadership:* Leadership is about inspiring and leading people. The key traits of a leader are vision, personal integrity and accountability, a willingness to trust others, and a mentoring/caring spirit. Unfortunately, although we have reviewed many texts on leadership, very few are worth their cover price. A landmark work, now about twenty years old, is *Servant Leadership,* by Robert K. Greenleaf. For a more recent treatment, see *Leveraging People and Profit* by Bernard A. Nagle and Perry Pascarella.[3]
- *Systems thinking:* Systems thinking is about understanding and managing complex systems. This is one of the most critical thinking skills that every executive should have but few actually do. Again, Peter Senge's *Fifth Discipline* and the *Fifth Discipline Field Book*[4] are fantastic resources for learning in this arena.
- *Organizational growth and maturation:* Every organization naturally passes through a lifecycle beginning with courtship and ending in death. Your job as an executive is to coach your organization, to "prime" and keep it there. Understanding and managing stages in corporate development and decay are fundamental prerequisites for serving in an executive leadership position. In this realm, the preeminent thinker is Ichak Adizes. His *Managing Corporate Lifecycles*[5]

is highly readable and thought provoking. If you don't read anything else we have recommended, read this book; we guarantee it will change the way you see your company and your role in it.

In Closing

We conceived this book convinced that if we could help executives and entrepreneurs think better about the employment of technology and, on a larger scale, about the way they build and run their businesses, we would consider the months of research and writing worthwhile. We hope that by now you agree, and that because of this book, you will think better as you approach your work. If we've helped you in this, we'd like to know. If not, we'd like to know that, too. We don't claim to have all the answers, or that the answers we have are the only valid ones. We're students of life just like you, and would love to learn from your experiences. Write us, e-mail us, or call us; let us know what you think. We will continue to learn and so will you. We wish you fewer losses, more wins, and a full and rewarding life at a tempo much slower than "the speed of stupid."

Contact Information

We are founding partners at Executive Thought, LLC (www.ExecuThought.com), an executive management consulting firm headquartered in Denver, Colorado. We may be reached by e-mail at Dan.Burke@ExecuThought.com or Alan.Morrison@ExecuThought.com.

NOTES

INTRODUCTION

1. Standish Group, *Chaos Report,* 2001, www.standishgroup.com.

2. Ibid.

3. Ibid.

4. It is important to note that it is impossible to reveal and discuss all factors surrounding each case story. We have taken care to ignore superfluous components of each and focus on those factors that best reveal problematic thinking. For the same reason, you will not find a one-to-one mapping of issues revealed in analysis to issues revealed in the story. As in the real-life cases and perspectives of their participants, only hindsight was 20/20.

CHAPTER 1

1. Rick Levine, Christopher Locke, Doc Searls, and David Weinberger, *The Cluetrain Manifesto* (Cambridge, Mass.: Perseus Books, 2000).

2. One way to find such companies is to do a Yahoo!® search for "information technology consulting," which will lead you to a listing of approximately 500 such companies.

3. See Alan Cooper, *The Inmates Are Running the Asylum* (Indianapolis, IN: Sams, 1999).

4. Note that the WebTrends site does a decent job of answering the questions we posed above. Follow the "Products" link as a good example of quality site design.

CHAPTER 2

1. *Mythical Man Month*, rev. ed. (New York: Addison-Wesley, 1995), 182–183.

2. "Static" relates to design limitations that do not allow for data level interactivity, transaction processing, or personalization. Some static sites are filled with Flash or other interesting dynamic components; however, the content still remains relatively stable.

CHAPTER 3

1. Personal communication with John Raeder, February 2001.

2. It would be tempting to point to Bill Gates and others like him to counter this argument, but people like Gates are not just technologists; they have uncanny business sense as well.

3. Personal communication with Frank Mendicino, March 2001.

CHAPTER 5

1. John Gray, *Men Are from Mars, Women Are from Venus* (New York: HarperCollins, 1992).

2. *Managing Corporate Lifecycles* (Paramus, NJ: Prentice Hall Press, 1999), 263–265.

CHAPTER 6

1. "Vision" defines the product you would build if time and funds were unlimited; "scope" defines the part of the vision that you plan to actually implement, given time and funding constraints.

2. *Adaptive Software Development* (New York: Dorset House Publishing, 2000).

3. Ibid.

4. Mary Beard (1876–1958), quoted in *Wisdom of the Ages* (software) (MCR Software, 1988–1998).

CHAPTER 7

1. Tom Ingram, "Managing Client/Server and Open Systems Projects: A Ten Year Study of 62 Mission Critical Projects," *Project Management Journal*, June 1994, 26–36.

2. "Why CRM Projects Fail," *CRM Journal*, www.crmcommunity.com/resources/journal/article2.htm.

CHAPTER 9

1. Many authorities on project management name only three constraints: features, schedule, and budget. Their position is that quality is not negotiable and thus is not subject to tradeoff. Although this sounds great, it is simply untrue in practice: When things go badly in a project, quality is often the first thing to suffer, a fact usually hidden from view. Admitting that quality is not an absolute allows us to make it visible and manage it, thus avoiding hidden quality loss.

2. It is important to note that time and cost are usually treated as independent variables, when in fact they are related. Given a fixed project team size, cost becomes a function of time.

CHAPTER 10

1. Rick Levine, Christopher Locke, Doc Searls, and David Weinberger, *The Cluetrain Manifesto* (Cambridge, Mass.: Perseus Books, 2000).

CHAPTER 11

1. A parallel can be found in the loss of confidence and general cynicism toward government and government officials by the U.S. public brought about by the Wa-

tergate scandal and other disclosures of ethical lapses on the part of high federal officials.

2. Daniel Montano, the CEO of the Denver-based creative firm Montano-Solaria, contributed greatly to our thought in this area.

3. There are obviously exceptions to this rule, but they are rare.

4. *Paradigm Shift* (New York: McGraw-Hill, 1993).

5. In 1965, Gordon Moore observed that the capacity of electronic chips was doubling every eighteen to twenty-four months, an observation that is still remarkably accurate.

6. On the surface, the Web more closely resembles old-fashioned host-centric computing than client-server or n-tier computing.

CHAPTER 12

1. It is important to note that what some would call "planning" we would call "knee-jerk." If planning for strategic projects does not consider the basic elements we provide in this framework, it is not planning.

2. For in-depth and powerful treatment of these concepts, see Peter Senge, *The Fifth Discipline* (New York: Doubleday Currency, 1990).

3. Stephen Covey, *The Seven Habits of Highly Effective People* (New York: Fireside Press, 1990).

4. It is rare to find a simple system in business that generates meaningful results.

5. "The Coming Depression," *PC Magazine* (April 25, 2000).

6. We use the term "presence" here to mean *everything* that establishes a company in the competitive arena. This includes products, branding, image, relationships, and so forth.

7. For in-depth treatment of the problem of emerging markets and disruptive technologies, see Clayton M. Christensen, *The Innovators' Dilemma: Why New Technologies Cause Great Firms to Fail* (Cambridge, MA: Harvard Business School Press, 1997).

8. *Corporate Lifecycles* (New York: Prentice Hall Press, 1990), *The Pursuit of Prime* (Santa Monica, CA: Knowledge Exchange, 1996), and *Managing Corporate Lifecycles* (Paramus, NJ: Prentice Hall Press, 1999).

9. The use of these questions in this context is best exemplified in Extended Business Modeling Language (xBML), a powerful business modeling methodology and language invented by Cedric Tyler and commercialized by his company, BusinessGenetics (www.businessgenetics.net).

10. *The Little Prince* (San Diego: Harcourt Trade, 2000).

CHAPTER 13

1. If probability ever becomes 100 percent, the risk has become a reality and is no longer a risk. It is now an issue.

2. Whether original or not, we're giving Tom Griffin credit.

3. Examples include Microsoft's "Process Model for Application Development" and Rational Software's "Rational Unified Process."

4. This refers to decisions made prior to project launch regarding schedule, budget, features, and quality.

5. Tom Ingram, "Managing Client/Server and Open Systems Projects: A Ten Year Study of 62 Mission Critical Projects," *Project Management Journal*, June 1994, 26–36.

6. Proponents of the traditional lifecycle will protest that these questions were covered by phases within the traditional approach. Our response is that they are only covered conceptually. Once the system is operational, there are always unanticipated consequences of the system and its impact on the user.

7. See, for example, www.gantthead.com and www.pmi.org.

CONCLUSION

1. You should recognize that people are systems as well. Everything stated here applies to people. In particular, regardless of how powerful you may be, you can't control people; you can only influence them.

2. Stephen Covey, *The Seven Habits of Highly Effective People* (New York: Fireside Press, 1990); Peter Senge, *The Fifth Discipline* (New York: Doubleday Currency, 1990); Roger Connors, Tom Smith, Craif R. Hickman, and Thomas Smith, *The Oz Principle* (New York: Prentice Hall Press, 1994); John G. Miller, *Personal Accountability* (Denver: Denver Press, 1999).

3. Robert K. Greenleaf, *Servant Leadership* (Paulist Press, 1983); Bernard A. Nagl and Perry Pascarella, *Leveraging People and Profit: The Hard Work of Soft Management* (Woburn, MA: Butterworth-Heineimann, 1997).

4. Peter Senge, Art Kleiner, Charlotte Roberts, and Bryan Smith, *The Fifth Discipline Fieldbook* (New York: Doubleday Currency, 1994).

5. (Paramus, NJ: Prentice Hall Press, 1999).

GLOSSARY OF
E-TERMS AND PHRASES

ASP 1. "Active Server Pages," a technology from Microsoft used to build Web pages. 2. "Application Service Provider," a company that provides access to applications hosted on the Web.

B2B Business to business.

B2C Business to consumer.

Brochureware In its simplest form, a Web-based version of a company's marketing materials. It is typically constructed through static Web pages with no user interactivity beyond links for navigating to additional details on specific topics.

Burn rate The rate of expenditure: "Our *burn rate* is hitting $50,000 per week."

Click and mortar A Web-based business that is spawned from and/or has a symbiotic relationship with an existing "brick and mortar" business.

DHTML "Dynamic HTML," a standard that allows animated objects to be placed within HTML Web pages. (See **HTML**.)

E-Tail Web-based retail sales.

ERP "Enterprise Resource Planning," software that supports the implementation of a business management system that integrates all facets of the business, including planning, manufacturing, sales, and marketing.

Executables A computer program in machine-readable (binary) form. See also **Source code**.

Flash A browser-based standard and supporting system for animated graphics, created by Macromedia Corporation.

HTML "Hypertext Markup Language," the language used to construct Web pages that can be viewed with a standard browser program.

Ilities* Short term for the following characteristics of a quality system:

Adaptability Ability to adapt easily to change.

Autonomy Ability to function both individually and as part of a whole.

Data accessibility Ability to access both local and remote data transparent to its location.

Flexibility Ability to grow and contract the architecture as required.

Interoperability Ability to move transactions and data cooperatively across heterogeneous environments.

Maintainability Ability to maintain the system.

Modularity Ability to easily add, remove, and change modules. Describes a "plug and play" architecture.

Openness/Support for standards Ability to interoperate with other systems.

Portability Ability to move applications in whole or in part between architectures.

Reliability Ability to operate correctly under circumstances for which the software was designed.

Resiliency Ability to sustain and recover from abnormal use or use outside of the circumstances for which the software was designed.

Robustness Ability to continue to operate under circumstances for which the software was not designed.

Scalability Ability to easily and linearly increase the capacity of a system to meet demands placed on it by things such as increases in transaction volume, increasing data storage needs, increasing numbers of active users, increasing numbers of total (active and inactive) users, and so forth.

Launch velocity Literally, the speed required for a spacecraft to escape the Earth's gravitational pull. For an Internet company, launch velocity refers to quickly achieving a high level of usage, revenue, profitability, or other similar metrics. This is essential to the survival of a dot-com company, because continued funding, market valuation, and other critical factors are highly dependent on these metrics.

Real time The time in which a system can detect an event, determine a course of action, and execute that action to control the outcome of the event. For example, a real time process control program might detect an above-normal pressure, determine that a valve should be opened, and

---

*Much of this comes from Boar, Bernard, "Implementing Client Server Computing," McGraw Hill, 1992

command the valve to open, all in time to reduce the pressure before it went out of limits.

Rigor   Describes the amount of detail, precision, policy, and methodological structure that is applied to any business discipline, in this case system development.

Source code   A computer program in human-readable (text) form. See also **Executables**.

SWOT   "Strengths, Weaknesses, Opportunities, and Threats." In the context of the EA Framework, strengths and weaknesses are derived from and relate to the organizational domain, whereas opportunities and threats are derived from and relate to the competitive domain. All four must be considered when forming vision, strategy, and plans.

Testing   Determining if something works as planned. Testing of new software usually progresses through three stages: 1) "unit testing," during which each program or system module is tested individually; "integration testing," during which all the parts are tested together; and "user acceptance testing," which is performed by actual future users of the system. In addition, "regression testing" should be performed whenever any modification is made to an existing system, the purpose being to ensure that nothing was "broken" by the changes.

INDEX